ATLA Monograph Series
edited by Dr. Kenneth E. Rowe

1. Ronald L. Grimes. *The Divine Imagination: William Blake's Major Prophetic Visions.* 1972.
2. George D. Kelsey. *Social Ethics Among Southern Baptists, 1917-1969.* 1973.
3. Hilda Adam Kring. *The Harmonists: A Folk-Cultural Approach.* 1973.
4. J. Steven O'Malley. *Pilgrimage of Faith: The Legacy of the Otterbeins.* 1973.
5. Charles Edwin Jones. *Perfectionist Persuasion: The Holiness Movement and American Methodism, 1867-1936.* 1974.
6. Donald E. Byrne, Jr. *No Foot of Land: Folklore of American Methodist Itinerants.* 1975.
7. Milton C. Sernett. *Black Religion and American Evangelicalism: White Protestants, Plantation Missions, and the Flowering of Negro Christianity, 1787-1865.* 1975.
8. Eva Fleischner. *Judaism in German Christian Theology Since 1945: Christianity and Israel Considered in Terms of Mission.* 1975.
9. Walter James Lowe. *Mystery & The Unconscious: A Study in the Thought of Paul Ricoeur.* 1977.
10. Norris Magnuson. *Salvation in the Slums: Evangelical Social Work, 1865-1920.* 1977.
11. William Sherman Minor. *Creativity in Henry Nelson Wieman.* 1977.
12. Thomas Virgil Peterson. *Ham and Japheth: The Mythic World of Whites in the Antebellum South.* 1978.
13. Randall K. Burkett. *Garveyism as a Religious Movement: The Institutionalization of a Black Civil Religion.* 1978.
14. Roger G. Betsworth. *The Radical Movement of the 1960's.* 1980.
15. Alice Cowan Cochran. *Miners, Merchants, and Missionaries: The Roles of Missionaries and Pioneer Churches in the Colorado Gold Rush and Its Aftermath, 1858-1870.* 1980.
16. Irene Lawrence. *Linguistics and Theology: The Significance of Noam Chomsky for Theological Construction.* 1980.
17. Richard E. Williams. *Called and Chosen: The Story of Mother Rebecca Jackson and the Philadelphia Shakers.* 1981.
18. Arthur C. Repp, Sr. *Luther's Catechism Comes to America: Theological Effects on the Issues of the Small Catechism Prepared In or For America Prior to 1850.* 1982.
19. Lewis V. Baldwin. *"Invisible" Strands in African Methodism.* 1983.
20. David W. Gill. *The Word of God in the Ethics of Jacques Ellul.* 1984.
21. Robert Booth Fowler. *Religion and Politics in America.* 1985.
22. Page Putnam Miller. *A Claim to New Roles.* 1985.
23. C. Howard Smith. *Scandinavian Hymnody from the Reformation to the Present.* 1987.

Scandinavian Hymnody from the Reformation to the Present

by
C. HOWARD SMITH

ATLA Monograph Series, No. 23

The American Theological
Library Association
and
The Scarecrow Press, Inc.
Metuchen, N.J., & London
1987

The author gratefully acknowledges permission to reprint the following:

Excerpts from George M. Stephenson's Religious Aspects of Swedish Immigration (Minneapolis: University of Minnesota Press, 1932). Reprinted by permission of the publisher.

Excerpts from Karl A. Olsson's By One Spirit (Chicago: Covernant Press, 1962). Reprinted by permission of the publisher.

Preface from the Covenant Hymnal (Chicago: Covenant Press, 1973), Reprinted by permission of the publisher.

Excerpts from J.C. Aaberg's Hymns and Hymnwriters of Denmark (Des Moines: Committee on Publication, Danish Evangelical Lutheran Church of America, 1945). Excerpts reprinted by permission of the Board of Publication of the Lutheran Church of America.

Excerpts from E.E. Ryden's The Story of Christian Hymnody (Rock Island, Augustana Press, 1959). Reprinted by permission of Fortress Press.

Excerpts from Oscar Lövgren's Psalm Och Sånglexikon (Stockholm: Gummessons Bokförlag, 1964). Reprinted by permission of the publisher.

Excerpts from Oscar Lövgren's Våra Psalm och Sångdiktare, (Stockholm, Gummessons Bokförlag, 1939). Reprinted by permission of the publisher.

Excerpts from G. Westin's De Frikyrkliga Samfunden i Sverige (Stockholm: Svenska Missions Förbundet Forlag, 1934). Reprinted by permission of the publisher.

Excerpts from Sånger och Psalmer (Stockholm: Svenska Missionsförbundet Förlag, 1951). Reprinted by permission of the publisher.

Excerpts from J. Nörregaard's Baptist Work in Denmark, Finland, Norway and Sweden (Stockholm: Westerbergs Förlag, 1967). Reprinted by permission of Libris Media A.B. Örebro, Sweden.

Excerpts from G. Westin's Den Kristna Friförsamlingen i Norden (Stockholm: Westerbergs Förlag, 1956). Reprinted by permission of Libris Media A.B. Örebro, Sweden.

Library of Congress Cataloging-in-Publication Data

Smith, Charles Howard, 1915-
    Scandinavian hymnody from the Reformation to the present.

    (ATLA monograph series ; no. 23)
    Bibliography: p.
    Includes index.
    1. Hymns, Scandinavian--History and criticism.
I. Title. II. Series.
BV489.5.S64 1987   264'.2'0948   87-1001
ISBN 0-8108-1938-4

Excerpts from the foreword of Psalm och Sång (Stockholm: Westerbergs Och Oms Förlag, 1966). Reprinted by permission of Libris Media A.B. Örebro, Sweden.

Excerpt from Veckoposten (Stockholm: March 17, 1966). Reprinted by permission of the editor.

Excerpts from Kenneth Scott Latourette's A History of Christianity (New York: Harper and Brothers, 1953). Reprinted by permission of the publisher.

• CONTENTS

Editor's Foreword

Preface

x

• EDITOR'S FOREWORD

Since 1972 the American Theological library Association has undertaken responsibility for a modest monograph series in the field of religious studies. Our aim in this series is to published two dissertations of quality each year at reasonable cost. Titles are selected from studies in a wide range of religious and theological disciplines. We are pleased to publish Charles Howard Smith's study of Scandinavian hymnody as number twenty-three in our series.

Following theological and musical studies at Eastern Baptist Theological Seminary in Philadelphia, Charles Howard Smith took an M.Mus. at the University of Southern California and completed a doctorate in musicology at the University of Minnesota. From 1948 until 1980 Dr. Smith served as Professor of Music at Bethel College and Bethel Theological Seminary in St. Paul, Minnesota. Author of several articles on church music, Dr. Smith, now Emeritus Professor of Music at Bethel College and Seminary, resides in Arden Hills, Minnesota.

Kenneth E. Rowe
Series Editor

Drew University Library
Madison, N.J.   07940

• PREFACE

There is a scarcity of detailed writings in English on the hymnody of the State Church and the Free Churches of Scandinavia. Ernest Ryden's The Story of Christian Hymnody is perhaps the only book to give a significant place to the hymnody of Scandinavia. Julian's Dictionary of Hymnology touches on various phases of Scandinavian state-church hymnody but could give no space to that of the free-church tradition. The year of publication, 1892, would preclude the possibility of any such inclusion. Even Albert Bailey's monumental work, The Gospel in Hymns, makes no mention of Scandinavian hymnody.

Dissertations and theses, such as Gerhard M. Cartford's "The Contribution of Ludwig Lindeman to the Hymnology of the Norwegian Church," Lee Olof Gustaf Olson's "History of Swedish Church Music," Brynolf Lundholm's "An Analysis of the Swedish Chorale," Carl T. Hjortsvang's "Scandinavian Contributions to American Sacred Music," and Henry Daquin's "Pietism and the Traditional Worship Practices of the Lutheran Church," all touch on the subject to a greater or lesser degree but not in any detail. Thus it is the purpose of this book to trace the development of hymnody in Scandinavia from the Protestant Reformation to the present time with special emphasis on free-church hymnody.

Chapter I presents a short history of the Reformation in in Scandinavia, particularly in Sweden, and its resultant impact on the hymnody of the church. The contribution of Olavus Petri and the Psalmbok of Jesper Swedberg receive special emphasis. This particular detail concerning the Reformation is justified because of its continuing influence on the hymnody of the Scandinavian Free Churches.

xiii

Chapter II deals with the rise and development of the Free Churches of Scandinavia which were influenced by Anglo-American Free Churches and Moravian Pietism. The Mission Covenant, Methodist, Baptist, and Pentecostal denominations are discussed in their relationship to the entire movement in the Scandinavian countries: Norway, Sweden, and Denmark.

Chapter III is concerned with the hymnody of the Pietist movement in the Scandinavian countries and its background in the hymnody of German Pietism. A sketch of the hymnody and church music practices of the Pietists in Germany is included in this chapter.

Chapter IV contains an examination, discussion, and evaluation of the hymns and hymn writers of the Free Churches of Scandinavia with a more detailed treatment of the contributions of the Baptists of Sweden.

The influence of state-church hymnody on the hymnody of the Free Church and a reciprocal influence is the concern of Chapter V. A study of both texts and tunes in representative hymnals was involved in the gathering of materials for this chapter.

Chapter VI presents an evaluation of the present status of free-church hymnody in the Scandinavian countries and the most recent developments in the hymnody of the State Church and the Free Churches of Scandinavia.

Chapter VII contains a short history of the free-church movement among the Scandinavian people in the United States. An analysis of denominational hymnals among the Scandinavian churches is also contained in this chapter.

Primary sources for this research include the three-volume set by the Swedish hymnologist, Oscar Lövgren, Våra Psalm-och Sångdiktare and his Psalm och Sånglexikon, as well as the forewords to the many hymnals and chorale books made available for this study. The three works by Gunnar Westin dealing with the free-church movement in Scandinavia provided most of the historical background material for the second chapter. The books by Waddams, Latourette, Karl Olsson and Grimm supplemented these detailed histories of Westin. Magazine articles on Scandinavian hymnody of the free-church variety plus the many items of personal correspondence from cooperative persons in Sweden, Norway, and Denmark furnished additional pertinent information, particularly concerning present-day Scandinavian hymnists. Materials from the abovementioned dissertations shed additional light on information gleaned from other sources, in addition to substantiating the information obtained from the same.

ACKNOWLEDGMENTS

The writer is indebted to Bethel Theological Seminary in St. Paul, Minnesota, for the use of the many old hymnals of Scandinavian origin housed in the archives of the library. This courtesy saved many hours of work in tracking down items of primary source materials. Pastors and church musicians in the Twin Cities area have been most gracious in lending hymnals and other books pertinent to this project. Pastors, denominational leaders, and publishers in Scandinavia cooperated to the fullest extent in locating and mailing many free-church denominational hymnals without which this research would have been impossible.

The writer's father-in-law, the late Rev. Joseph E. Tanquist, spent scores of hours in the translation of materials from the Swedish, Norwegian and Danish languages. Without his help, the completion of this project would have been impossible.

Heartfelt thanks and appreciation are expressed to the writer's advisor and counselor, Johannes Riedel, Professor Emeritus of the University of Minnesota. Dr. Riedel gave of his time in many sessions in offering helpful suggestions as to the scope of this study as well as materials and procedures. His encouragement over the many years of graduate study has kept the final goal in sight at all times.

Mr. Bertil Franzen, Rektor of Betelseminariet in Stockholm, Sweden, provided help by making the historical material in Chapter II more accurate and complete. The author is also indebted to Mr. Bernie Erickson, also of Sweden, who translated much of the materials in the section on recent developments in Scandinavian hymnody in Chapter VI. Mr. J. Irving Erickson of Chicago, an eminent hymnologist on Scandinavian hymnody, offered many helpful suggestions along the way toward the completion of this work. His words of encouragement have been much appreciated.

The author's wife, Dorothea, spent many hours typing the first draft of the original study. The author is indebted further to his daughter, Lois Jacobs, for her typing the final draft of the manuscript.

C. Howard Smith

Arden Hills, Minnesota

CHAPTER I

THE REFORMATION IN SCANDINAVIA
AND ITS HYMNODY

The Church in Sweden in the
Sixteenth Century

The main developments in the Swedish Reformation occurred between the years 1523 and 1593. In 1523 Gustavus
Vasa was crowned king of Sweden, an event which ushered
in a new era in Sweden's religious and political history. In
1593 the great Council of Uppsala established Lutheranism as
the official state religion.

The sixteenth century was a period of unrest in Sweden.
There was growing dissatisfaction with the Papacy because of
its involvement with Denmark in its invasion of the country
and because of its effort to bring Sweden under the Danish
crown. The Danish king Christian II was able by deceit to
emerge victor in his struggle with Sweden. His victory was
celebrated in a massacre which occurred in Stockholm in 1520.

Gustavus Vasa, who had been a participant in this rebellion, escaped from incarceration in Denmark in 1520 and
returned to Sweden to free his country from Danish rule.
This self-styled, zealous emancipator received allegiance from
many of the Swedish people and established his first army in the
Province of Dalarna. By June of 1523, Sweden had fallen to
Gustavus, and he was elected king by the Swedish Parliament
on June 4. His final confirmation as king had to wait until
1528, due to persistent unrest in foreign and domestic affairs.
During this five-year period, Gustavus formulated plans and
policies which were to transform thoroughly the Church in
Sweden. Bergendoff thus evaluates the significance of these
years:

The decade 1521-1531 witnessed some of the most important, if not the most important, events in Swedish
history. This was the period of the foundation of
the modern Swedish State, which had its beginnings
in the reign of Gustavus Vasa. During these years,
too, came the transformation in language and literature, for the literary productions of this period determined the cultural character of the new nation.
And that which is the subject of this investigation,
the nature of the Swedish Reformation, can be understood only against the background of these years.
This decade saw the transformation of the Church
from a wealthy and powerful organization, obedient
and loyal to Rome, into a body dependent upon the
king for its support and authority, and in matters
of doctrine pledged to preach an evangelical faith.
The period is full of dramatic interest, and its leading personalities are virile. Our study centers in
the man who gave the new nation its spiritual training, and influenced its religious and cultural destiny.
But his work would have been impossible without the
king, who built a new State and remodeled the ecclesiastical structure.[1]

That the Church "was the most united, the most powerful and the wealthiest body in the country at the opening of
the sixteenth century cannot be doubted."[2] In the year he
was elected king, Gustavus realized that the power of Rome
had to be reckoned with. This was to be his principal mission in the ensuing years.

In 1523 Gustavus made the acquaintance of three men
who were to be influential on him and the whole Reformation
in Sweden: Laurentius Andrae, the archdeacon of the Cathedral Church; Olavus Petri, a teacher at the Cathedral School;
and Laurentius Petri, the younger brother of Olavus. Olavus
was to have the greatest influence on Gustavus. He was
called to Stockholm in 1524 to serve as preacher, an appointment which shows how willing the king was to listen to his
message attacking the temporal power of the Church. More
will be mentioned concerning Olavus Petri and his contribution to the Reformation in Sweden. In passing, it should be
noted that he spent time in study at the University of Wittenberg and brought many of Luther's ideas and Scriptural inter-
pretations back with him upon his return to Sweden.

Correspondence between Gustavus and the pope was carried on quite extensively during the latter part of 1523. Neither the king nor the pope were to compromise or move from their respective positions. According to reputable historians, the severance from Rome can be dated as of November 1523, although it was to take four more years of discussion and correspondence before the crisis came. Olavus Petri caused some consternation when, in addition to his preaching of Reformation doctrine, he married. In spite of the bishop's letter of protest, Gustavus upheld the action of Olavus Petri. He was persistent in his overcoming of opposition, and the archbishop was increasingly aware of his impotence to stem the tide of the Reformation as it was slowly but surely being carried out by the king.

Protestant advances in the sixteenth century were many and significant. A few of the rules set forth by the Parliament of Vesterås provide background for this study:

1. The Word of God was to be taught in simplicity.

2. The Gospel was to be taught in all schools.

3. The ability to preach was to be the criterion for ordination.

4. The election of bishops was to be confirmed by the king.

5. The church and the nobility were to derive their power from the crown.[3]

The Parliament of Vesterås brought the power of the king into focus in no uncertain terms.

Other significant advances in the Protestant cause are worth citing. In February of 1526, the first Protestant book, Een Nyttwgh Wnderwijsning (An Useful Teaching), was published, and in August of the same year, a translation of the New Testament, ordered by the king, was ready for distribution. Bergendoff says, "In their quiet but increasingly strong influence on public opinion, these books laid a foundation in public opinion on which the king continued to build a new State and a new Church-order."[4]

It had been nearly four years since Gustavus Vasa had been elected to the throne of Sweden; and although he had often been reminded of the propriety of a coronation, he wanted to make absolutely sure of his position before proceeding with that pompous ceremony. When his position was believed to be secured, he set the coronation for the Epiphany season of 1528. After further negotiations and appeasements were made with the party of the opposition, the coronation of Gustavus took place on January 12, 1528. Bergendoff describes the procedure at the coronation:

> The preacher of the day was Olavus Petri, and in clear, almost stern, language he read the law of obedience to the people, and the law of responsibility to the king. Five years earlier, at Strengnäs, when Gustavus Vasa had been elected king, he had heard Olavus Petri proclaim the Lutheran doctrines. Since then the king had put some of those doctrines into practice, and on this day an evangelical preacher preached the coronation sermon for an evangelical king in the archepiscopal church of Sweden.[5]

The opposition to the king was not at an end by any means. Even though church polity was only moderately changed, charges were leveled against the reformer-king. Waddams has made this observation in his short history of the Church in Sweden:

> At Ephiphany 1528 three bishops were consecrated by Petrus Magni, according to the old ritual, and thus the Apostolical Succession was retained at the beginning of the movement for reform. The same year saw the coronation of Gustaf, who called a Church council in Örebro in the following year, 1529. This Council is interesting in showing the slow way in which developments came. Saints' days were reduced to reasonable proportions, but there was no idea of doing away with the old habits and religious customs. As to ceremonies, most of them were retained and the main emphasis was put on the need for explaining them, so that they should not be superstitious habits. Various steps were taken to improve the knowledge of the clergy; the town priests were to be learned, and able to teach their country brethren.[6]

After the Council at Öbrebro, revolt continued particularly in the southern part of Sweden. Gustavus was charged with introducing Lutheran heresy, despoiling cloisters and churches, and degrading and debasing the sacraments.[7] Among other charges, it was declared that he ate meat during Lent and encouraged others to do the same. Complaints were forthcoming because it was told that the Mass was celebrated in Swedish, the Virgin Mary was no longer venerated, and priests, monks and nuns were forced to marry. To these charges the king replied that whatever was wrong would be righted in due time. A quote from the book by J. G. H. Hoffmann, L'Eglise vit et ne se rend pas, concerning the state of worship and theology at this time had been included by Waddams; it partly refutes the charges leveled at the Reformers by those loyal to Rome:

> There was no desire to destroy at any cost: the newly found faith of the Northern people would not allow it; it wanted to christianize, to evangelize, to construct. Catholic customs were retained with the exception of certain practices like the use of holy water and incense, and the blessing of palms. The feasts of the Saints and the Virgin Mary were kept and also the elevation in the Mass, the services of Matins, Vespers and Compline as well as the use of priests' vestments.... At the same time the Reformation proclaimed the principle of the absolute authority of Holy Scripture in the Church, God's salvation of sinners by grace alone through Jesus Christ, the necessity for prayer and reading of the Bible, which had been completely translated into Swedish in 1541. The Reformation totally rejected all formal and mechanical piety and the traces of paganism which remained in the veneration of relics.[8]

The opposition to the decisions of the Parliament of Vesterås and the Council at Örebro testify of the resistance to the Protestant Reformation. Gustavus was yet to encounter more opposition to his reforms ere the church of the Reformation became recognized and tolerated by the party of the opposition.

Olavus Petri and the Swedish Reformation

As had been indicated previously, Olavus Petri is considered to be foremost among those who sowed the seeds of

reform in the Church in Sweden. Because of his contribution
in many areas, he is accorded a major place in this brief summary of the Swedish Reformation.

Olavus Petri was born on January 6, 1493, in the town
of Örebro, which was an important commercial and military
city. Little is known about his parents or concerning the
early life of either Olavus or his brother Laurentius. In the
city of Örebro was a Carmelite monastery which was established in 1418. In all probability it was in this school that
the Petri brothers learned much about the teachings of the
church in addition to the ordinary curriculum in reading and
writing. Instruction was also given in various parts of the
liturgy, and memorization of the same part of the educational
procedure.

His formal training, about which comparatively little is
known, included two years each at the universities of Leipzig (1514-1516) and Wittenberg (1516-1518). The years at
Wittenberg were important not only to Olavus but to the entire world. During this time Martin Luther preached against
the sale of indulgences, and on that eventful day of October
31, he nailed his ninety-five theses to the door of the church
at Wittenberg. Subsequent developments concerning Luther
and the Church no doubt made deep and lasting impressions
on the young student. His contact with the "great reformer"
in the classroom had great effect and manifested itself in many
ways in Olavus' contribution to the Reformation. Bergendoff
has evaluated the influence of these years in Wittenberg:

> What had Olavus Petri received in Wittenberg from
> 1516 to 1518? We cannot know. But it is hard to
> believe that Luther had not left enduring marks on
> his development. He must have lost faith in Scholas-
> ticism and come to see in the Bible the only source
> of spiritual truth. His eyes had been opened to the
> abuses existing in the Church, and the events of
> 1518 had shaken the doctrine of the supremacy of the
> pope. Above all, he had heard of a righteousness
> of God that is given freely to those who believe, and
> cannot be earned by any number of kind of good
> works. At the same time, it should be remembered
> that he had heard of no division of the Church. The
> problem was not one of breaking away from the Church;
> it was rather one of restoring what had been lost or

forgotten during the development of abuses and foreign doctrines. Throughout his career Olavus held
that in Sweden there had been no falling away from
the Church. When, ten years later, he wrote, "We
will always claim to be part of that Christian communion which is not limited only to Rome, but exists
throughout the whole earth," he was consistent with
what he had heard and learned in Wittenberg.[9]

Olavus returned to Sweden sometime in 1519, but the
reason for his return cannot be precisely determined. The
autumn of 1520 was a most crucial time in Swedish history.
It will be remembered that this was the time of the great
Blood Bath under the Danish king. According to tradition,
both Olavus and Laurentius nearly lost their lives, but this
cannot be fully substantiated. His later description of the
gruesome events indicates that at least he was an eyewitness.

Before his ordination to the ministry, Olavus was appointed teacher of the Cathedral School in Strengnäs by Laurentius Andreae, a high administrative office in that city. This
appointment was confirmed in the same year, 1520. In this
strategic post he was also given the privilege of preaching in
the cathedral. Because of his years of study under Martin
Luther, quite naturally the teachings of the great reformer
colored the preaching of Olavus. He soon attracted attention
and also brought down the wrath of those loyal supporters
of the Roman Church.

Olavus' attitude toward Scripture and his concept of
the church and the mass definitely colored his ministry.
Whether his accusers "read in" more to his beliefs and ut-
terances than Olavus really meant to say is open to question
and speculation, but one thing is certain--he was to influence
Sweden to a great extent in these days of religious upheaval
and reform. As teacher in the Cathedral School, he greatly
influenced Laurentius Andreae, who was several years his
senior. While the younger was concerned with enriching the
Church through a renewed emphasis on the Bible, the older
saw far-reaching implications for both the Church and the
State.

The sphere of Olavus' influence extended to Gustavus
Vasa who, as indicated previously, was elected king of Sweden
in 1523. As the king heard Olavus preach, he was impressed

with the fresh doctrine which was presented in the sermons.
He inquired of the Archdeacon Laurentius concerning the young
preacher and his message; in reply Laurentius traced the origin of the movement under Martin Luther and no doubt made
clear to the king what he had previously heard about the
events and controversy in Wittenberg. Thus it seems that
Laurentius was actually the first to enlighten the king and
sow seeds of reform in his heart and mind. Laurentius was
to be his guide for five years in the "transformation of the
structure and spirit of the Church."

In 1524 Olavus was appointed by the king to a new post
as secretary of the City Council in Stockholm. He also served
as preacher at the St. Nicholas Church in the capital city.
When the new pastor, Hicolaus Stecker, came to St. Nicholas,
it meant that two former students of Luther were in strategic
posts in Stockholm. The atmosphere was now conducive to
the continuation of the work of the Reformation, and great
things were to be accomplished in the ensuing years.

The year 1526 was important in the history of the Swedish Reformation. As has been previously mentioned, An Useful Teaching appeared in February and proposed the basic
Biblical doctrine concerning man and God's dealings with him,
and in August 1526 came the first translation of the New Testament in Swedish. The royal coat of arms was printed on the
last page indicating the king's approval of the work. The
authorship of these volumes has been disputed over a period
of years. Since the sixteenth century, credit for the Biblical translation has gone to both Laurentius Andreae and Olavus
Petri. Scholars have credited both Laurentius and Olavus with
the authorship of An Useful Teaching, although Olavus is
generally conceded to be the author. The 1908 discovery of
an unknown work by Olavus Petri shows a close identity to
An Useful Teaching. The difference in language between
this volume and Olavus' court records presents still another
problem in the authenticity of its authorship. It still remains
an open question with some reputable scholars. There are
those who have even had questions concerning the translators
of the New Testament. It has been good intellectual exercise
for those who have pursued these questions, but, in the final
analysis, they are not crucial to this particular study.

In Olavus Petri, Martin Luther had one of the greatest
exponents of his doctrines. Like Luther, he was called upon

on many occasions to defend his faith with all of its implications for the Church and State. His first polemical writing, Reply to an Unchristian Letter, appeared in March 1527, directed to a Danish monk, Paulus Eliae, who had strong sympathy with the Roman Church and tried to refute the teachings of Luther in a letter which had wide circulation.

In the work Olavus defends Luther and challenges the accusations of Paulus dealing with such matters as Luther's teaching on faith versus works, the sacraments, the temporal power of the Church, the nature of revelation, and the doctrine of the saints.

Besides his defense of Luther, other polemical works by Olavus appeared between 1527 and 1528. Again, the authorship of some is questionable. The following are among those credited to Olavus:

A Little Book concerning the Sacraments

A Short Instruction Concerning Marriage

A Little Book on Monastic Life

Concerning the Word of God

It is evident from all of Olavus' activity in the Swedish Reformation that his writings had a definite purpose in his defense against charges and for religious and political reform. Their purpose was to enhance the progress of the Reformation in his own country.[10]

Olavus Petri's Contribution to the Liturgy

Of basic interest to this particular study is the contribution of Olavus Petri to the whole area of liturgies. Bergendoff has evaluated his contribution in the opening paragraph of chapter five of his book:

In regard to the form and material of the service in the Swedish Church no one had had so directive an influence as he. The form of service suggested by him is in use today, with few modifications, in the Established Church of Sweden. His collections of songs laid the foundation of the Swedish Hymn Book.

His Manual of Service, or "Handbook," has the distinction of being the first of its kind to appear in
any Protestant Church. His Postils went far to create
the body and soul of the preaching of the Church of
his own country. To the determination of the form
of worship and of the character of religious instruction Olavus Petri meant to the Swedish Church what
Luther meant to the Evangelical Church in Germany.
The genius of the Swedish Reformer, here as elsewhere, manifests itself not in creation of new forms
and doctrines, but in selection of material produced
by the German Reformation and emphasis on what he
considered essential and best.[11]

The Swedish Mass (Svenska Messan) first appeared in
Stockholm in 1531, although from its subtitle we learn that it
was in use before that, probably by 1528. In the same year,
Olavus Petri defended the use of the vernacular in a pamphlet,
Why the Mass Ought to Be Held in Swedish. Many consider
the Svenska Messan to be the Swedish counterpart of Luther's
Deutsche Messe. This can be readily understood. Bergendoff
has made an interesting comparison between the two in his
monumental work. Similarities between the Swedish Mass and
others in the German have also been discovered. Bergendoff
goes into great detail in comparing it with one found in Sluter's Low German Songbook of 1531. The Swedish Mass by
Olavus contains an appendage of the Seven Pentetential Psalms
translated into Swedish, with the suggestion that these be
used as Introits to the service.

Bergendoff suggests that Olavus' work was not merely
a translation from the German, but that he selected the form
in accordance with the needs of his own people, excluding
and including certain items of the liturgy and offering suggestions as to the execution of those which were used. He
has been accused of Calvinistic tendencies in his desire to
drop the singing of the mass, but these charges cannot be
fully substantiated. He did attempt to adapt the mass to the
conditions in Sweden at the time. The Roman Mass was still
popular and continued to be used as late as 1539 when the
Swedish Mass was finally accepted and approved.

Bergendoff has asserted that the collection of songs of
Olavus Petri became the foundation of the Swedish Hymn-Book.
After a rather cursory discussion of the introduction of Chris-

tianity into Sweden and the Swedish Reformation under Gustavus Vasa, the brothers Petri, and other leaders, it is natural to follow with the early hymnody of the Reformation
Church and ultimately to show its influence on the hymnody
of the Free Church of Scandinavia.

One of the works by Olavus Petri published in 1526
was the first collection of Swedish hymns which later became
the Psalmbok. There is some disagreement as to how many
hymns were contained in this pamphlet-type book, but it is
believed that there were as many as twelve, including five
or six originals and an equal number of translations from
Luther's first collection of 1524. The book passed through
at least three editions in which some changes were made from
the original. The edition of 1530 is believed to have contained
mostly originals by Olavus and some additional stanzas to one
of the original number in the 1526 book. According to Lövgren, complete copies are extant of the edition of 1536. This
contains forty-six songs of which Olavus wrote no more than
eight. Probably this was the last book of its kind published
under his sponsorship.[12]

The 1536 song book bears a most interesting and complete title: Svenska Sånger eller Wisor nu på nytt pretade
forökade, och under en annan skick ä tilforenna utsatte (Swedish songs or hymns newly printed, enlarged and published
in a different form from the preceding one). The inclusion
of the "Wisor" would indicate a carry-over from the edition of
1531. The book with this title went through two more editions in 1542 and 1543. In 1549 the last and an enlarged edition of this series was printed with the title Then Svenska
Psalmboken, which today remains the official title of the State
Church hymnal of Sweden.

An examination of the available hymns of Olavus Petri
reveals a close affinity between the German and Swedish Re-
formations. In the 1530 edition some of the hymns are translations of their German models found in several German collections. This would be a natural procedure due to Olavus'
close connection with Martin Luther and German hymnody.
The books which appear to have been the most influential in
the compilation of the Swedish hymnal seem to come from Low-
German sources, i.e., those of Speratus (1526) and Sluter
(1531). It is not possible to include a detailed analysis or
comparative study between the German and Swedish sources

at this juncture, but it is worth noting that in the 1526 book
are to be found hymns based on well-known psalms from the
German, among them "A Mighty Fortress." Occasional hymns
are included such as were to be used for special portions of
the Mass and seasonal celebrations.

Again it is difficult to ascertain that Olavus Petri edited,
translated, and published these books, but a lack of evidence
to the contrary seems to point to him as the logical person.
The strongest argument in his favor, as Bergendoff points
out, is that the Swedish originals are parallel to passages in
other of Olavus' prose writings.[13]

Lövgren has indicated that in the 1530 Psalmbok there
is a supplement of four ditties (visor) about the Antichrist
and his characteristics. These are polemics directed against
the pope and the practices of the Roman Church. No doubt
they were written when "defamatory outpourings were freely
repeated in daily on-going, at a time when the battle was
waged between Catholicism and Protestantism in Sweden."
The author appears to have been Olof Svensson, a school
teacher in Stockholm.[14]   (See Appendix A.)

Before the Reformation there was an abundance of Latin
hymns peculiar to the Scandinavian countries. G.E. Klemming
of Stockholm collected enough hymns for a four-volume set
and published them in 1885-1887 under the title Latinska
Sånger Fordom Använda i Svenska Kyrkor och Skolor. No
doubt some were sung between stanzas of sequences as well
as during some of the office hours of the church. These
continued to be used in the worship of the Lutheran congregations.

During the early days of the Swedish Reformation, the
Latin was not always displaced by the vernacular in the singing of hymns. In one of the letters of Gustavus Vasa, he
makes a comparison between the two choices in singing, an
indication that Latin was still used on occasion in the singing
of hymns as well as in the regular service of the Mass. But
singing in the vernacular was firmly entrenched in the church
in Sweden and gained in popularity as did the Swedish New
Testament.

Regarding the practice of singing in the church, it
should be pointed out that Olavus defended the singing of

hymns by the people on scriptural grounds in his preface to
the 1536 edition. In Germany books were primarily for use
by the officiating clergy and perhaps the choir, and it may
be assumed that the Swedish books, as well, were for the
same purpose. Basically, however, Olavus' idea was the same
as Luther's: people should be permitted to express their
faith in both private and corporate worship by participating
in the singing of hymns. Lövgren has set 1571 as the year
when the hymns came into general usage. Many people, prior
to this time, did not seem to understand the purpose of the
old and new songs and degraded them by chanting them while
drinking in the ale houses "without regard for godliness or
Christian discipline aimed for in the churches."[15]

But singing was a "must" at this time of reformation
and renewal, and the new-found faith attained expression in
outbursts of prayer and praise. Thus, like Martin Luther,
Olavus Petri contributed to their spiritual development and
edification in many ways, not the least of which was his supply
of Christian hymns in their native tongue. Although Julian
gives credit to Laurentius Petri as the father of Swedish hymnody, the honor must go to Olavus.

Bergendoff has paid tribute to Olavus Petri at the end
of his book in a most fitting manner:

> It is not too much to claim for Olavus Petri that he
> was the prophet of the Swedish evangelical communion.
> In the days of disintegration and destruction of the
> old, he saw clearly the character of a new church.
> His writings reveal an understanding of the fundamen-
> tal principles of the Christian community, and his en-
> deavor was to put first things first. The extreme
> measures adopted by Gustavus Vasa toward the ma-
> terial organization of the Church, time and wiser de-
> cisions could remedy. But had the period of the
> transformation lacked the spiritual truth and wisdom
> and candor of Olavus Petri, it would have lacked a
> soul, and the Reformation would have destroyed spiri-
> tual as well as material treasures. Olavus Petri knew
> the power of destruction. He preferred the power of
> construction. The heart rather than the altar must
> witness the first reformation. He set himself to the
> task of making available the treasures of Scripture,
> liturgy, and song of the Christian Church to his

fellow countrymen. He pointed out more insistently
the things that should be kept than the things that
should be abolished. Patiently, fearlessly, humbly,
faithfully he used every mode of expression in his
power to build up the true invisible realities of Christian religion. The further history of the Swedish
Reformation, and of the Swedish Church, was a reali-
zation of the ideals presented by Olavus Petri long
before that Church understood the nobility and ful-
ness of those ideals. He taught the Swedish people
to read, but more than that, he taught them the
relationship of the Book to their life in home and
Church and State.[16]

Hymns and Collections of the Late Reformation

After the death of Olavus Petri, his brother Laurentius
(1499–1573) succeeded him as the spiritual leader of Swedish
Protestantism and the first evangelical archbishop. Olavus
had radical leanings as leader of the Swedish Reformation,
whereas Laurentius tended to be more conservative. Like
Luther, he desired to retain what was good in the Roman
service. His efforts to save Gregorian Chant were not successful due to the problem of accent and the new language,
a situation which the Roman Church has had to face today in
its liturgical reforms. The Roman Mass had officially been
forbidden in Stockholm around the year 1539, and in 1571
Laurentius suggested some six chorales as substitutes for the
Introit and the Graduale. However, Gregorian melodies were
used with vernacular words for a considerable time, but finally
gave way to Protestant songs; purely Latin hymns continued
to be used into the seventeenth century. According to Brynolf Lundholm, the Gregorian Chant continued to lose ground
over a period of thirty years, and with the Radical Handbook
of 1614, the Latin texts were thrown out, the roots of Gregorian elements were cut off, and the way paved for congregational participation.[17]

Laurentius continued the work of his brother in issuing
several editions of the Psalmbok. The first under his sponsorship was published in 1567 and was the most complete to
date, containing approximately 102 and 114 hymns respectively,
which represented a great deal of new material. (The growth
in size and quality in fifty years is worth noting.) In the

1572 book, there appeared a song against drunkenness. That evangelical preachers needed to be admonished in this respect is indicated by the content of the song!

Laurentius Petri was succeeded as archbishop by one of similar name, Laurentius Petri Gothus (1530-1579), his son-in-law. While the elder Laurentius is considered to have been one of the best interpreters of Luther's psalms, Gothus and Olavus Petri rank highest as Swedish psalm writers.[18] Their psalms have appeared widely in Swedish hymnals.

Laurentius Joane Gestritius (d. 1597) is credited with the publication of a songbook, Psalms, Spiritual Ditties, and Songs of Praise, which was published twenty years after his death. For the most part, its contents consists of translations from German and Latin sources.

An edition of the Swedish Psalmbok appeared in the year 1586 in which there was appended an almanac and a home physician section containing the twelve signs of the Zodiac and their relation to the different parts of the human anatomy.[19] A much later edition in 1642 included, among several interesting items, some Danish originals and a "Birchbark song" called Nävervisan. Evidently the latter was so called because the tune was played by blowing on birch bark placed between the hands. Another novelty connected with this song was the arrangement of the fifteen verses in an acrostic spelling the author's name, a practice which was common at the time.[20]

Hymnody in Post-Reformation Sweden

The seventeenth century witnessed an increased interest in the hymnody of the Church. Congregational singing was now an accepted and enthusiastic practice, and music became prominent in the Church and school. Lundholm has pointed out that many books like those of Petrus Rudbeck were published, which contained psalms that were suitable for the texts of each Sunday and had greatly extended melodies. These Italian-style melodies were popular among the Swedish people. The chorale developed into an accompanied chant-like song as in Germany, and the rise of part singing also played an important role in the development of congregational songs in Sweden.[21]

In the seventeenth century there was continued interest in the texts of the German church songs. The church
in Sweden, as well as Germany, was still on guard against
Catholicism, and the inroads of Calvinism were of great concern. Lövgren has observed that the Church was

> ... contending for pure doctrine but with scant em-
> phasis on the spiritual life. But even in these dark
> days there appeared a number of psalm writers who
> dwelt on the passion of Christ. It is remarkable that
> a time when men tried to objectify spiritual things
> the new songs of individual experience came into
> prominence.[22]

At this time a number of German originals were translated into the Swedish language for use in corporate worship
or else were used as a basis for new evangelical songs. Among
the German writers appearing in Swedish books are the following:

> Basilus Fortsch (d. 1619)
> Johann Arndt (1555-1621)
> Martin Rutiluis (1550-1618)
> Johann Gross (1564-1654)
> Johann Heermann (1585-1647)
> Johann Rist (1607-1667)
> Paul Gerhardt (1607-1676)

Prominent among the Swedish translators of German psalms are
the following:

> Andreas Petri Amnelius (1638-1692)
> Hakan Ausius (d. 1653)
> Jacob Boethius (1647-1718)
> Petrus Brask (1650-1690)
> Bishop Johannes Geselius Jr. (1647-1718)

Besides translations from the German texts, more and
more interest was being shown in supplying the Swedish
Church with native hymnody. Lövgren has included several
names among the writers of seventeenth-century Sweden in
his first volume:

> Haquin Spegel (1645-1714)
>   Spegel held bishoprics in Skara and Lindköping

and was one of the foremost song writers previous
to J. O. Wallin. Only a few of his verses have
survived.

Israel Kolmodin (1643-1709)
>   Kolmodin was a Lutheran pastor and the author of
>   numerous Swedish psalms.

Jacob Arrhenius (1642-1729)
>   Arrhenius, a layman, and professor at the Univer-
>   sity of Uppsala, composed songs of pietistic flavor
>   and published a popular collection, many of which
>   centered around the person of Jesus.

Gustaf Ollon (1946-1704)
>   Ollon was another layman whose songs were criti-
>   cized as being too enthusiastic, mystical and fanati-
>   cal.

Erik Lindschöld (1634-1690)
>   Lindschöld was a member of the Swedish Parliament,
>   court poet and the writer of a few songs used by
>   the Church in Sweden.[23]

Jesper Swedberg and the Psalmboken of 1695

The seventeenth century in Sweden, as had been mentioned before, was a time of great productivity in the field
of hymnody. Clergy and laity alike were expressing their
new faith in poetic outbursts, resulting in both worthy and
unworthy poetry "on the market." The increase in hymns
naturally led to the compilation and publishing of new books
to be used officially and unofficially by the Church in Sweden.

Mention has already been made of the editions of 1586
and 1642 in which supplemental verses were included, but
the next "official" hymnbook was Gamla Uppsala psalmboken
of 1622, or the "old" Uppsala Psalmboken as it later became
known. Although this hymnal has no royal confirmation, it
was accepted by the Swedish church until 1645 and became
a model for future books. It contained most of the psalms in
use in that day. More officially recognized was the hymnal
of 1645, Then Svenska Uppsalapsalmboken (The Swedish Uppsala Psalmbook). A committee was appointed by the Swedish
Riksdag to oversee its publication; and while it was accepted
as the "official" hymnal, the use of others was not forbidden.
One other hymnal mentioned by Hjortsvang and Olson is entitled Åbopsalmboken of 1673. Little information has been

available concerning this book, but Olson has evaluated it
as the most important of the several which followed that of
1645.[24]

Uppsala Psalmboken, according to Lövgren, was to
serve the churches of the entire Swedish kingdom, but as
was previously the case, more and more songs were being
written and coming into use with a resultant confusion. He-
quin Spegel had been entrusted with the overseeing and
editing of a new book, but nothing came of this appointment
by the "committee" because the king had approached Jasper
Swedberg (1653-1735) to be chairman of the new project.
Swedberg was an ordained minister and had also been conse-
crated as bishop of Skara in 1732. As preacher in the king's
court, he was loyal to the Lutheran faith but showed signs
of sympathy toward the pietistic movement.

Work on the new book began in 1691 when Swedberg
conferred with Spegel concerning it. He was careful not to
make drastic changes in the old and well-loved psalms but
took more liberty with those of newer vintage. In 1694 the
book was sanctioned by the king after careful scrutiny by
duly appointed "readers" and officially published. This Gamla-
Psalmboken, as it later became known, contained 413 "psalms,"
of which Swedberg was supposed to have composed sixteen,
with twenty translations also by him.

As soon as the book was put on the market, a storm
of protest and criticism arose concerning it. It was attacked
for its heretical teaching, and Swedberg was accused of propa-
gating doctrines contrary to the Lutheran faith. Swedberg
did not deny the charges but simply stated that the "psalms"
that were cited had, for the most part, been included in early
books. Lövgren feels that the critics were stirred up by
some leading jealous preachers of the day who had personal
grievances against Swedberg. However, the king ordered
the book withdrawn and Swedberg, who had invested much
of his personal funds in its publication, sustained considerable loss. He related later that his work had come to good
use in the United States where the Swedes did not detect
errors in the songs.[25]

The archbishop of Uppsala was charged with the revision
of the 1694 book. This revision consisted of the deletion of
seventy-eight songs and the addition of nine others selected

by the archbishop and the theological faculty of the University of Uppsala. The work of Swedberg is in bold evidence, especially in the translations. Completed in 1695, the revised edition was adopted in 1698 and declared to be the "authorized book for the entire realm." The Swedberg psalmbook remained unsurpassed in usage and popularity until the J. O. Wallin edition of 1819.[26] (See Appendix B.)

Waddams' estimate of Swedberg's monumental volume is here quoted:

> The Swedish Hymn-book of 1695 owed much to Svedberg's inspiration. This book had a great influence on Church life, and also deeply affected Christian life in the homes of the people. In addition it also influenced cultural and artistic development, and stands in the forefront of a great Swedish tradition of hymnody.[27]

The Reformation in Denmark and Norway

Outside of Germany, the popularity of Luther's teachings is seen almost solely in the Scandinavian countries where the Reformation was closely linked with the political, social, and economic life of the people. Students such as Olavus Petri, who had studied at Wittenberg and returned to Scandinavia, plus German students who had settled in the north countries spread the teachings of Lutheranism in these localities. The main impetus for the spread of this new religious movement, however, came from the rulers themselves, as had been seen in the great part Gustavus Vasa played in Swedish religious life.

The Union of Kalmar in 1397 was supposedly an agreement that would unite the three Scandinavian countries under the Danish king. Each country retained its laws and customs, and the Swedes especially were rebellious against foreign rule. The Danish king, Christian II, was merely a figurehead as he continued to lose power, and quite generally the nobles and clergy increased in power and wealth. By the time of the Reformation, half the land in Denmark was in the hands of the clergy.

The king had more success in Denmark than in Sweden.

Although he ignored his promises made before his accession
to the throne, he declared in favor of the peasants and towns-
men by his actions toward the nobility. Rebellion ensued;
in 1523 he was deposed by the nobility and the clergy, and
Duke Frederick was proclaimed king.

The new king was divided in his loyalty between clergy
and nobility. He made use of Lutheranism to attain his own
desired ends by encouraging the spread of Reformation teaching. In 1524 the first Danish version of the New Testament
appeared followed by a new version in 1529 which was edited
by Christian Petersen, the "father of Danish literature."

Frederick virtually assumed the position of the pope
when, in 1526, he "repudiated the papal nominee to the archbishopric of Lund, and with the consent of the royal Council
confirmed another candidate and retained the confirmation
fees instead of sending them to the pope."28

The Lutheran cause was further strengthened in Denmark when Frederick's son, Christian, who began to introduce
the Lutheran service into the duchies of Schleswig and Hol-
stein, became ruler in 1526. He appointed court chaplains,
thus freeing them from the control of Rome. Although he
made some concessions when his accusers rose up against
him, the Reformation spread rapidly in Denmark as it did in
Sweden. When Christian III became king in 1536, Lutheranism was declared the state religion at the national assembly
in Copenhagen. The Church Ordinance approved by Martin
Luther was adopted by the National Assembly of Odense in
1539 as the basic law of the Church of Denmark. The king
became head of the church; schools, hospitals, and churches
came under the jurisdiction of the appointed bishops.

Most church historians agree that no preparation had
been made for the Reformation in Norway. The reform in
the early stages took the form of plundering of wealthy churches and monasteries rather than the preaching of any new
Reformation doctrines. Norwegian antipathy to Frederic I
and Duke Christian was exhibited by Norway's participation
in the Danish civil war which grew out of the attempt of Christian II to regain his throne. Upon the victory of Christian
III in Denmark and the institution of the Lutheran Church as
the state religion, Norway was compelled to become a province
of Denmark.

The advent of Lutheranism in Norway followed naturally. The propagation of the faith was somewhat thwarted because teachers and preachers were few and the Danish language was not understood by the rank and file of the Norwegian people. They resented the imposition of the new faith, and unrest and dissatisfaction resulted. In reality the religious awakening in Norway had to wait until the eighteenth century, although, by order of the king, Lutheranism was established as it had been in Denmark.

The ordinances of the Roman Church forbade the laity to preach or sing in the services of the church, so, in all probability, hymns were not sung in Denmark except perhaps on special occasions. It is presumed that such singing could not be prohibited in the homes or private gatherings. Hans Thomisson includes five "old hymns" in his hymnal which was one of the important early hymnals in Denmark. He explained that these hymns were proof "that even during recent times of error there were pious Christians, who by the grace of God, preserved the true Gospel. And though these songs were not sung in the churches--which were filled with songs in Latin that the people did not understand--they were sung in the homes and before the doors."[29]

Alternating lines of Danish and Latin indicate that in all probability the hymns were sung responsively. Hymns to the Virgin Mary, as well as those of legendary character, were favorites among the earliest of Danish hymns. Of the latter type is one of the favorite Christmas hymns of Denmark which, in its beautiful recast by Grundtvig, is still a favorite among the Danish people:

> Christmas with gladness sounds,
> Joy abounds
> When praising God, our Father,
> We gather.
> We were in bondage lying,
> But He hath heard our prayer.
> Our inmost need supplying,
> He sent the Savior here.
> Therefore with praises ringing,
> Our hearts for joy are singing:
> All Glory, praise and might
> Be God's for Christmas night.

Right in a golden year,
Came He here.
Throughout a world confounded
Resounded
The tidings fraught with gladness
For every tribe of man
That He hath borne our sadness
And brought us joy again,
That He in death descended,
Like sun when day is ended,
  And rose on Easter morn
  With life and joy reborn.

He hath for every grief
Brought relief.
Each grateful heart His praises
Now raises.
With angels at the manger,
We sing the Savior's birth,
Who wrought release from danger
And peace to man on earth,
Who satisfies our yearning.
And grief to joy is turning
  Till we with Him arise
  And dwell in Paradise. [30]

Early Danish hymns, like the Swedish, were translations from
the Latin. Two of these were "Stabat Mater Delorosa" and
"Dies Est Lactilia in Ortu Regali," the latter recast by Grundtvig as "Joy Is the Guest of Earth Today."

Among the earliest of Danish originals before the Reformation are the following: "I Will Now Hymn His Praises Who
All My Sin Hath Borne," "On Mary, Virgin Undefiled Did God
Bestow His Favor," and "O Bride of Christ, Rejoice" (Advent
Hymn). "All ... breathe a truly evangelical spirit and testify
to a remarkable skill in the use of a language so sorely neglected."[31]

The best known of all the pre-Reformation hymns from
Denmark is entitled, by Thomisson, "The Old Christian Day
Song." Three manuscript copies are preserved in the library
at Uppsala, Sweden, the oldest of which is dated around 1450.
The song itself is thought to have been written before the
fifteenth century. Both Denmark and Sweden claim its possible origin.

Aaberg has included Grundtvig's revision in his book:

> With gladness we hail the blessed day
> Now out of the sea ascending,
> Illuming the earth upon its way
> And cheer to all mortals lending.
> God grant that His children everywhere
> May prove that the night is ending.
>
> How blest was that wondrous midnight hour
> When Jesus was born of Mary!
> Then dawned in the East with mighty power
> The day that anew shall carry
> The light of God's grace to every soul
> That still with the Lord would tarry.
>
> Should every creature in song rejoice,
> And were every leaflet singing,
> They could not His grace and glory voice,
> Thought earth with their praise were ringing,
> For henceforth now shines the light of life,
> Great joy to all mortals bringing.
>
> Like gold is the blush of morning bright,
> When day has from death arisen.
> Blest comfort too holds the peaceful night
> When skies in the sunset glisten.
> So sparkle the eyes of those whose hearts
> In peace for God's summons listen.
>
> Then journey we to our fatherland,
> Where summer reigns bright and vernal.
> Where ready for us God's mansions stand
> With thrones in their halls supernal.
> So happily there with friends of light
> We joy in the peace eternal. [32]

The significance of this song in pre-Reformation Danish hymnody is expressed by Aaberg thus:

> In this imperishable song, Pre-Reformation hymnody
> reached its highest excellence, an excellence that
> later hymnody seldom has surpassed. "The Old Chris-
> tian Day Song" shows besides, that Northern hymn-
> writers even "during the time of popery" had caught
> the true spirit of Evangelical hymnody. There songs

were few, and they were often bandied about like
homeless waifs, but they embodied the purest Christian ideals of that day and served in a measure to
link the old church with the new.[33]

As was the case in Sweden, hymnody played a large
part in the Danish Reformation. The Romanists were caustic
in their criticism of the use of Danish "ballads" in the service
of worship. Since these songs of pre-Reformation vintage
proved to be so popular in Denmark, the leaders of Lutheranism used them to great advantage in the Protestant cause.

The earliest collection in Danish hymnody and perhaps
the first complete hymnal of the North was published by Hans
Mortensen in 1528. Julian considers him to have been the
first evangelical preacher in Malmö and the father of Danish
hymnody. Included in the collection are translations from
Latin, German, and Swedish plus some Danish originals and a
liturgy for the morning service. The book grew in popularity, and in 1529 a new edition was published by Mortensen
in Rostock. He was aided in this revision by Arvid Petersen
and Hans Spendemager. It contained thirty new hymns and
liturgies for the various Sunday services and is entitled Een
Ny Handbog med Psalmer og Aandelige Lofsange (A new handbook with psalms and spiritual songs of praise ...). Simul-
taneously with the various editions of this more or less official Danish hymnal small collections were made by Hans Tau-
sen, Arvid Petersen, and others. At a meeting of the Protestant leaders in Copenhagen, it was decided to revise these
collections and combine them into one book. Thus the first
common Danish hymnal was published in 1531. This was used
until 1544 when it was revised by Hans Jensen. The Danish
Psalmebog of 1569, compiled and revised by Hans Thomisson,
succeeded the 1544 edition. Known as Thomisson's Psalmbog,
it contained some 268 hymns, psalms, and sequences in both
Latin and Danish, set to appropriate tunes. Its popularity
is shown by its numerous reprints and general usage in the
Danish church for almost 150 years.

Aaberg decries that although in less than fifty years
the Reformation in Denmark had produced one of the finest
hymnals of the period, it did not produce a single hymn
writer of merit.[34] As had been indicated, the final hymnal
contained translations and some originals but no poems of
real merit. Aaberg has observed that although people loved

these new hymns and clung to them for many years, when
the newer and more worthy hymns appeared the old ones came
into disuse and very few are now in the Danish hymnal.[35]

The first notable hymn writer of the Danish Church
was Hans Christensen Sthen who failed to be accorded a place
by Julian. He was born about 1540 in Roskilde. Little is
known of his early life, but he is thought to have been well-
educated, excelling in oratory, writing, and translating. Des-
pite many adversities, he was for a long time the very successful pastor of the Lutheran Church in Malm. He became
famous as a writer through two small volumes of poetry entitled A Small Handbook Containing Diverse Prayers and Songs
with Some Rules for Life (1578) and A Small Wander Book
(1591).

Aaberg has provided translations of three of his very
fine hymns which reflect the deep Christian devotion and
humble spirit of their author:

MORNING HYMN

The gloomy night to morning yields,
So brightly the day is breaking;
The sun ascends over hills and fields,
And birds are with song awaking.
Lord, lend us Thy counsel and speed our days,
The light of Thy grace surround us.

Our grateful thanks to God ascend,
Whose mercy guarded our slumber.
May ever His peace our days attend
And shield us from troubles somber.
Lord, lend us Thy counsel and speed our days,
The light of Thy grace surround us.

Redeem us, Master, from death's strong hand,
Thy grace from sin us deliver;
Enlighten us till with Thine we stand,
And make us Thy servants ever.
Lord, lend us Thy counsel and speed our days,
The light of Thy Grace surround us.

Then shall with praise we seek repose
When day unto night hath yielded,

And safe in Thine arms our eyelids close
To rest by Thy mercy shielded.
  Lord, Lend us Thy counsel and speed our days,
  The light of Thy grace surround us.[36]

DEVOTIONAL HYMN

O Lord, my heart is turning
To Thee with ceaseless yearning
And praying for Thy grace.
Thou art my sole reliance
Against my foes' defiance;
Be Thou my stay in every place.

I offer a confession
Of my severe transgression;
In me is nothing good.
But, Lord, Thou wilt not leave me
And, like the world, deceive me;
Thou hast redeemed me with Thy blood.

Blest Lord of Life most holy,
Thou wilt the sinner lowly
Not leave in sin and death;
Thine anger wilt not sever
The child from Thee forever
That pleads with Thee for life and breath.

O Holy Spirit, guide me!
With wisdom true provide me;[37]

STHEN'S "NAME" HYMN*

Lord Jesus Christ,
My Savior blest,
My refuge and salvation,
I trust in Thee,
Abide with me,
Thy word shall be
My shield and consolation.

---

*In its unabbreviated form the first letters of the eight stanzas spell his name.

I will confide,
What 'e'er betide,
In Thy compassion tender.
When grief and stress
My heart oppress,
Thou wilt redress
And constant solace render.

When grief befalls
And woe appalls
Thy loving care enfolds me.
I have no fear
When Thou art near,
My Savior dear;
Thy saving hand upholds me.

Yea, help us, Lord,
With one accord
To love and serve Thee solely,
That henceforth we
May dwell with Thee
Most happily
And see Thy presence, holy.[38]

One more author deserves a place among Danish hymnists, although he did not make a lasting contribution to the field. In 1623 Anders Christensen Arrebo, Bishop of Tronhjem, published a metrical psalter containing a few hymns in addition to the Psalms of David. The volume never received wide acceptance or usage. The Danish Church clung tenaciously to the "old favorites" of Thomisson's hymnal which songs "were no longer imprinted on the pages of a book but in the very heart and affection of a nation."[39]

During the Reformation and well into the eighteenth century, Denmark and Norway had the same hymnody. This is understandable in the light of the previous discussion concerning the lack of a real enthusiasm in Norway for the Reformation and the strong ties between the two countries. According to Julian, although the Norwegians have allowed themselves considerable freedom in their choice of hymns, they have in the main followed the lead of Denmark.

Summary

From its inception, the Christian Church has been
known for its use of music, especially hymnody, in the propagation and expression of its faith.   In all three countries of
Scandinavia, the Church has witnessed a continual development in the writing and use of hymns from the time Christianity was introduced to the present day.

In Sweden one of the great contributors to the cause
of the Reformation was Olavus Petri who not only inspired the
reformer-king Gustavus Vasa by his preaching but also laid
the foundation for the hymnody of the Swedish Church through
his translations, original hymns, and the compilation of the
earliest hymnbooks. Some of his hymns survive to this day
in the State Church, as well as in the Free Churches of his
native land. His immediate successors carried on the work
begun by him, and the heritage of Swedish hymnody has continually been enriched by their dedicated efforts.

The Reformation in Norway, and more particularly in
Denmark, produced works in the field of hymnody just as
significant as those in Sweden, though less in number. From
the Mortensen hymnal of 1531 to the hymns of Hans Christensen Sthen, the Church has been edified by the poetic writings of men, limited in talent, but nevertheless intent on expressing their faith. The aim of this study is to trace the
development of Scandinavian hymnody from the early beginnings of this chapter to the present day.

NOTES

1. Conrad Bergendoff, Olavus Petri and the Ecclesiastical
       Transformation in Sweden (New York: Macmillan,
       1928), pp. 1, 2.
2. Ibid., p. 5.
3. Ibid., pp. 36, 37.
4. Ibid., p. 22.
5. Ibid., p. 44.
6. H. M. Waddams, The Swedish Church (London: Society
       for Promoting Christian Knowledge, 1946), p. 14.
7. Bergendoff, op. cit., p. 49.
8. Waddams, op. cit., p. 19.
9. Bergendoff, op. cit., p. 75, 76.

10. Ibid., p. 146.
11. Ibid., p. 147.
12. Oscar E. Lövgren, Våra Psalm Och Sångdiktare. 3 vols. (Stockholm: Svenska Missionsförbundet Förlag, 1937), I, p. 65.
13. Bergendoff, op. cit., p. 165.
14. Lövgren, op. cit., I, p. 70.
15. Ibid., p. 69.
16. Bergendoff, op. cit., pp. 250, 251.
17. Brynolf Lundholm, "An Analysis of the Swedish Chorale" (unpublished Master's thesis, Eastman School of Music, Rochester, New York, 1937), pp. 14, 15.
18. Lee Olof Gustaf Olson, "History of Swedish Church Music" (unpublished D.S.M. dissertation, Union Theological Seminary, New York, 1945), p. 39.
19. Lövgren, op. cit., I, pp. 77, 78.
20. Ibid., pp. 78, 79.
21. Lundholm, op. cit., p. 16.
22. Lövgren, op. cit., p. 81.
23. Ibid., pp. 125-140.
24. Olson, op. cit., p. 41.
25. Lövgren, op. cit., p. 81.
26. Ibid., p. 124.
27. Waddams, op. cit., p. 24.
28. Harold J. Grimm, The Reformation Era, 1500-1650 (New York: Macmillan, 1954, 1965), p. 238.
29. J. C. Aaberg, Hymns and Hymnwriters of Denmark (Des Moines: The Committee on Publication of the Danish Evangelical Lutheran Church in America, 1945), quoting from the hymnal by Hans Thomisson, p. 10.
30. Ibid., pp. 10, 11.
31. Ibid., p. 11.
32. Ibid., p. 12.
33. Ibid.
34. Ibid., p. 14.
35. Ibid., pp. 14, 15.
36. Ibid., p. 16.
37. Ibid., pp. 16, 17.
38. Ibid., pp. 17, 18.
39. Ibid., p. 18.

CHAPTER II

THE RISE AND EARLY DEVELOPMENT OF THE FREE CHURCHES IN SCANDINAVIA

The Pietistic Movement

Just as the Lutheran Reformation was a reaction to the status and practices of the Roman Church, so Pietism was a reaction to conditions, emphases, and practices of established Lutheranism. It could be considered a "counter reformation" in the broadest meaning of the term.

The Book of Concord had been accepted in 1580, and the worship practices of the State Church flourished during the sixteenth century. Following this period of prosperity and growth, the Reformation church went through a period of decline during the Thirty Years War (1618-1648). During this time churches were plundered and destroyed, pastors were persecuted and killed, and the spiritual life of the Church dropped to a very low level.

There followed in the wake of the Thirty Years War what was known as the period of Orthodoxy. The activity and emphasis of the Church during this time is summarized by Henry Daquin:

1. Church orders were reissued and legalistic and disciplinary measures were taken to enforce them.

2. Attendance at services was compulsory and fines were imposed for lack of attendance.

3. The people were compelled to go to confession and receive the Sacrament.

4. The "Herr" Pastor had to be obeyed.

5. Congregational participation in the service was
    limited because people were not familiar with the
    music of the liturgy. The choir and cantor took
    over the major portion of the service.

6. The doctrine of faith was almost forgotten and
    when emphasized it was of an intellectual type.

7. Theology had become scholastic and the sermon
    was pedagogical.

8. Emphasis was on the externals of worship, and
    many people came just before the sermon and left
    immediately following it.[1]

Pietism appeared as a reaction to these conditions within
the Lutheran Church of the seventeenth and eighteenth centuries. It must be kept in mind that it was the desire of
the leaders to purge the Church from within and not to form
a separatist group. Some Orthodox leaders laid stress on
some of the same things as did the Pietists. Theophilus Gorsz-
hauer, one of the Orthodox group, complained about the pre-
valent conditions in the Church and can thus be considered
one of the forerunners of the pietistic movement.

Pietism was actually founded by Philip Spener (1635–
1705) as a protest against the deterioration of Orthodoxy to
meaningless codes. He was a graduate of the University of
Strassburg where he pursued studies in history, philosophy,
and philology. He was interested in the writings of Luther
and was accused of Calvinistic leanings by those who opposed
him. The basic intent of the pietistic movement was to awaken
the cold orthodox Church, reform the clergy, and regenerate
the Church in every aspect of its life and ministry. Though
the movement was begun by Spener, the subsequent organization was to be the work of August Francke of the faculty of
the University of Halle.

The followers of Spener were organized into the Collegia pietatis, or small gatherings of like-minded people who
met periodically to study the Bible, Luther's writings, and
other devotional materials, for their own personal edification
and spiritual enrichment. Emphasis was placed on the inner
life of personal holiness, discipline and morals, and the strict
observance of the Lord's Day. In these early days, there
was no intention of disrupting the established church orders

but merely of bringing new life into its fellowship and ministry. However, because of the strong emphasis on these
"home" gatherings and personal devotion, interest in corporate worship in the sanctuary waned and the emphasis was increasingly toward separatism. Eventually the police complained
against the Collegia pietatis, and even though some of the
meetings were transferred to the church building itself, troubles
ensued. Consequently, many began the actual break from
the Church and absented themselves from the services and
the sacraments.

Besides the implied separatism, the Pietists stressed
regeneration of church membership and clergy and the distinction between the true saints and the unconverted. To a
greater or lesser degree, a spiritual pride and self-righteous
attitude developed among them. Emphasis was placed on lay-
leadership, and many of the Pietists did not see the necessity
for the clergy at all. It was felt that all believers were
"priests unto God" and could administer the Sacraments under
divine unction as well as the clergy.

The practical side of Christianity was another aspect
and emphasis of Pietism. Brotherly love was stressed and
practiced with the result that a period of great benevolence
was seen in the establishment of missions, orphanages, etc.
The Pietists were concerned with the spiritual and temporal
well-being of their "flock," a concern expressed in such vital
and practical ways.

In addition to the meetings of the Collegia pietatis, members were encouraged to practice daily private devotions in
the form of Bible reading and prayer. Spener's Pia Desideria
(1675) depicts the Christianity of this period and stresses
the need for personal Bible study for the training and growth
of piety, not only of the laity but also of the clergy. Although this book met with mixed reactions in the eighteenth
century, it is still being published and read today.

As with any reform movement, Pietism was to experience
its share of opposition and criticism. Although many of the
Pietists broke with the Church, Philip Spener did not leave
the Lutheran communion. He accepted a call to Dresden as
chaplain to Elector John George II of Saxony, but while there
he opposed the low morals of the court and criticized the conditions at the Universities of Leipzig and Wittenberg. This

opposition brought considerable disfavor on Spener. Under
the protectorship of Elector Frederick III, he established the
theological school of the University of Halle, where an influential center for Pietism flourished. August Francke, a pupil
of Spener and the founder of the Collegia biblica at the University of Leipzig, caused a great deal of unrest and stirred
up opposition to himself by his lectures. As a result, conventicles were forbidden, and he was obliged to leave his
post at Leipzig. A similar situation obtained in Erfuhrt, and
he was obliged to leave there in 1691.

As was mentioned previously, Francke later joined the
theological faculty at the University of Halle in 1691. Strife
developed between him and the clergy of the city, and "literary battles" between Pietism and its opponents were waged
outside of Halle.[2] At Halle, however, they developed and
spread, and historians claim that the whole Lutheran Church
in Germany was affected by them. Francke, who was more
aggressive than Spener, encouraged the devotional life of
the students and many of his lectures were nothing more than
"revival sermons."[3] Although Halle was a stronghold of Pietism, the movement did begin to decline in the ensuing years,
and by the latter part of the eighteenth century, it was lost
there.

Spener's influence was felt in cities like Württemberg,
where Pietism acquired many adherents with much less opposition than in other places. Although this city was never widely
influential in the cause, it did produce notable leaders such
as Christian Gottlob Pregizer (1751-1824) and the Hofacker
brothers, Ludwig (1798-1828) and Wilhelm (1805-1848). Its
influence was also noteworthy in Switzerland, where a training school for missionaries was established.

As for Philip Spener, in the wake of a divided church
in Germany, the ecstatic phenomena of the Pietists, and the
polemics against Pietism, he abandoned the struggle as early
as 1698.[4] His desire was to remain an orthodox Lutheran and
make his witness count "within the fold." Separatism continued to grow, and early in the eighteenth century the
clergy's attitude toward established Pietism was much more
moderate than was previously the case. By the middle of the
century, meetings (which did not hinder the peace) were
allowed to be held.

While Pietism endeavored to keep its reform activities within the State Church, by its practice of small assembly meetings, it became fertile soil for separatist groups. The first to become really independent from the Lutheran Church were the Moravians around the year 1691. The Moravian Church traces its beginning to the ministry of John Hus in pre-Reformation time. After his martyrdom, his followers organized and became known as the Bohemian Brethren. The Thirty Years War almost extinguished them, but a small remnant found refuge on the estate of Nicholas Ludwig, Count of Zinzendorf (1700-1760) in 1732. Zinzendorf had been reared in strict Pietism. His godfather was Philip Spener and his tutor, August Francke, so he was steeped in the traditions of this reform movement. Latourette has summarized the activities and outcome of this association as follows:

> He also had an intense desire to spread the Christian faith throughout the world. In the handful of persecuted refugees he saw the means of fulfilling that vision. They founded the village of Herrnhut on his property, he identified himself with them and became a bishop of their church, and through him missionaries from among them went to various parts of the world. Zinzendorf wished them to become members of the state church of Saxony, but in 1745, while being a section of that church, they were formally organized with their own bishops, in the succession of those of the Unitas Fratrum, and with their distinct services, liturgy, and hymnology.[5]

The Spread of Pietism

Sweden

Religious life in Sweden at the beginning of the eighteenth century was in precisely the same condition as that of Germany when Philip Spener began his reform. When foreign nationals came to Sweden to practice their faith, they found a church controlled by the Crown; and although they were allowed to carry on their religious activities, they were forbidden to propagate their faith. The Church in Sweden is open to criticism during this period. Karl Olsson's translation from two eminent church historians aptly describes the conditions of the time:

The church was hyperorthodox and intolerant, objective and formal; it left little room for personal
piety or spontaneous worship; it was mediated by
a hierarchy not so pretentious or complex as that of
the Roman Church but just as unbending in its authority and in its suspicion of lay interference. It
was structured by a static theology which was un-
affected by the new discoveries in science and hence
open to the irrationality of superstition, magic, and
demonology.[6]

Furthermore, the contact between pulpit and pew was very
impersonal, and the clergy exhibited little concern for the
spiritual welfare of the people. Preaching was abstruse, and
cruel disciplinary actions were meted out to those who came
under the scrutiny of the Church.

With the negative aspects of church life and practices
duly stressed, in all fairness it should be mentioned that the
established Church did much to encourage literacy by establishing schools for the laity. It exerted influence in the civil
life of the community in the "suppression of sexual immorality,
drunkenness, irreligion and blasphemy...."[7]

Interest in the mystical side of Christian devotion was
evident even before Pietism became firmly established in Sweden.
The Church as the Bride of Christ, as well as the mystery of
His passion, occupied the minds of Christians in the seventeenth century. A devotional book, A Spiritual Wellspring,
was published in 1641. In 1642, in close succession, appeared
a translation of Johan George's Prayer Book and Lewis Bayly's
The Practice of Piety. "Thus, while the official orthodoxy
of the church grew more unyielding, a new tradition of piety
formed in the deeps, preparing the way for the evangelical
endeavors of the following century."[8]

Pietism began to infiltrate into Sweden as early as the
latter part of the seventeenth century. By the eighteenth
century, the ecclesiastical powers were strongly opposed to
the conventicles which seemed to be inspired by the German
pietists. Measures were taken to suppress these conventicles
but they were continued. The more conservative element in
Pietism was tolerant and understanding of the attitude of the
established church, but the radicals took an unmitigated stand

against the church because of its intolerant attitude toward
the Pietists and the persecution it inflicted on them.

The central figure among the radical Pietists was Sven
Rosen from Västergötland, a student at Uppsala and the son
of a prominent clergyman. His early contact with Pietism was
in the person of Andreas Hellerstrom, dean of the cathedral
of Göteborg. Although his ardor for Pietism cooled while he
was a student at Uppsala, his interest revived when he became tutor for a family of nobility near Stockholm in 1728.
Another one who influenced Rosen in the cause of Pietism was
the young German physician Johan Conrad Dippel, who came
to the capital city early in 1727. Originally a Halle Pietist,
he was dismissed and disowned because of his radical views.
After a series of arrests and imprisonments, and finally a
pardon, he made his way to Sweden. Eventually, upon invitation to Stockholm, Dippel became a popular but controversial figure in that city because of his denouncement of
the Church. Although Dippel himself was banished from
Sweden, his influence continued to be felt in the person of
such men as Sven Rosen. Rosen became the leading man
among the radical movement.

Peculiar to the radicals was the emphasis on the inner
spiritual experience and the expectation of the imminent return of Christ. They continually absented themselves from
the Church and the Lord's supper and lived in a rather peni-
tent mood as they looked with disdain on the luxuries of the
world. They dressed in gray, drab clothing called "vadmal"
and, as a consequence, became known as "gray jackets." The
group separated themselves from the world in 1734 by moving
into one dwelling which became famous as "Mamma's House."
This conventicle and the year 1734 are notable because they
marked the establishment of the first free group of the radical separatists. Though only fifteen or sixteen in number,
they were to exert strong influence on Rosen. During his
association with them, he wrote many of his strong theological
works.

After a comparatively short term, the radicals were
scattered through a series of arrests and imprisonments in
which their very lives were threatened. Sven Rosen himself
was brought to trial and finally banished from the country
in 1741. Two years later he joined with the Moravians in
London. This association may account for the moderation in

Rosen's attitude toward the established Church. After re-
canting from his radical position, he was reinstated in 1746.
Although he requested to be allowed to return to Sweden,
this request was not granted, and in 1747 he emigrated to
North America with a group of Moravians. In 1748 he was
ordained a deacon in the Moravian Church in Bethlehem,
Pennsylvania. Two years later he died.

Thus, the activities of the radical Pietists as the first
of a free-church type in Sweden became merely an episode.
However, their concept of voluntary assemblies of Christians
and other tenets and beliefs had a lasting effect on the entire church life of Sweden.

The first missionaries from Herrnhut, Melchior Zeisber-
gen and Tobias Frederick, came to Sweden in 1731, where
they too had contact with the "Dipplians." Zinzendorf himself came to Sweden in May of 1735 after a rather unhappy
experience in Denmark. While the visit of Zinzendorf did
not seem to kindle any new "reformation fires," his writings
did exert a powerful influence and were read far and wide
throughout the length and breadth of the land. Although the
leader of a separatist group, Zinzendorf remained loyal to
the Lutheran Church and urged the Moravians in Sweden to
work through the local churches and pastors in their missionary endeavors. During the decade of the 1750's, Herrnhutism
gained much ground, and during succeeding years, he was
instrumental in a great awakening in the Church of Sweden.

Thus two influential groups were at work in Sweden at
this time, the Pietists and the Moravians. Both were to be
of great influence through their writings and preaching. The
spiritual outlook of both has been preserved in the hymnody
each produced which will be discussed at length in the next
chapter.

Although Pietism flourished in the eighteenth century,
as was mentioned previously, it did not go unchallenged by
the Church or the Crown. In 1726, the Edict against Conventicles was enacted in an effort to thwart the spread of
what were considered antichurch views. A new Conventicle
Edict was later enacted and remained in force as late as 1858
as an attempt to clarify the status of conventicle meetings.
The idea behind the edict was to preserve the unity of the
State Church, to keep all devoted to church and King, and

to insure a "solid social structure in which political and religious cohesions were intermingled."[9]

The religious awakening in Sweden in the eighteenth
century began to show evidences of decline as the century
drew to a close. However, the revival broke out again in
the nineteenth century, and this era was one of great prosperity in the religious life of Sweden. The Church again had
been faced with spiritual decline, an undue emphasis on materialism, disregard for Sunday, and a disintegration, and
almost dissolution, of family life. Evidences of renewal began
to appear early in the period. Evangeliska Sällskapet was
formed in 1808 for the production of Christian literature. In
1811 Jacob A. Lindblom, Archbishop of Uppsala and primate
of the Church of Sweden, published his new catechism. The
Swedish Bible Society was organized in 1815 after the pattern
of a "similar organization in Great Britain." By the combined
efforts of the above-mentioned publishing concerns, religious
life was stimulated following the period of apparent decline.

The awakening of the nineteenth century in its "full
tide" was felt in the southermost and northernmost sections
of Sweden. In the South the rather serious minded clergyman, Henric Schartau (1757-1825), was an active leader. He
began his ministry during a period of rationalism in preaching.
In his early years he leaned toward the Moravian position,
stressing the wounds and blood of Christ, but later reacted
against this and turned more to sanctification. He was very
critical of the sentimentality in Pietism and laid stress on the
sacraments of the Church. Schartau created a large following
of those who came to hear him preach although he was not
a separatist in any sense of the word. His convictions and
influence were carried on by those who followed him.

In the north of Sweden, circles of läsare ("readers")
gave their attention to the writings of Martin Luther and
Arndt's True Christianity. Like the movement under Schartau, this group, though church-related, was of a legalistic
pietistic character. After the läsare had held forth for considerable time, a group known as the Nya Läsare ("new readers") sprang up in the northern port town of Pitea. Largely
farmers, they were influenced by the Herrnhut emphasis on
grace and redemption through Christ. In time, they denounced
the old läsare for their Pharisaical self-righteousness and an
undue emphasis on keeping the law. Under the leadership of

a former soldier, Erik Stalberg, they formed separate conventicles, and the separation became final in the middle of
the century when they took upon themselves to administer
the sacraments.[10]

Sweden was again to feel another impact from England
in the ministry of George Scott (1808-1874), a Scottish Methodist, who carried on a very successful ministry in Stockholm
from 1830-1842. He preached in a chapel erected by the
Methodists of Great Britain in 1826. Gunnar Westin relates
concerning the ministry and significance of this Methodist
Mission:

> Around the Methodist Mission was created a highly
> important center for the free evangelical activity with
> its energetic conversion-preaching, conventicles, the
> use of laymen, the distribution of Bibles, books, and
> tracts, temperance propaganda, foreign mission, city
> mission, Sunday schools, and publication of periodi-
> cals. Through his position as unofficial legation Pastor
> Scott won for himself a place of great possibilities.
> It was now that the influence of piety of the Anglo-
> American type began to make itself felt with force
> hitherto unknown. George Scott's work in the Stock-
> holm Methodist Mission (1830-1842) became of prime
> importance for the Swedish revival and became the
> factual starting-point for the subsequent free-church
> movement.[11]

Although Scott as a foreigner had no rights whatsoever
to preach to any others than English-speaking Methodists,
he drew a large following of people who flocked to hear him.
He declared himself to be against separatism and, by this
stand, emulated the practice of Wesleyan Methodism. Westin
dogmatically asserts that Scott must have seen impending separation because of the lines he was following and the ultimate
formation of free-churches in Sweden:

> Just as assuredly as the Wesleyans of that day in
> their practice were free-church people, so was Scott
> while in Sweden a free-church preacher, even though
> he was not inclined to admit this. Scott, as a non-
> Swedish citizen preacher for hundreds of listeners
> in the English Church in Stockholm, was no more
> than an intruding conventicle preacher without any

right whatsoever to shepherd souls among the Lutherans of the land.[12]

Although he was forced to leave the country, his influence was widely significant. His work and its far-reaching
implications is lucidly set forth by Westin:

> There were other distinguishing traits in Scott's work
> which served as preparation for the free-church move-
> ment. His Methodistic revival preaching, which towards
> the close of his sojourn in Stockholm was not as force-
> ful as at first, was of the kind that attracted both
> those who formerly had found their way to the hall
> of the brethren church, as well as those who were
> under the legalistic-Pietistic influence. The large
> throngs that crowded around Scott's pulpit, since the
> autumn of 1831 when he began to preach in Swedish,
> were drawn there by the powerful message of sin and
> grace, full atonement in Jesus and free access to sal-
> vation and righteousness. Thither came many who
> were in anguish regarding their spiritual state, and
> Scott began to hold special classes for those who
> were worried and seekers. Many conversions took
> place. A revival broke forth in Stockholm, which
> fact made glad the heart of Scott and came in for
> growing public attention.... During the 1830's the
> interest increased to the extent that when in the autumn
> of 1849 he could dedicate his large church edifice it
> was already incapacious of accommodating the crowds
> that came. Thus the revival movement that had sprung
> up as a result of Scott's preaching had led to the
> building of the first free church edifice in Sweden
> for the promotion of revival and mission among Swedes,
> but wholly outside the frame of the State Church
> system.[13]

By-products of Scott's ministry include the formation
of an agency for Bible and literature distribution, the formation of a Temperance Society, and a foreign missionary advance, all connected with his work in Sweden.

The successor to Scott in the interest of the free-church
movement was Carl Olof Rosenius (1816-1868), the son of a
pastor in upper Norrland and a friend of the Readers. (Lövgren considers him to have been a member of the Nya Läsare

group.) For a time he was a student at the University of
Uppsala, but adverse circumstances including ill health prompted
his withdrawal. In time he came in contact with George Scott
and became almost an assistant to him in the pulpit of the
Methodist chapel, and editor of the journal Pietisten, which
had a circulation of several thousand. When Scott was forced
to vacate his pulpit in 1842, Rosenius continued in the preaching ministry and assumed the editorship of Pietisten. In due
time friends of Rosenius purchased Scott's Chapel, and Rosenius continued to preach there until his death. He became a
very popular preacher and many of his disciples associated
together in Evangeliska Fosterlandsstiftelsen (National Evangelical Association), founded in 1856. This group was influenced
by the Inner Mission Movement in Germany in its colporteur
work and its establishment of a deaconess institution.[14]

Rosenius did not leave the Established Church and
strongly advised his followers against a separatist position.
Even though he had great grievances against the Lutheran
clergy, he took Communion and had his children baptized as
Lutherans. He was popular as a journalist and devotional
writer not only in Sweden but in Norway and Denmark as
well.

Scott had another disciple in Anders Wiberg, who was
a priest of the State Church. Because of his separatist views,
Wiberg and Rosenius parted company, and the former was to
take his place later with the Baptist movement, which was
coming to the fore at this time. According to Westin, the
radical position of the Baptists on many issues caused Rosenius to take a more conservative position.

Although, outwardly, Rosenius was not a separatist or
a Pietist, at heart he espoused the cause of Pietism and encouraged its followers by his preaching and the ministry of
his pen. Small groups and societies sprang up over Scandinavia which carried out the traditions of Scott and Rosenius
and encouraged the tendency toward the free-church movement on a grand scale. More will be said concerning the work
and influence of Rosenius in the next chapter.

Denmark

On the eve of the nineteenth century in Denmark, the
State Church was suffering from the inroads of rationalism,

a condition which prevailed in many of the European countries.
The writings of Kant had come from Germany, stimulating
thinking among the intellectuals in the Church.   The clergy
became enamoured with neology and the enlightenment.   On
the other hand, Pietism and Moravianism had exerted wide
influence in the country.   Latourette describes the situation:

> From Germany had entered Moravianism and Pietism
> and both had begun to have effect not only in limited
> circles but also widely through outstanding churchmen,
> hymnody, and the renewal of confirmation with the
> accompanying instruction.   Pietism had brought a
> deep sense of sin, sometimes so great as to produce
> an attitude of helplessness and despair.   Moravianism
> had given an assurance of God's love and of salva-
> tion.[15]

Thus a sharp antithesis existed in the religious life of
Denmark at the dawn of the century in the presence of both
liberal and conservative elements in Protestantism.   Church
attendance declined as State Church pastors preached an ethi-
cal Gospel, and even though Pietism and Moravianism were
still enlisting followers, their active ministry was not as dy-
namic as in former days.

The situation might have been cause for alarm, but
the Danish Church was far from dead.   The hymnody of such
men as Thomas Kingo and the Pietist Adolf Brorson, and the
leadership of many outstanding clergymen kept the Church
alive during these critical days.   Pietism and Moravianism,
even though represented by comparatively small groups, continued to hold forth effectively.

The years following 1815 were to be the most creative
for Danish Protestantism.   Preceding the general awakening,
many activities pastored the revitalization of the entire church
life of Denmark.   In 1801 the Danish Evangelical Society, which
promoted the printing of the New Testament, was formed.   In
1814, the Danish Bible Society was organized by Ebenezer
Henderson, a missionary appointee to India.   Rationalism was
challenged by the preaching of such men as Henrik Steffens.
Much of the inspiration for these developments, as well as
financial support, came from Anglo-American sources.

The success of this returning "tide of faith" in Denmark

naturally was due to some of the strong leaders in the church.
One of the very early leaders was Nicolaj E. Balle (1744-1816),
for several years the Bishop of New Zealand. In his lectures
he strongly opposed rationalism and urged a return to biblical preaching. He published a textbook on the catechism as
well as a hymnal, both of which aroused criticism. Another
leading figure in these early years was Jakob Peter Mynster
(1775-1854), also a strong opponent of rationalism. In his
early ministry, he strongly adhered to the writings of Kant
and was vehemently opposed to revivalist preachers and conventicles. His emphasis changed when he was thirty years
of age because of a deep religious experience. An eloquent
preacher, he became a strong influence in the Church of Denmark; however, he was charitable in his attitude toward the
rationalists. His sermons and devotional books influenced the
entire nation, although sin and repentance found little place
in either. He remained loyal to the State Church because of
its emphasis on "individual freedom for prayer and meditation."

A name which has become immortal in Danish Church
history is that of Nikolaj F. S. Grundtvig (1783-1872). His
father came from a long line of Lutheran pastors and his
ministry was not influenced by rationalism. Following the line
of least resistance, Grundtvig prepared for the ministry at
the University of Copenhagen. He went through a period of
intellectual and spiritual struggle during his university years
and broke away from the orthodoxy in which he had been
reared. As the time drew near for him to become curate to
his father, he went through a period of spiritual crisis from
which he emerged victoriously to be a leader of great repute
in the Danish Church.

One of Grundtvig's early contributions to the spiritual
awakening in Denmark was his History of the World, in which
he attacked rationalism and declared Christ to be the focal
point of history and the unifier of the human race. He as-
pired that Denmark should have a rebirth and that Christians
should be Christians in every aspect of daily life.

Because of their part in the awakening in Denmark,
many Pietists and Moravians were arrested in accordance with
the Conventicle Act of 1741. While some ministers of the State
Church showed a kindly attitude toward them, Grundtvig
tended to be critical of their separatistic views. Nevertheless, even though he was not a Pietist, he was a constant

source of inspiration to the Pietist and Moravian pastors, and
his ideas and attitude found expression in their sermons.
More will be said concerning his relationship to the free-
church movement later in this chapter.

One of Grundtvig's greatest contributions to Danish
Church life was in his hymns. He edited a hymnal, largely
of his own hymns, and the note of joy in most of them caused
them to be received by the Danish people with great enthusiasm and profit. Chapter III will deal in detail with his hymnody.

As a statesman and patriot, Grundtvig sought to edu-
cate the Danish people in their heritage as "God's chosen
people." He was an educator and introduced new ideas into
the educational system in his country. In politics his followers followed both the conservative "right" and the demo-
cratic "left" positions. Some of his later followers divided
into the moderates and liberals, the former organizing the
Church Society of 1898 and the latter establishing agricultural
and high schools. Thus his influence both in the civic and
religious life of Denmark is evident; and as Latourette has
pointed out, "Grundtvigism" became a potent and characteristic strain in Danish life."[16]

The name Kierkegaard has long been associated with
the church and theology of Denmark. Søren A. Kierkegaard
(1813-1855), in spite of his brief life-span, became famous
for his contributions not only in his native country but also
far beyond its borders. He was reared and prepared for
confirmation in Copenhagen. Following many vicissitudes of
his early life, he had a transforming emotional experience
when he was assured of God's love for him.

The death of his father and his subsequent inheritance
created financial independence for him. He was able to complete his theological studies and in time became a controversial figure in the theological world through his voluminous
writings and lectures. In his polemics he denounced the
State Church and refused its communion because he felt that
it had "watered down" the Gospel and had made its main message merely a "code of ethics." He desired to make the
Church reflect on its position in the world. His estimate of
the Christian Church in Denmark is summarized by Latourette:

While Denmark was a Christian nation, not one Dane, so he insisted, had the character of a New Testament Christian. Christ had said that narrow is the gate which leads to life and broad is the gate which leads to destruction, yet the state church acted as though the reverse were true and that all in the country had entered the way to life. The state church, so Kierkegaard declared, had prostituted the sacraments. Men who had no real Christian faith brought their children for baptism and others with as little faith stood as godfathers to the children. Confirmation, in which the adolescent took on himself the vows made for him in baptism, was an even more ghastly travesty. Men who on week days lied in their business took Communion on Sundays and returned, unconcerned to their old practices on Mondays. Although blessed by the Church, marriage was far from meeting New Testament demands. Thus ran the indictment.[17]

While not considered a separatist as such, unofficially he did leave the communion of the State Church and criticized men like Grundtvig for not leaving also. By his standards of Christian living, and because of his attitude toward the State Church, he added greatly to the advance of Pietism.

The influence of both Grundtvig and Kierkegaard was expressed most fully in the Inner Mission. The movement endeavored to lead people into a full Christian life on an individual basis and to assemble them into small groups within the church for the purpose of study and mutual spiritual edification. Latourette describes the ideals of the Inner Mission as "closely akin to those of the Continental Pietists and of British and American Evangelicals."[18] It developed extensively but remained within the confines of the State Church.

The Association of the Inner Mission was organized in 1853 for the spiritual renewal of the church in Denmark. Lay leadership was stressed, and many preachers were sent out into the realm as heralds of the cause. Because of internal trouble the organization was dissolved, and in 1861 the Church Association for the Inner Mission in Denmark was formed. As its name indicates it was to work within the State Church. The outstanding leader of the new organization was Wilhelm Beck (1829-1901), who had been influenced both by Kierke-

gaard and Grundtvig in his early years. He was ably assisted
by Johannes Clausen in "revival" campaigns in Denmark and
in the sending of missionaries, colporteurs, and other workers
to various parts of the country. While still operating within
the Church, by 1900 they had erected nearly 400 meeting
places for their converts.

The Inner Mission conducted a vigorous program which
resulted in the usual opposition from the leaders of the Church.
It grew, however, and spread out over all of Denmark. It
expressed deep concern for the social condition of the day,
established Sunday schools and various types of projects for
youth, and inaugurated many day schools which specialized
in instruction in agriculture, handicrafts, and related subjects.

The Lutheran Mission in Denmark began as a result of
the preaching of P. C. Trondberg, a pastor who had been
influenced by Kierkegaard concerning the State Church. One
of the lay preachers of the movement was Christian Moeller,
who founded the mission and by the suggestion of Rosenius
remained and worked within the Church. In later years the
Luther Mission became pietistic in emphasis, and missionaries
were sent out in affiliation with the Moravians. Their dif-
ferences with the Inner Mission began to fade, and soon there
was even an exchange of leadership and workers between the
two groups.

Nineteenth-century Protestantism in Denmark is summarized by Latourette in this way:

> Fresh organizations arose, partly for the deepening
> of the faith in the nominally Christian multitudes,
> partly in education, partly in various forms of service
> for the underprivileged, and partly to spread the
> faith in other lands. The overwhelming majority of
> the population were baptized and confirmed in the
> Church of Denmark. In it various parties contended,
> the chief of which were the Grundtvigians, the Inner
> Mission, and the middle, sometimes called the high-
> church, element. The Church of Denmark was offi-
> cially Lutheran. It was a folk or national church,
> with an increasing degree of participation by the laity
> on the parish level. Dissenting bodies were very
> small minorities.[19]

Norway

The condition of the religious life of Norway in the nineteenth century was one of contrast. On the one hand, the agnostics were hostile to the Christian cause and vocal in their opposition to it. Writers were scornful and satirical toward the Church, and secularism was on the increase. On the other hand, the Church was carrying on a vigorous ministry in spite of its critics and was being nurtured and encouraged by both Denmark and Sweden, especially Denmark.[20]

The revival movements in the nineteenth century were prepared by Pietism and Herrnhutism. Bishop Pontoppidan of Bergen strengthened the cause of Pietism by his textbook which was a preparatory study for confirmation. Confirmation theoretically was compulsory from 1736 to 1911 through the influence of Pietism. The Inner Mission movement of Denmark inspired a similar one in Norway, and at the same time Lutheran Orthodoxy was undergoing a revival. In 1842 the Conventicle Act of 1741 was repealed, thus paving the way for more activity and growth of the dissenting groups. Again we see the strong course of Pietism and Moravianism in Scandinavia.

Just at the turn of the century there appeared on the scene one of the foremost leaders of Norwegian religious life, Hans Nielsen Hauge (d. 1824). He felt inspired after a deep spiritual experience to preach the Gospel without any interference or restrictions from a governing body. Westin considers him to be the greatest leader in the religious life of Norway in his day and has expressed it in this way:

> He, more than any other, left his imprint on the indigenous Lutheran folk movement during the first part of the 1800's. Until 1804 he travelled about a great deal, and he also authored several publications of religious content.... A certain characteristic of old time Pietism was inscribed on the whole movement. In this respect he went against the Herrnhutian persuasion or viewpoints.[21]

The movement which grew up around Hauge was known in the Norwegian language as "venneflokker" or "friend-flocks." Hundreds of such groups were formed which could not be suppressed even by the Conventicle Act. These became lay-movements and as a result of their widespread influence many of the lay preachers were persecuted and imprisoned. Hauge himself was apprehended and spent long periods in jail awaiting the outcome of the long deliberations against him by the civil and religious authorities. These proceedings continued over a ten-year period, and when he was finally freed, he was a broken man. These draconian measures against their leader became a cause of concern on the part of many of Hauge's disciples, and they became reticent to preach as freely and openly as before.

After Hauge's reinstatement in 1814, the movement experienced a renewal but with a stronger and more Lutheran character. Hauge advocated that the meetings be held within the church and that the sacraments be administered there also. In this respect, he reflected the views of Rosenius in Sweden. The movement was at its peak in the year of Hauge's death (1824), and for the next twenty years it continued to grow and extend itself. Some of the early radicalism was modified, and it became increasingly difficult to distinguish the Haugeans from the other clergy.

The Haugean awakening was supplemented in many ways with related organizations coming into being. The Norwegian Bible Society was formed in 1816, followed by the Tract Society in 1820. A mission circle was begun in 1826 under the leadership of Carl Bülov of London; and abiding by the principle of Hauge, it was contained within the church. Although Bülov was forced to leave Norway, the mission societies spread and developed into a very efficient layman's movement. Det Norske Misjonsselskap was organized in 1842 and was followed by many others of its kind in the ensuing years. The direction of this development is described by Westin:

> This society movement could even under these circumstances have eventuated into a folk movement self-regulated and more independent of Church leadership. Such separation did not come to pass, however, even though certain societies were strongly colored by the layman attitude. Instead through Haugeanism there devolved in the middle of the century a more solid cooperation with the churchly movement, which was a home mission movement of great moment. There was Theology Professor Gisle Johnson, the great man with a teaching career of forty years, who more than

any other was instrumental in causing the Church to
capture the revival.[22]

Gisle Johnson (1822-1894) was strongly influenced by
the early emphases of Kierkegaard but had little time for
Grundtvig. He was a preacher of unusual ability, and his
preaching made a lasting impact on the Norway of his day.
He was instrumental in the inauguration of the Inner Mission
and had considerable to do with the founding of the Luther
Foundation and the periodical Luthersk Kirketidende. The
awakening under the professor of theology influenced clergy
and laity alike and reached even to the United States and
Great Britain in the form of pietistic and evangelical movements.

Both the Haugeans and the Johnsonians appealed to
all classes of people alike. Large number of "prayer houses"
were built for holding informal meetings, the first one being
erected in Skien in 1850.

Moravian Pietism exerted a strong influence on the
Danish clergyman Gustav A. Lammers (1802-1878), who settled
in Skien after his theological training in Norway. His preaching attracted large crowds of people; as a result a rather
comprehensive revival broke out in 1849 with accompanying
separatist tendencies. In addition to questioning his own
position as a clergyman, he believed that pedo-baptism was
the root of all the evils in the church. As a consequence of
these struggles within his own thinking, he withdrew from the
State Church and founded the Free Apostolic Christian Church
in Skien. The church expanded, and Lammers in his travels
made many contracts in Scandinavia. It seemed that he was
destined to become one of the great leaders in the free-church
movement but this was not realized. Disturbed by the radical
views held by some of his followers concerning baptism, and
in a state of turmoil and indecision himself concerning his own
stand, he returned to the State Church in 1860. Many of
his followers became Baptists, and others formed a dissenting
church of another order. In spite of these existing conflicts,
the free-church movement gained and went forward on a very
solid basis.

Finland

Although the country of Finland does not receive a major

emphasis in this study, some significant aspects to the religious life there are worthy of comment. Westin has observed that

> in no other country in the Northland did the different shades of Pietism come to mean so much to the Lutheran national church as in Finland. The older church life here was closely tied to the vicissitudes in Sweden. Pietists and Herrnhutians suffered persecution.... The Finnish people were very susceptible to a radical form of spiritual manifestations where ecstacies were in evidence. The revivalists however remained within the framework of the Finnish State Church.[23]

Another leader who made a significant contribution to the religious life of Finland of that day was Fredrik G. Hedberg, who struck out on a new path in his preaching. Unlike the legalistic Pietism, his message was more of the "free grace" type with the "come as you are" invitation. Hedberg became editor of a publication known as Evangelisten, which because of censorship and other complications was printed in Sweden.

The forward thrust of Pietism is also seen in the literature distribution work in Finland under the direction of John Peterson. The Lutheran Evangel Association, similar in intent and purpose to Evangeliska Fosterlandstiftelsen in Sweden, did much to foster the cause of Pietism in the country. Laws which militated against the non-state religious beliefs were annulled near the end of the 1860's, and thus greater religious freedom was afforded the dissenting groups, though not without some limitations.

Although Finland conserved a great deal of its Lutheran heritage and tradition, it did experience a great awakening in the nineteenth century. During the latter part of the century, the Church "was not only solidly Lutheran but also, to a greater extent than the state churches of Denmark, Iceland, Sweden, and even Norway, Pietist."[24]

The Free Churches of Scandinavia

To appreciate the growth of the free-church movements

in the eighteenth and nineteenth centuries, one must look at
them against the background of the severe compulsion laws
of both centuries. As we have seen, the progress of the
separatists, typified mainly by the Pietists and Moravians,
was a constant course of irritation and concern to the Lutheran
Church. The following partial list of laws, culled from several
sources, indicates one type of obstacle against which the dis-
senters worked in the quest for religious freedom. Most of
these were Swedish laws but similar ones were in force in the
other Scandinavian countries to a greater or lesser degree:

Conventicle Notice of 1726 (konventikelplakat)

This law forbade the small group meetings for Bible
study and prayer. It was annulled in 1858.

The Draconian Religion Law of 1735

According to this rule, one could be accused of
"secretly harboring some deviating idea" and not
necessarily having attended a conventicle.

The "Pass" Law of 1812

This law was directed against the activity of the
colporteur and required a pass for anyone to travel
outside of his home precinct. It was annulled in
1860.

The Law of March 1855

The implications of this law were that anyone officiating at a communion service without special permission and who was not a priest of the State Church
was given a heavy fine. A smaller fine was imposed
upon those who participated in the communion under
such circumstances. This was only one of several
laws enacted in the 1850's which were burdens to
those of the free-church persuasion. It was annulled in 1864.

The Royal Order of 1858

Although the State Church has enacted strict laws
"to hold itself together," even these were power-
less to stem the tide of free-church growth and
spread. This Royal Order represents one of the
early attempts to ease the laws against conventicles.

The Law of 1860

By this law permission was granted to separatist
groups by the Riksdag to petition the king for the
privilege of forming new organizations.

The Dissenter Law of 1873

In this law some of the heaviest restrictions of the
early laws were annulled, though not all. Pastors
were given the right to perform marriages by the
provision of this law, but they had no legal validity.
It was possible for one to get married by a civil
act.

This is just partial documentation of laws enacted concerning dissenting bodies and their relationship to the State
Church. Even when the tide was turning in the direction of
moderation toward the separatists and laws were enacted in
their favor, in some locales the feeling was still strongly unfavorable toward these minority groups. Consequently, complete liberty for them could not be realized for some time, in
fact, not until the Law of Religious Liberty was passed in
1857.

Attitudes toward the fringe groups varied within the
constituency of the State Church. In 1859 Archbishop Reuterdahl expressed his feelings toward them by the statement,
"Rejoice those who can do so. I cannot rejoice over this religious confusion and place in this old Sweden."[25]

A more tolerant attitude was exhibited by Bishop G.B.
Bjork at his pastors' meeting in Göteborg when he pointed out
that there should be a closer cooperation between the State
Church and the new evangelicals, because "there is a need
for people whose faith is not genuine to find ground for such
in such endeavors of others, for which our church has not
offered sufficient hope."[26]

At a conference for pastors in Lund in 1858, the sunder-
ance of the church was reported with the Baptists being the
most eager, aggressive, and progressive. The presiding bishop
was H. H. Thomander, who had succeeded Reuterdahl in 1856
and was more liberal in his views. He could not advocate
drastic measures when it could readily be seen that no good
would come of such actions.

A summary of the Central Bureau of Statistics for the
period 1856-1860 notes that in one coastal area, besides the
parish church, several houses of prayer and separate meeting
places for worship and lectures had been erected. Although
the prevailing conditions were a matter of concern for many

officials of the State Church, others were ready to admit that
in many instances great good had come from these private
gatherings.

The Free Churches of Sweden

The free-church movement broke through in Sweden in
the latter part of the nineteenth century. It is noteworthy
that as early as the end of the seventeenth century Pietism
was preparing the way for this development.

This was also a time of religious darkness and uncer-
tainty as it was viewed by many of the church leaders. Archbishop Söderblom of Uppsala sounded a clarion call for unity,
understanding, and cooperation between the two church bodies
when in 1921 he said:

> Shall we here in Sweden need go through the same
> process as did the Christendom in England through
> many generations before the self-evident insight dawns
> upon us, that all of us who seek God's kingdom and
> His righteousness above all, in spite of our differences
> and habits, still are called to stand side by side in
> the church of Jesus Christ. My heart is consoled and
> strengthened when matters are taken seriously and
> we find that Church people and free-church people
> can stand as one man in defense of Christian faith
> and Christian nurture.[27]

The free-church movement received impetus, encouragement, and new ideas from the Methodists in England, the Pres-
byterians in Scotland, and the Baptists in Germany and America. These all contributed to the disquietude of the Church.
The cause of Orthodoxy was championed by the followers of
Kierkegaard, the Swedenborgians, and the liberals.

Considerable emigration to America during this period
resulted in thousands of Swedes coming into contact with the
revival movements among American Baptists and Methodists.
Many were converted to the new faith and returned with glow-
ing reports of the situation in America and an enthusiasm to
see the same religious awakening in Sweden. American influence of a similar nature was felt in Norway and Denmark.

Church historians agree that the protracted line of the

pietistic and Herrnhutian movements led to the free-church movement in the middle of the nineteenth century. Developments prior to the 1850's, as had been indicated, were only the beginnings of the separation that was to come. The reports of bishops and other church leaders indicated tendencies toward separation rather than a firmly established free-church existence. Westin is dogmatic when he maintains that the Swedish free-church movement is the "outflow of the old Swedish movement called 'readers,' though strongly stimulated by Anglo-American piety, not so much by way of theology, but rather in godliness and outlook upon life and especially in methods of conducting evangelical work."[28] The first of the separatist groups worth the name was the Norrland Hyper-Lutherans. They were a type of "reader" group who had undertaken to administer the communion apart from the regulations of the handbook, and around 1860 comprised approximately 1,000 members.

Westin declares the "first clear free-church movement of any importance in Sweden, and which also broke through the barriers of hindering laws during this time, was that of the Baptists."[29] By the end of 1859, they numbered about 4,000 baptized members. It should be borne in mind that this was before any official permission had been given so that anyone could identify himself with any free-church group. The movement gained support from Baptists in America and carried on an agressive ministry under the able leadership of Anders Wiberg.

In point of time, an important step in the Swedish Free Church movement can be reckoned from the year 1857 when the first national Baptist Conference was held in Sweden, at which time the denomination began to take definite shape. The Methodist Episcopal Church appeared on the scene around 1866; by 1876, after much struggle and organizational difficulties, it became a permanent organization. The Mission Covenant was organized in 1878.

With all the laws in vogue which were unfavorable to the free-church ideal and the whole community steeped in church tradition, this hardly looked like the time for the appearance of the free-church. On the contrary, history has proved that the time was ripe and the separatists became firmly established. Also, the Lutheran State Church "in its lower as well as higher religious instruction furnished the

ground work and structure for the general Christian tenets
of the free-church movement."[30]

The Baptist movement, like most of those of the free
church, was influenced greatly by George Scott about whom
much has been said already. Almost without exception, everyone of the early Baptist leaders had come into contact with
the Wesleyan missionary. Many heard him preach, while others
had contact with him in less formal ways. When Scott was
forced to flee the country, the Baptists drew inspiration from
his successor, Rosenius. The Baptist advance in Sweden in
no small part was inspired and helped by Swedish Baptists
in America, who returned to their native country to carry on
the work. Financial aid to educational and other institutions
was coming from the American churches.

Two sailors, Gustav W. Schroder and F.O. Nilsson,
were pioneers in the establishment of the Baptist faith in their
own land. Nilsson (1809-1881), formerly a Swedish sailor and
then later an American seaman, experienced a deep spiritual
crisis during a storm of Cape Hatteras. When he returned
from this particular voyage, he visited the Baptist Mariners'
Church in New York, and after an assurance of his own spiritual well-being, he began a colporteur work among the Swedish and Norwegian sailors in that city. Inspired by the success of these efforts, he returned to Sweden in 1839. Here
he began a similar work in which he was engaged until he was
invited by the Seamen's Friend Society of New York to work
among the sailors in Gothenburg. In 1840 he met George
Scott and Anders Wiberg in Stockholm. These men greatly
encouraged Nilsson in his work.

In 1845, Nilsson met the sea captain, Gustav Schroder,
who had previously become a Baptist and joined the Baptist
Mariners' Church in New York. In Gothenburg, they studied
the question of baptism, and when Schroder left for work in
Chile the same year, he encouraged Nilsson to write to one
of the prominent German Baptists, J.G. Oncken, concerning
this subject. The result of this correspondence was that Nilsson
traveled to Hamburg and in August of 1847 was baptized by
Oncken in the River Elbe. In the face of impending danger
and in the knowledge that the Conventicle Act was still in
force, he returned to Sweden.

The work in Sweden proceeded very slowly, and at the

end of a year, five persons were baptized at night in the sea
at Vallersvik near Gothenberg on September 21, 1848. The
officiating clergyman was a Dane, A.P. Forster, who had been
sent from Hamburg. This event caused a great sensation,
and the coming days were difficult for Nilsson. As a result
of this and other of his missionary activities, he was brought
to trial; by the provision of Conventicle Law, he was convicted
and banished from the country. An appeal to the high court,
as well as to the king, was of no avail in his case.

Nilsson left Sweden for Copenhagen in 1851, where he
served as pastor until 1853; when further persecution developed, he left for America. Here he became a circuit rider
in the Mississippi Valley until 1860, when he returned to
Sweden--still an outlaw. The Conventicle Act was modified
in the same year, and a pardon was granted to him by Charles
IV on December 11. Nilsson's case had attracted attention
from far and near, and although the original decision seemingly was not in his favor, in due time sympathy was to turn
to the Baptist cause and led ultimately to its prosperity.

Before Nilsson left for Copenhagen in 1852, he baptized
a former State Church clergyman, Anders Wiberg, one night
in July. Reference has already been made to Wiberg, who
became one of the strong leaders of the young Baptist Church
in Sweden. He had been well acquainted with Rosenius, Scott,
and many of the läsare group. When the State Church officials became suspicious of his activities and religious beliefs,
and after having suffered some degree of persecution for his
separatist leanings, he resigned from the formal ministry.
His future service consisted of preaching and administering
the communion at the small group meetings. In spite of the
Rosenius' attitude toward separation, he was kind to Wiberg,
and as Stephenson suggests, "he probably wished to save
him for the cause of evangelism within the State Church."31

Religious liberty in the United States fascinated Wiberg,
and as a result of this interest he made a journey across the
ocean where some significant developments took place. Their
importance is expressed by Stephenson:

> The years of Wiberg's residence in the United States
> are as much a part of the history of the Baptists in
> Sweden as of the Swedish Baptists in America. In
> fact, the foundations of the Baptist church in Sweden

were laid in the United States; above all it was the
financial support that Wiberg obtained from individuals
and organizations that made it possible for the sect
to increase from a score or more at the time he went
to the United States to about six thousand in 1863.[32]

His activities in the United States included work as a
colporteur among the sailors and immigrants. This work was
sponsored by the American Baptist Publication Society. Besides this appointment, he traveled among the Swedes in the
various settlements, encouraging them in the faith. Truly
he was a Swedish missionary working among his fellow countrymen in a foreign land.

His work in America was interrupted by an urgent call
to return to Sweden and help organize the work there. He
did return in 1855, and the same year he became pastor of
the First Baptist Church of Stockholm. One of his first tasks
was to organize the Baptists in Sweden. Delegates came from
various parts of the country from the forty-five churches
which had been established. There were well over 2,000 members in these churches; in 1857 alone, nearly 1,300 were baptized into the Baptist fold.

Another of the early leaders of great stature was Gustav Palmquist, a name synonymous with the Baptist cause in
Sweden and America. He had come into contact with the spiritual movement in Stockholm connected with the ministry of
Rosenius and had read some of the writings of Wiberg. Another important episode in Palmquist's development was a con-
versation he had with Nilsson in Stockholm in 1850. While in
America, he had become a Baptist, and during Wiberg's visit
to the States, the two met and traveled extensively together.
One of the significant contributions Palmquist made to the
Swedish Baptist cause in America was the founding of the
first church in the U.S. at Rock Island, Illinois, in the early
fall of 1852.

When Wiberg was going through a period if ill health,
he urged Palmquist to return to Sweden to help develop and
expand the work of the Baptists. Among his significant contributions was the leadership of a school for colporteurs which
had been established a year before his return to Sweden.
The Sunday school, which developed in America, had influence
in development in Sweden as well. However, the first impulses

toward Sunday school work in Sweden came from personal
contacts Per Palmquist, brother of Gustav, had with Robert
Raikes, its founder from England. Under Per Palmquist's
leadership, it developed into a reputable institution in Sweden.
Men who were to take places of leadership in both America
and Sweden among the Swedish Baptists were inspired and
taught by both Wiberg and Gustav Palmquist. The latter died
in 1867 after a most successful ministry for the cause of the
Baptists in his native Sweden. His contribution to the cause
of Baptist hymnody will be discussed in the next chapter.

The aggressive spirit of the Baptists in Sweden during
the early years of their struggle for religious liberty was commendable. In spite of persecutions and reverses, their zeal
was unabated, and they were determined to carry on what
they believed was a God-given mission. By 1860 they numbered well over 4,000 in membership. American help was
extended in that when Wiberg returned to Sweden in 1855,
he was still under the support of the American Baptist Publication Society. In 1866 the American Baptist Missionary Union
took over the support of his work.

In 1866 Wiberg returned from another visit to the United
States with funds and plans to start a theological seminary.
Although the school for colporteurs had done a commendable
job in the training of workers under Gustav Palmquist, Wiberg
felt the need for a more adequate training for the Baptist
ministers. After much discussion and debate following the
proposal, it was decided to inaugurate a seminary, and in
1866, "Betelkapellet," which was to become the center of Swedish Baptist activities, was founded. In June 1966, the cen-
tennial of Bethel Seminary was celebrated with the dedication
of the new quarters in one of the suburban sections of Stockholm.

In 1857 the first national conference for Baptists was
held, and in 1889, in Stockholm, a more centralized organization became a reality in the formation of the Baptist Union of
Sweden. That such a central organization was not begun
sooner is explainable in the light of the Baptists' known fear
of any kind of dictatorship. The work was divided into various departments under respective leaders, each with its own
budget. By this organization, the work had progressed with
various departments of the Union carrying on an aggressive
ministry and program at home and abroad.

Around 1860 the doctrine of sinless perfection was preached and, in many congregations, readily accepted. In 1870 a new separation took place which led to the formation of the Free Baptist demonination. Doctrinal and practical matters such as holiness and the education of pastors were the dividing issues. After several years as pastor in America, John Ongman (d. 1931) returned to Sweden in 1890 to begin an active work in the city of Örebro which was one of the centers of free-church activity. He brought with him a zeal for the type of holiness movement he witnessed in the United States and was influential in his leadership in that direction. He organized Bible schools, young peoples' societies, and missionary groups. The Örebro Mission Society founded by him actually became the foundation for the Örebro Bible School.

Great emphasis was placed on the gifts of the Spirit, i.e., the speaking in tongues, and the imminent return of Christ in His second advent, although speaking in tongues was not a part of Ongman's holiness emphasis. A fresh impetus was given this Baptist group following the start of the Pentecostal movement around the year 1907. Opposition broke out against Ongman and the emphasis of his church, which led to his resignation in 1807 and his assuming the pastorate of the largest free church in Örebro the Philadelphia Church, which he had founded with members of his former church.

After Ongman's death of 1931, real division came, and many churches left the Baptist denomination. Quite a number have declared since then that such a division was not necessary. Ongman's group has continued as the Örebro Mission Society with its own schools, paper, publishing house, and missionary program. Its members number upwards of 20,000 while the Baptist Union has approximately 21,000. The Örebro group has maintained a definite independence from the latter group since Ongman's passing. A future relationship between the two is a matter of speculation. (It is of passing interest to note that the most recent hymnal of the Baptists of Sweden represents a cooperative effort by both organizations.)

Another smaller Baptist fellowship (known as the Holiness Association) emerged during the 1880's. This developed out of a spiritual revival in the province of Narke. Besides its emphasis on holiness, great stress has been laid on the missionary outreach of the church and the encouragement of lay leadership within its ranks. The denomination has never

been strong and at the present time its membership is about
5,000 people.

The Methodist Church in Sweden, like the Baptist movement, is a product of the Anglo-American free church, and
indebted to the great revivalists such as Moody, Wesley,
Whitefield, and Spurgeon. Men such as these exerted a powerful influence on the thinking and activity of those who were
sympathetic to the free church cause.

The influence of Wesley and Whitefield can be seen in
the Swedish preacher from Philadelphia, Dr. C.M. Wrangle.
As pastor of the Swedish Lutheran Church in Philadelphia
in the 1760's, he read the writings of Wesley and came in
contact with the revival movements connected with the preaching of George Whitefield. On his return to Sweden in 1768,
he had the experience of meeting personally the founder of
Methodism at his headquarters in London. Although he cannot be credited with the actual founding of Methodism in
Sweden, he was instrumental in the organization of the Scripture Distribution Society, whose activity is indicated by its
name. Wrangle's ministry and sphere of influence were felt
in the court of King Adolph Frederick when he was appointed
to be its chaplain.

Other Swedes had contact with Wesley. These, if even
in an indirect way, had much to do with the establishment
of Methodism in Sweden. In 1769, J.H. Liden attended meetings at Wesley's Chapel in London and became interested in
the spread of Wesley's doctrines in Sweden. When N.S. Swe-
derus, a parish priest in Ervalla, heard that a Methodist mission had been started in Stockholm by Joseph A. Stephens,
he wrote a letter to Stephens stating that he too had become
a close friend of the Wesleys during his stay in London. Another Swedish Methodist, Christoffer Sundries, married one of
Wesley's stepdaughters during a time of residence in London
and became an officer of the City Road Chapel. Through
relatives in Skåne, he informed the Swedish people concerning
the spread of Methodism through its missionary activities.

George Scott, the Wesleyan Methodist, was of exceptional
importance in the establishment and spread of Methodism during his twelve-year ministry in Stockholm and its environs.
His activities in the cause of Pietism have already been discussed. In 1833 he published a pamphlet on Methodism, which

was informative and widely read. Westin mentions that for a
time Methodism and the läseri came to be regarded by the
press as synonymous because of the extensive reading on
the part of both groups.[33]

Scott's stand against formal separation from the State
Church was commended by the clergy in 1859. His attitude
in regard to separation is summarized by Westin:

> When the American Methodist Episcopal church started
> direct Mission in Sweden, Scott came out in opposition
> to this and wrote letters to friends in Sweden assert-
> ing that this work did not represent true Wesleyan-
> ism. The Superintendent of the mission, V. Witting,
> wrote to the leaders in New York saying that the
> "worst enemy" the new Methodist mission in Sweden
> had was Scott.... The superintendent of the Metho-
> dist mission in Scandinavia in his report of 1860 re-
> lates that George Scott in his visit to Sweden in 1859
> in a large ministerial meeting had publicly advised
> believers not to leave the State Church but to remain
> in it. This had been published in a number of news-
> papers and it had militated against the growth of
> Methodism.[34]

Stephenson traces the actual origin of the Methodist
Church in Sweden to the ministry of Olof Gustaf Hedstrom.
As part of a South American expedition in 1825, Hedstrom
found himself in New York when the expedition was abandoned.
After marriage to an American woman, he came into contact
with some Methodists. He was converted to the cause and became an enthusiastic Methodist. With his wife, he returned to
Sweden on a mission to his parents and close friends. On his
second visit to America, he was accompanied by his brother,
who became the founder of Swedish Methodism in the western
part of the country. Two years after his return to the States,
Hedstrom became a recognized pastor of the New York Conference of the Methodist Episcopal Church and served for ten
years as pastor of English-speaking congregations. His position in relation to Swedish Methodism is evaluated by Stephenson:

> Through the importunity of friends Hedstrom was in-
> duced to take up the work that not only gave him the
> distinction of being the founder of Swedish Methodism

in the United States and indirectly the father of
Methodism in Sweden but caused his name to be
blessed by thousands of Swedish immigrants who, at
a time when kind words and friendly advice were
worth more than silver and gold, met the Methodist
missionary for the first time as they landed at Castle
Garden, gateway to the "Promised Land."[35]

For a period of thirty years, from 1845 to 1875, Hedstrom was pastor of the Bethel ship in New York Harbor.
His ministry was one of encouragement and counsel to Swedish
immigrants upon their arrival in their new country. He ex-
tolled the American way of life and urged them to become
good citizens. They were presented with Bibles and sent on
their way.

While pastor in New York, Hedstrom had been instrumental in the conversion of two of the first missionaries to
Sweden, namely, Albert Ericson and Victor Witting. Ericson
was the son of a Lutheran pastor in Stockholm and had served
as pastor in the Methodist Church in the United States before
returning to Sweden in 1866. He had been elected president
of the new Scandinavian Methodist Seminary in Chicago and
went to Sweden for further preparation for this important and
significant position. He became a much sought-after preacher
in Sweden's capital. His enthusiastic followers requested that
they be allowed to retain him as a regular pastor; but this
request did not reach the mission board in time, and Ericson
returned to the States.

Simultaneous with this development was the arrival in
Sweden of Victor Witting who came on a purely social visit to
relatives in Skåne. Witting was born in Malmö on March 7,
1825. He arrived in New York in 1845 as a Swedish sailor
but two years later abandoned his career in the navy. After
twenty years of traveling about the country, much of the
time in search of gold, he returned to New York, a destitute
man. At this time he came under the influence of Hedstrom
and in 1855 entered the Methodist ministry. He later became
editor of Lilla Sändebudet, the first official organ of Swedish
Methodists in the United States.

"Witting's visit in Sweden inaugurated ten years of
active ministry, during which the Methodist Church was organized."[36] He was induced by Bishop Calvin Kingsley, whom

he had met in Copenhagen, to accept the position as Superintendent of Methodist missions in Sweden. He accepted,
and from 1867 until 1876, Witting worked tirelessly in the
organization and expansion of Swedish Methodism. He began
with small groups, and the first congregations were formed
in 1868, one in Stockholm and a second in Göteborg. The
Swedish Methodist Missionary Society was organized in September of 1868, numbering in its constituency "7 congregations, 15 preaching places, 424 members and 5 Sunday schools
with 34 teachers and 354 children."[37] Several publications
were instituted including an official organ, pamphlets, and
Sunday school materials. Wesley's sermons were advertised
and read widely.

The spread of Methodism in Sweden was "eyed" by those
who were friendly and unfriendly to the cause. The Methodists were accused of catering to the less intelligent among
the Swedes and of emulating the colporteurs of the National
Evangelical Foundation in their speaking. The work of the
colporteurs was credited with the progress of the Methodist
church in Sweden. George Scott was most vocal in his denunciation of the movement, insisting that it had nothing to
do with Wesleyan Methodism. The Baptists were included in
the opposition, taking issues in the matter of pedo-baptism.

The church continued to grow. Already in 1873 Witting
had the idea that a conference should be organized, but it
was not until 1876, the year that Witting returned to America,
that the American Conference sanctioned such a move.

The Methodist church in Sweden was a well-organized
denomination by the turn of the century, still with close ties
with America. An American was always the presiding officer
at the annual conference until 1904, when a bishopric (which
included Sweden) was established in Zurich. American ties
continued to be strengthened by the attendance of four delegates at the American yearly conference. Westin elaborates
further on the Anglo-American relations of Swedish Methodism:

> Methodism has doubtlessly more than any other free
> church denomination reflected the Anglo-American
> religiosity, such as it appeared in revivals and free
> church formation. Wesley's dominating influence pre-
> vailed through his writings and practical work methods
> and became the norm for Methodist preachers....

Financial support and interrelationship served to
deep the anchorage in American Methodist views and
methods of work. The Methodist literature in Sweden
also became rapidly infused with the impulses from
the great revivals in the middle 1870's under the
direction of Moody and Sankey. During the summer
of 1876 the Book Concern gave notice that it was sell-
ing Sankey's song book, and later, a Supplement
to Sankey's songs. Sankey was himself a Methodist.
The Methodists like the Baptists suffered decline in
numbers because of emigration. Many of their best
pastors moved away not to return, as well as a large
part of the membership.38

The formation of Svenska Missionsförbundet (Swedish
Mission Covenant) in 1878 had a long prehistory. The work
of the colporteurs which stemmed from the läsare and the
various freewill societies and meetings opened the way for
"Evangeliska Fosterlandsstiftelsen," the strong arm of the
Lutheran free-church movement. When this organization was
formed by followers of Rosenius in 1856, a new phase of the
colporteur work in Sweden began. High church officials,
mostly in the university at Lund, tried to suppress this venture, but again without success because of the leadership of
men like Victor Rydberg, who early in the 1850's began the
struggle for religious freedom. At the time of Rosenius' death
in 1868, the new group had nearly 300 workers out in the
various districts. This was the only organization with which
the Lutheran evangelicals could unite. Many of the converts
sought fellowship with the Baptists and Methodists who had
more semblance of organization at this time.

Because of the different doctrinal emphases among the
free-church groups, controversy was much in evidence. It
was at this time that the free-church leader, Paul Peter Waldenström, began to assume a position of prominence. He was
to become one of the greatest leaders in the free-church
cause and a powerful religious voice in the country. Like
his great teacher and predecessor, Rosenius, he sought reform within the confines of the State Church. At one time
he was offered a position on the faculty of the Augustana
Theological Seminary in Chicago, but because of family pressures declined the position. He became editor of Pietisten
after the death of Rosenius, but unlike Rosenius he sanctioned
conventicles and the administration of the sacraments outside

of the Church, and he himself proceeded to officiate. His
writings in Pietisten met with a storm of protest and inquiry,
particularly his views on the atonement. Waldenström expressed hope that all of the evangelicals, including the Baptists and Methodists, could unite in one body, presumably
the Lutheran. The baptismal issue stood in the way, and
eventually he became convinced that such a consolidation
would never materialize. Nevertheless, the entire evangelical cause experienced great growth and prosperity during the
1880's.

A combination of developments brought about the forming of the Covenant. Besides espousing Waldenström's theological views (particularly his view on the atonement) and
consenting to conventicles, the preacher committee, of which
Waldenström was chairman, began to accept mission contributions apart from the Fosterlandsstiftelsen. This was the
start of an independent mission organization. Missionary
candidates who adhered to Waldenström's theories and church
polity were rejected by Fosterlandsstiftelsen, and in due time
Waldenström was expelled as a representative of the group.
The "proverbial" committee was formed to establish a new organization with its own seminary for the training of its leaders. The committee drew up a plan for church order, and
the new organization Svenska Missionförbundet came into being
on August 2, 1878, in Stockholm in connection with the third
preachers' meeting. Twenty-three delegates, not including
Waldenström, met in a little room in the Bethel Chapel; without much fanfare the new church was born. Waldenström had
hoped that the new organization might remain in the National
Evangelical Foundation; however, when he realized there was
little hope for this, he joined the Covenant and was its greatest member until his death in 1917.

The various independent societies within the Förbund
made consolidation necessary, but this came about very gradually. Disagreements arose between Waldenström and E.J.
Ekman, the conference chairman. Under Ekman's leadership,
the denomination grew and at the twenty-fifth anniversary
in June 1903, he reported the following statistics:

> 1,100 churches
> 84,000 members
> 500 preachers
> 105,600 Sunday school pupils

Trouble ensued when in 1903, Ekman published his book, The Fullness of the Gospel and the Endless Punishments. His whole theological slant was a cause for a general uneasiness, and consequently Ekman could not retain his position, whereupon the elder Waldenström assumed again the leadership of his denomination. He continued to exert powerful influence not only in the matters of organization and expansion but through his sermons and writings. In 1894 the first common songbook of the Covenant was published, and its use was a unifying factor for Missionförbund.

The relationship of the Förbund to the State Church has been one which has challenged the thinking of church historians. In a technical sense, the members of the Förbund remained within the Lutheran fold and continued to pay their taxes, even though, in fact, they became a distinct and separate organization. (Even the Baptists remained in the State Church until 1952, and the majority still have remained in it, at least in spirit.) Karl Olsson comments on this relationship as follows:

> In its eighty some years of history, the Swedish Mission Covenant has never become the full-orbed church suggested in this process. It has vacillated between the society and the church concept. Its members are still, to an overwhelming number, nominally affiliated with the Church of Sweden. It could hold this anomalous position because it lived in the shadow of an establishment which indirectly gave content to the Covenant. The theology and even the liturgy of the Church of Sweden have had a profound effect upon the development of the Swedish Covenant. This is not to deny that other agencies have played their part. For example, the Pentecostal movement has served to define the role of the Swedish Covenant to a considerable extent. But the overarching fact has been the church. [39]

The Pentecostal church in Sweden is perhaps the most loosely organized of any of the groups considered thus far; at least it started out to be such, and even in the advancing years it has remained thus. Stephenson traces its origins to the ministry of the Swedish-American evangelist, Fredrik Franson, a native of Nora, Vastmanland. He was born on June 17, 1852, and when he was seventeen, his parents moved

to America and settled in Kansas and later in Nebraska. In
1872, Franson was converted and joined the Baptists. Almost immediately he became an evangelist, patterning his ministry after that of Moody and Finney. His appeal was mainly
to the three groups discussed in our study, and he did not
hesitate to cross denominational lines to make converts. His
message emphasized the "gifts of the Spirit" and the second
advent of Christ. In the autumn of 1881, he visited Sweden
and, within the space of two years, visited more than half
of the cities and hamlets with his message of the "baptism of
fire." The Swedes responded to his message and were prepared for the several succeeding ministries which were of
similar emphasis. Some have questioned Stephenson's assertion that Franson was the "originator" of the Pentecostal movement in Sweden, although recognizing at the same time that
he greatly influenced the movement.

Another impetus in the direction of Pentecostalism came
from T. B. Barratt of Oslo about whom more will be said in
connection with Pentecostalism in Norway. The impact of
his ministry was felt deeply in Sweden. Representatives from
different denominations in Sweden came to hear him preach
and to receive his message.

The Baptist denomination became the center of this "new
and radical" Pentecostalism in Sweden. The movement involved
some of the oldest Baptist churches as well as several younger
congregations (e.g., the Seventh Baptist Church of Stockholm,
which was organized in 1910). In 1911, a young preacher
by the name of Levi Pethrus (1884-1974) came to be pastor of
the Baptist congregation. Pethrus was not denominationally
minded. The Philadelphia Church, as it is now known, became independent of denominational control and under Pethrus
developed a ministry along Pentecostal lines. Because of its
Pentecostal leanings, the church was excluded from the Baptist group in 1913. Through the leadership of Pethrus and
his congregation the movement developed its publication, its
corps of preachers, a Bible school, and other cooperative
enterprises. [40]

Levi Pethrus, without a doubt, was the greatest leader
of the Pentecostal movment in Sweden. In the book commem-
orating the fifty years of Pentecostalism in his native land,
Pethrus recounts its development in a graphic way. He traces
the tremendous growth within the span of fifty years and

declares its potential in the future. Pethrus emphasizes that
the industrialism, materialism, and unbelief which followed
the free-church movement led to a weakening and downgrad-
ing of the churches. The element of the supernatural in
Christian experience was relegated to the apostolic age, and
spiritual drought was the result.[41]

The Pentecostal revival developed with great momentum,
and according to one historian, Professor Emanuel Linderholm,
it spread rapidly in Sweden as no other movement had experienced. It emphasized Spirit baptism and the supernatural
in Christianity shown in the gifts of the Spirit, especially
tongue speaking and healing.

The concept of a free church has been exercised throughout its history, and the churches have held together without
central organization. In 1943 a school was begun comparable
to those in the public school system of Sweden. It is a folk
high school, of which there are three sponsored by the Pentecostals in Sweden. The Philadelphia Church, in particular,
has taken every advantage and opportunity of television and
radio to extend its ministry. This aspect of its growth has
been phenomenal.

The Pentecostal movement has far surpassed the hopes
and aspirations of its early founders. The varied aspects
of its ministry--including the churches, missions, musical
program, literature, publications, radio, television, etc.--
still challenge its leadership. An active ministry characterizes
the Pentecostal churches in Sweden.

Another group which might legitimately be placed close
to the Pentecostals is Helgelseförbundet (Holiness Covenant).
It is an outgrowth of the Methodist emphasis on an emotional
experience of sanctification and sinless perfection. C.J.A.
Kihlsledt, a clergyman of the State Church, became one of
the early evangelists in this holiness movement. Another
early leader was Miss Nelly Hall, a disciple of Fredrik Franson.
In 1887 after ten years of ministry, there were 158 evangelists in the field. Helgelsförbundet remained a missionary
organization working in cooperation with the free churches
as much as possible.[42]

The Free Churches of Norway
and Denmark

"The oldest principle-clear, continually on-going free-
church movement in Norway is Methodism."[43] So writes Westin
concerning the work of the Methodist church in that country.
Its progress was due to its connection with the Methodist
church in the United States, and its development into a rather
solid, free-church organization is the result of the guidance
and oversight of the American bishops. The Methodists carried
on a system of pastoral exchange with America, which procedure greatly strengthened the churches.

Naturally opposition grew as was true in all phases of
the establishment of free churches in Scandinavia. Many believers could not see the necessity of missionaries being sent
to Norway, the same as to the so-called heathen countries.
As was true with the Baptists, the American Methodists considered the work in Norway as a foreign mission project.

O.G. Hedstrom had a part in the Methodist witness in
Norway in that many sailors and emigrants were converted
in the Bethel Chapel in New York and returned as missionaries to their native Norway. One such person was O.P.
Petersen who in 1849 returned to Norway to preach, making
many converts during his one-year stay. Near the close of
1853, Petersen returned to Norway as a missionary followed
by Danish-born C. Willerup, who came to strengthen the
Methodist cause. These two men established the first congregations for the Methodists in Sarpsborg and Fredrikshold.

Most of the preachers of the first generation of Methodists were emigrants who returned to their country from
America to preach the Gospel. There were some exceptions
to this situation, however, and the first man of importance
among the native preachers was Martin Hansen, who later was
made a district superintendent by the new denomination. The
work of the Methodists progressed, and a church was begun
in Oslo in 1864; in 1869, Petersen became the general superintendent of the Methodists in Norway.

The cause of Methodism in Norway was greatly strengthened by the ministry of one of its native sons, T.B. Barratt.
He joined the Methodist church in Bergen in 1881 and was

officially received into the conference in 1889. In 1892 he
became pastor in Oslo, where he remained for six years. Barratt will be considered later as a great leader among the Pentecostals in Norway, but in the 1890's he stood foremost among
the greatest preachers and leaders among the Methodists.

The Baptists of Norway did not experience a spectacular
beginning nor a phenomenal growth. Norwegian seamen and
emigrants in the United States played a significant role in
the Baptist cause here as elsewhere. The Baptists of Sweden
were more influential in the Baptist cause in Norway than
were the Swedish Methodists in theirs.

The first Baptist preacher in Norway was a Danish seaman, Fredrik Rymker, who was converted and baptized, like
so many others, in New York. He first served as preacher
in Denmark, then, under the auspices of American Baptists
and the Seaman's Friend Society, came to Norway and settled
in Skien. His labors took him also to Porsgrund and Larvik
where Baptist churches were established in the 1860's.

At the beginning Rymker was a welcome guest in the
pulpit of the Lammers Free Church, and, in general, a cordial
relationship existed between Rymker and this group. Lammers
had maintained a strong feeling against rebaptism and when, as
a result of Rymker's preaching, people began to ask for rebaptism, this relationship cooled off. Many of those who were
thus rebaptized did not become Baptist but formed themselves
into a Christian Dissenter Church, which also practiced open
communion. Some of the influential leaders did become very
capable and effective leaders in newly organized Baptists churches.

Rymker realized after a time that his work in Norway
had come to an end, so he withdrew to Sweden, and his support from America was cancelled. Before he left, however,
the Baptist cause in Norway was strengthened by the preaching of F.O. Nilsson who came in 1861 and preached for nearly
six weeks. Converts were made and several baptismal services were held during this time.

At the suggestion of Nilsson for a strong preacher to
be sent to Norway, Ola Hansson of Skåne was sent to carry
on the work in Skien when Rymker left. Hansson's territory
included southern Norway where he labored until the close of

the 1860's, when he began a pioneer work in the northern
part of the country.

The first native Norseman among the Baptist preachers
was the seaman G. Hubert, who after his conversion in the
United States began to preach and in 1862 came to Norway
to do missionary work. He was supported by the English
Baptist Missionary Society for several years and carried on
a ministry in various places in southern Norway. In the latter
1860's he went to the West Coast where he labored in Bergen
and Stavanger. A church was organized in Bergen in 1870,
and with help from English Baptists, a chapel was erected in
1872. By his efforts, support was also forthcoming from England for the work of several pastors from Sweden. Hubert
remained in Bergen until 1879, at which time he took up the
work in Skien. The church there purchased the Lammersian
House of Prayer in 1890.

Two other Swedes were responsible for the ongoing of
the Baptist cause in Norway: Olof Larsson from Dalarna, who
labored in the 1860's in the vicinity of Bergen, Trondheim,
and Troms; and Olof Palm, who was one of Wiberg's colporteurs. Several others from Sweden followed in subsequent
years and made significant contributions to the Baptist work.
At the time of the twenty-fifth anniversary of the Norwegian
Baptist Conference in 1902 in Skien, there were thirty-five
churches with 1,700 baptized members and a combined total
in the Sunday school of approximately 1,770. This was a
substantial growth in numbers since the formation of the conference in 1877, when there were just a little over 500 members.

The impact of the Baptist church on the religious life
of Norway is expressed by one of its strong leaders, Arnold
T. Ohrn:

> The Baptists of Norway are a small, but united and
> well organized body. Their influence on religious
> life in Norway has been immeasurably greater than
> their numbers would indicate. Their witness to Gos-
> pel truth has penetrated far within other circles.
> There are several times as many immersed believers
> outside the Baptist denomination as there are within
> it. Many others have broken with the state church
> principle. But even more important is the influence

of the Baptist message within the state church itself.
Dr. P. Stiansen writes: "The evangelical message,
the denial of sacramentalism, and the necessity of
entering into a personal relationship with God, have
been accepted by a large number of people within
the state church among both laymen and clergy....
Even the methods of work have been adopted; Sunday schools, prayer and testimony meetings etc. are
found today within the church as on the outside of
it. The result is that while the state church at the
beginning of the nineteenth century had very little
evangelical life, today it is most likely true that the
strongest spiritual life in Norway is found within the
state church. It is evident that some of the other
dissenting bodies share with the Baptists in this influence upon the state church."[44]

The Norwegian Mission Covenant Church had its roots
in the Lutheran Free Church, as we have seen was the case
in Sweden. The activities of Lammers had brought into focus
the condition of the State Church and the need for reform.
At a national Meeting in Oslo in 1873 attended by over 600
people, debate was carried on concerning church reform, and
demands were made of the government in lectures and motions
for such reform. The government showed little interest or
concern in the matter.

Growing out of the situation came serious consideration
for a Lutheran free-church organization. Two pastors left
the establishment and in 1876 went to Scotland to study the
free-church organization and activity in that country. After
long and thorough preparatory work in large assemblies, the
Lutheran Free Church of Norway was organized in 1878. It
was a hard blow to the new organization that one of the delegates to Scotland, J.S. Munch, re-entered the State Church
as Lammers had done previously.

The influence of Rosenius was seen in the new group
in the preaching of free grace. It had a Presbyterian polity,
but was strictly Lutheran in doctrine.[45] (An early form of
ecumenicity!) The progress of the free church was good,
although there were instances of radicalism and separatism.
The individual churches were autonomous, although basically
the ideas of the general church prevailed. The denomination
is not now classified as a dissenter group, and its members

are permitted to teach religion in the public schools. By the
1940's the group had grown to a membership of 6,000 among
fifty-eight churches, with its own youth schools, book concern, and publications.

The group which more nearly represented the Lutheran
free-church idea was the Norwegian Mission Covenant, which
drew its inspiration from the Covenant Church in Sweden.
Det Norske Misjonsførbund was organized in the middle of
the 1880's. Westin credits two major factors which led to its
appearance. One factor was that several churches of the
Lammers' movement in Skien still existed but there was no
common organizations and members found it very easy to join
the Førbund. These churches were located in Oslo, Skien,
Bergen, and Larvik, to cite just a few.

More immediate in influence, according to Westin, was
the revival effort of Fredrik Franson in 1883. His continued
ministry during several periods well into the twentieth century gave added strength and encouragement to this, another
free-church development. His influence was strong and lasting over Norway, and this assistance in the formation of the
Førbund was decisive.

The neo-evangelism of C.O. Rosenius in Sweden was
held in high regard in Norway, and his sermons and other
writings had wide circulation and ardent readers. The Lutheran missionary groups which sprang up over the country
held views for the most part comparable to those of Svenska
Fosterlandsstiftelsen. When the movement under Waldenström
spread to adjoining provinces in Norway, many Swedish preachers became active leaders there. In Oslo a crisis with the
Lutheran Mission Society ensued in 1870 and resulted in the
formation of the Kristiania Ansgarii Mission Society. The
Lammers church in Oslo joined this new enterprise in 1881.
Membership could be maintained within the new society without severance from the State Church. Divergent views concerning baptism and the communion did not play an important
role in membership requirements, only a simply Christian faith.
This was Waldenström's concept of the New Testament church.

These free societies were reluctant to organize into a
denomination, but the passing of time showed the necessity
and advisability for some type of organization. B.C. Flock,
an itinerant preacher from Oslo who had been connected with

the Lammers group, agitated for organization in his publication, "Morgenroden." Thus a combination of circumstances
led to the formation of the "Mission førbund" in 1883, six
years after the counterpart in Sweden. Several Swedes participated in this organization.

As the denomination grew, a more structured organization was deemed necessary. Young people joined the church
through the revival activities of Franson, thus necessitating
the building and staffing of Bible and theological training
schools. Through the bequest of a friend of the Førbund,
a school was started in 1913. Besides Flock's "Morgenroden",
another paper the "Talesmonden" (The Spokesman), appeared
in 1903. In 1924 the name was changed to "Misjonsbladet."
Through the instrumentality of Franson, a songbook, Evangelii
Basun, was published and in the ensuing years went through
several revisions. More will be said in Chapter III concerning this volume. The Norwegian Publication Society was
formed in 1933. In one brief period, the membership of the
Førbund doubled from 500 to 1,000. Missionary outreach was
a vital part of the program, and by 1940 the Førbund could
count seventy-eight churches with more than 6,000 members,
and sixty full-time preachers.

Free Congregationalism in Norway fostered the formation
of many smaller groups which shunned membership in the
Førbund and well as any type of unity among themselves.
They were mostly of the revival-type emphasis. One of the
preachers, Albert Lunde, spoke to as many as 5,000 or 6,000
persons in the Cal Meyerstree Mission House. This work continued as the "Evangelical Church's Own Mission House."

"It was the Methodist pastor, T.B. Barratt of Oslo, who
more than anyone else merited the name of pioneer for the
Pentecostal movement in the Northlands."[46] So writes Westin
of the man whom we have already met in connection with Methodism in Norway and the Pentecostal activity in Sweden.
Barratt had followed with keen interest the preaching of Evan
Roberts and the revival in Wales under his ministry. On the
way to America to seek funds for the erection of a Methodist
mission, he experienced a thorough-going change in his life,
with the accompanying gifts of the Spirit, in particular speaking with tongues. Through his reading of Roberts, Charles
Finney, and other revivalists, he had directed his thinking
toward some unusual spiritual experience for himself.

Suffering humiliation at not receiving the financial aid
he sought, he set out for Los Angeles in the fall of 1906,
and there became acquainted with the "Spirit baptism" movement which made a drastic change in his life and outlook.
The result of this contact was that he became the outstanding
apostle of the Pentecostals in the North Countries.

Barratt's position in the Methodist church added strength
to the Pentecostal revival in Norway. His publication "Byposten" (The Village Post) became the mouthpiece for the new
movement. True to form, opposition came from both Sweden
and Norway via the papers, but this only helped the cause
by attracting people to it. As had already been mentioned,
people came from Sweden to see the working of the new denomination. Some of Barratt's worst antagonists were among
the Methodists in Norway. At the conference meeting in the
summer of 1907, he asked to withdraw from the pastors' organization in order to enjoy freedom to carry on the work
which had had such a noteworthy beginning. He did indicate
his desire to retain his membership in the Methodist church,
however.

His missionary endeavors took him as far away as India
in 1908. Upon his return he assumed his work in Norway in
the interest of spreading Pentecostalism among his people.
In the fall of 1910, a Pentecostal congregation was organized
in Oslo, and "Byposten" had its name changed to "Korsets
Seier" (The Cross Victorious). This became the official organ
of the Pentecostal church in Norway.

It took some time for Barratt to clarify his thinking
on church polity. The question of baptism was a crucial one
with all of the free-church groups and the most difficult on
which to achieve unanimity. On a visit to Örebro in 1913,
he requested baptism of John Ongman but was refused on the
ground that he had no intention of becoming a Baptist. Pastor Levi Pethrus was less apprehensive about the implications
of such a baptism and so baptized Barratt. When Barratt
himself began to administer baptism in his separate church,
his position in the Methodist church became untenable. In
1916 he declared his intention to sever his connections with
the Methodists with whom he had been associated since childhood. In a very real sense this decision might be considered
the beginning of the first Pentecostal church in Norway. In
1921 the church in Oslo assumed the name Filadelfia and, at

this time and in a real sense, became the "mother" church of
the Pentecostals in Norway, comparable to the church in
Stockholm by the same name.

The denomination grew rapidly with many similar churches joining the ranks. In less then twenty years, Pentecostalism had become the largest free-church denomination in
Norway. The foreign mission program was organized in 1915
with responsibility for the work in half a dozen countries.
Barratt lived to see the Norwegian Pentecostal churches grow
in number to 258 with a combined membership of 30,000. To
the time of his death in 1940, he remained their "unchallenged
leader and example."[47]

The revival movements of the 1800's reached to the
country of Denmark as they had in other Scandinavian countries. Like Norway, Denmark had experienced a time of
awakening around the year 1700, but opposition in the form
of conventicle acts and various other types of regulations
tended to thwart the spread of revivalism. Most of the revivalist activities were carried on within the national churches.
Now, at the turn of the century, there was a renewed interest introduced partly through a resurgence of Pietism and
Moravianism and partly through the influence from similar
movements in England and America. Both of these countries
extended financial support for evangelistic efforts in Denmark.

Reference has already been made to the life and ministry of Nikolaj Grundtvig in Denmark. From the movement
he led, small free-will type congregations developed; however,
for the most part they remained within the limits of national
Lutheranism. A law enacted in 1849 granted limited religious
liberty in that it provided for a voluntary separation from the
State Church, although at the same time the state could pre-
vent the recognition of the smaller free denominations. Baptists in Denmark were not recognized as a denomination until
1952, while the Methodists received recognition in 1865. This
law did not precipitate a large-scale severance from the established Church, mainly because the revival movements from
a theological standpoint were conservatively Lutheran. "They
were led either by the genial Grundtvig with his national
pathos and enthusiasm for popular education, or by the pietistic Beck and his men. These came by and large to put
their imprint on religious life and to recapture the church."[48]

In Sweden a more fragmentary development resulted in
many more free-churches being established than in Norway
and Denmark. Even though in the latter two countries a
movement for the establishment of free-churches came forth,
it never became as significant as in the church-life of Sweden.
Free-church congregations began to appear in Denmark in the
middle of the 1850's under the leadership of U.P. Grunnet.
His previous plans to become a missionary did not materialize,
and upon his return to Denmark, he set about to establish
free mission societies. The first free church in Denmark was
established in Copenhagen in 1855. Under the influence of
Kierkegaard, Grunnet became critical of the State Church and
strongly advocated self-government for the individual congregation. He was ordained in an English free church in Hamburg and until 1897 was a strong leader in the free-church
movement in Denmark. For forty years he traveled in the
interest of free churches, but the movement never had any
unusual strength. In a period of thirty-five years to 1890
there were only ten such churches with a membership of about
700. This particular movement, although it was a start, did
not play a significant role in the religious life of Denmark.

Westin considers the Baptists to be the real pioneers
in the free-church movement in Denmark as they were in
Sweden. Unlike Sweden, its early leaders were not seamen
or emigrants who had been converted in America. The real
forerunner of the Baptist movement in Denmark was P.C.
Mönster, a goldsmith and engraver, who came to the Baptist
position simply by his own private study of the Bible. He
had been associated with one of the revival movements of
Fyn as one of its strong leaders. Baptism and other church
matters were lively topics of discussion in these circles, and
questions arose and issues came to the fore regarding many
phases of State Church life and teachings. Mönster's conducting of many conventicles brought him before the law
courts and resulted in his moving to Copenhagen in 1835.
While there he came to know Grundtvig and to appreciate the
latter's stand on the matter of the state church order but
was in complete disagreement with him on the subject of baptism.

In the capital city were small groups which met for
Bible study and other religious exercise. Mönster joined himself to these and became an active leader as did P.E. Ryding,

in whose home such meetings were conducted.   Another leader
in these early days was Julius Köbner, a man of Jewish de-
scent, who had come into contact with Baptists in Germany
and had been baptized by the German Baptist leader, J.G.
Oncken. He had much to say on the subject of baptism at
these gatherings. Soon Mönster believed that he ought to
identify himself with the Baptists, and others came to the
same conviction.   In 1839 Oncken came to Copenhagen and
baptized eleven converts to the Baptist faith. P.E. Ryding,
who was destined to become a strong leader among Danish
and Swedish Baptists was in this first group to be baptized.
Thus was formed the first free church in Denmark of any
real and lasting significance. Mönster was elected to serve
as the leader for this small group. The first organizational
meeting took place in Mönster's home, which is still standing
at Hummergade Nr. 6 in Copenhagen. At this time the First
Baptist Church of Copenhagen came into being.

There followed times of persecution and stress in which
many of the Baptist leaders were fined and imprisoned.
Bishop Mynster led the attack in insisting that the laws of
repression should be strictly enforced. During the 1840's
children of Baptists were gathered up and taken to the State
Church where baptism was forced upon them. Such action
aroused protest even among the Lutheran clergy, and even
before the law of 1849 this practice was abandoned. Enforced
baptism was not officially annulled by law until 1857, however.

In spite of opposition and persecution, the Baptist work
in Denmark continued to grow, and new churches were organized in various parts of the country. One of the earliest
to be organized was in the city of Aalborg under the leadership of O.N. Föltved. This church grew in strength during
his term of ministry which extended from 1840 until his death
in 1856. It has been one of the strongest for the Baptist
witness in Denmark even to the present day.

Though comparatively few in number in the early days,
the leaders among the Danish Baptists have been strong and
efficient. Köbner became pastor of the church in Copenhagen
in 1865 and also served as leader of the entire Danish Baptist constituency for thirteen years. His theological works
as well as his books of poetry were a source of encouragement
to the whole Danish Baptist cause. His leadership in these
early crucial days was a stabilizing and unifying factor in the

progress and development of this new group. Among the
pioneers and early leaders was Marius Larsen, who served
the Copenhagen church for nearly a quarter of a century,
and N.P. Jensen, a Danish-American, who brought about a
close contact with the American Baptists. The latter endeavors
resulted in financial aid from America.

The formation of the First Baptist Church in Copenhagen
paved the way for other free churches in Denmark of which
there is quite a variety. Though recognized officially in comparatively recent years (1952), the presence of the Baptist
church in Denmark has been a stimulus to the Danish people
whether they are members of the free or State Church. A
spirit of tolerance and understanding between the two groups
was exhibited at the Baptist Centenary in 1939 when officials
of the State Church participated actively in the program, at
which time they acknowledged the need for religious liberty
for all peoples of their country.

An early representative and leader in Danish Methodism
was Christian Willerup who, like so many others, was converted in the United States and at once became active in the
Methodist Church. In 1850 he was called to assist in the
ministry of the famous Bethel Ship in New York harbor, where
he contacted many seamen and emigrants from the northern
countries. His interest in Methodist missions resulted in his
going to Copenhagen, where he worked in the organization of
the Methodist church in that city. He solicited funds from
America to be used in the building of a church edifice. Organization was troublesome because of so few charter members
with which to begin a church. Eventually in 1865 the needed
funds were provided and the edifice was completed. The
church in time became known as the Jerusalem Church, and
a Norwegian-American preacher, P. Rye, was called to assist
Willerup, especially in the English services.

Willerup continued as superintendent of the Danish
Methodist Church until 1872. During building operations he
became involved in misunderstandings and difficulties of various
kinds; this together with writing and teaching responsibili-
ties, caused a breakdown in his health. In 1873 he was succeeded by a young man Karl Schou, also a Danish-American.
Because of the progress of Methodism during his term of office, many feel that he is the real founder of Methodism in
Denmark. Another early leader of this denomination was J.J.

Christensen, who died in 1904 after several years of fruitful
work among the Methodists.

The church experienced a continued growth during the
1880's, and at the twenty-fifth anniversary in 1883, its membership numbered about 1,000, which was to be doubled
in the next five years. In 1888 a preparatory school for the
training of ministers was established in the formation of Ep-
worth Societies, work for young people, and the erection of
church buildings and parsonages. Much interest was shown
in social work, including the cause of temperance. One of
the early leaders in the temperance movement in Denmark was
Pastor C.F. Eltzholtz. He founded an absolutist society in
1879 in the Vegle Methodist Church. Children's and conva-
lescent homes under Methodist auspices were numerous throughout the country. One of the largest social agencies sponsored
by the Methodists was the Central Mission in Copenhagen,
where an extensive welfare work was carried on by its founder,
Anton Bast. He was the choice of the American Methodists
for the Bishop of Scandinavia. Troubles which arose in the
mission forced Bast's resignation in 1928 and his ultimate
severance from the Methodist body. In more recent years,
the Jerusalem Church has had the direction of the Central
Mission's program.

In spite of struggle and reverses, particularly in the
1920's, the Danish Methodist Church continued to exert a
positive influence. Strong missionary work is being carried
on in parts of Asia and the Congo, and its present membership is in the neighborhood of 4,000.

As was true in the other Scandinavian countries, the
Missionforbundet had its roots in the Lutheran free-church
movement in Denmark. The Forbund was a long time in formation, and when it came into its own it was of "humble proportion" in comparison with the other free-church bodies.
Another of Kierkegaard's disciples, M.A. Sommer, played a
decisive role in preparing the way for the free church by
influencing certain circles against the State Church. It remained for a Danish-American, N.P. Lang, to become the real
free-church pioneer in Denmark. Westin describes his ministry as follows:

> In 1882 he returned to the homeland and in Copen-
> hagen started to hold meetings among Lutheran Mission

Friends. Lang had before going to the U.S.A. been
influenced by Lammers' free-church movement, and
had also become acquainted with Oscar Ahnfelt's songs.
He had done preaching in the U.S.A. and had been
inspired by D.L. Moody and the movement centering
around him. He now agitated eagerly for a clear revival preaching of a kind that was not favored by
all. A schism ensued between Lang and the leaders
in the Lutheran Mission House where he conducted
his work. Those around Lang withdrew and held
meetings in another meeting-house. Even there dis-
sensions arose and Lang proceeded to Norway on a
preaching tour. In the meantime the said free-church
group organized a tract society which became the
focus for the Moody inspired revival movement.[49]

Lang returned to Denmark and resumed his work during
the winter of 1883-84 when some Swedish evangelists were
"holding forth" in Copenhagen. Real headway in the revival
movement was made through the ministry of Fredrik Franson
and, as was true of his preaching elsewhere, opposition to
his fiery message developed, which only furthered the evangelical cause. As in Norway, Franson may be considered the
one who inspired the formation of Missionforbundet. Miss
Catherine Juell, one of Franson's converts from Norway and
a lady of high social standing, participated in revival campaigns in Denmark. The presence of a woman revivalist of
the type of Franson caused quite a sensation and much opposition.

Another personality of note to appear on the religious
scene in Denmark was a Dane, Jens Jensen-Maar, who became an outstanding leader in the Forbund. After his conversion he began to preach and was considered by the rank
and file of those who heard him to be a promising evangelist
and preacher. His contact with the men of the free-mission
group was of great inspiration to him, and in time he himself was to become a highly esteemed preacher among them.

Thus the spiritual awakening inspired the formation of
many free societies in the country of Denmark, and the new
denomination was taking shape and needed organizing. A
conference was called in Aalborg in 1888 and the Danish Missionforbund was organized, patterned on strictly congregational principles. Some adherents did not want to use the

name as such and so it was not used uniformly; others preferred to be known merely as the "free Mission" Society.

Quite naturally the subject of baptism came up for discussion, a question on which some of the leaders were divided. In 1899 denomination pronounced that "baptism and
communion is to be observed by all the Forbund's preachers
in accordance with each one's interpretation of the Scriptures."[50] In time members were urged to sever connections
with the State Church in matters of baptism, communion and
marriage, although complete severance was not mandatory.

Just at the turn of the century, the young denomination was beset with teachings such as sinless perfection and
Russelism, and in 1902 there was a split in the ranks. Those
who remained with the Forbund showed real enthusiasm coupled
with stability, and the work progressed even though the members were fewer. The first songbook of the Forbund, Evangelii Basun, was published in 1885 and contained many translations from Swedish, Norwegian, and English.

Pentecostalism in Denmark can be traced to the preaching of its great leader, T.B. Barratt, and his meetings in
Copenhagen. Derogatory writings concerning him in the press
only helped to strengthen his ministry and draw the crowds.
A noted opera star, Anna Larsen, joined the movement, and
this alone proved to be quite sensational and a means of attracting others. According to Barratt's own account, during
his visit to the capital city in 1909 and 1910, disturbance
and violence erupted. In the midst of this turmoil, the Philadelphia Church was formed, though it was not until 1915 that
it was fully organized.

When the Baptist view on baptism became predominant,
some withdrew from the group. One, Pastor Mygind, labored
as an independent missionary. Upon his return to Denmark
in 1917, he opposed violently Baptistic views and as a consequence joined the State Church and fought this "heresy" from
there. Lt. and Mrs. Sigurd Bjorner were baptized among
"Swedish Pentecostal Friends" in 1919, and like Barratt before them, they were no longer welcome in regular church
circles. As a result of their witness and its resultant treatment, the Evangel Church was formed in Copenhagen and
drew its membership from among many of their sympathizers
in the Philadelphia Church. This move was made after a

Pentecostal conference in Copenhagen in 1919, at which time
no reconciliation was possible. Subsequent to this event was
the breaking away of many churches because of doctrinal
emphases and the formation of new groups of Pentecostals.
Finally, the Elim Church became the largest and most regular
in Danish Pentecostalism.

Summary

The rise of the free-church movement in Scandinavia
had its beginnings in the Pietist and Moravian movements in
eighteenth-century Europe. Even a cursory study of both
movements reveals that the foundation principles of each agree
with the basic premises of the free churches, namely, the
centrality of the Bible and the correctness of doctrine issuing
in practical righteous living. The meeting of the pietists in
conventicles became the pattern for the beginning of the
various free-church groups. While Pietism did not form free
churches or become a separate organization, the Moravians
were separatists and thus became the pioneers and the pattern for the separatist groups. According to Westin:

> It is therefore significant to note that the fellowship
> which the Moravians had developed in Germany and
> which spread to many countries became in its practi-
> cal development a type of a free-church--"a gathered
> church." The type of work among the Moravians be-
> came a pattern for the Continent and Scandinavia
> and prepared the way for conventicles and congrega-
> tions of believers.... The Moravians won followers
> not the least by their songs of fellowship--Zion's
> songs.... However, this movement with societies,
> preachers, meeting halls, and literature did little to
> organize people in a succession of new local assem-
> blies. The entire Moravian movement from an organ-
> izational standpoint was very limited, and besides
> this, in the Lutheran countries it had an uncertain
> position. It accepted the Augsburg Confession and
> wanted to be recognized as Lutheran, but it carried
> on its own ministry alongside the legal state church
> worship. There was thus a restraining element in
> the Moravian free church and its ministry.[51]

The "classes" established by George Scott in his ministry in

Stockholm (1830-1842) had a free-church character similar
to the Wesley class meetings in London.

Prominent in the development of the free-church movement in Scandinavia were C.O. Rosenius and Peter Walden-
Ström. The National Evangelical Society, (Fosterlandsstiftelsen), with which they were associated, was the forerunner
of the Mission Convenant group. The other groups were
greatly indebted to American influence and Scandinavian-
American and English leadership, for their establishment.
The Baptists, in particular, were indebted to Germany and
to men like Oncken for their encouragement in the dark beginning days in Scandinavia.

The Pentecostal movement with its emphasis on spiritual gifts has become a rather strong force in the religious
life of Scandinavia. Its position in the free-church movement
in the North is enunciated by Westin:

> The group is so young that it has played a small role
> in free-church development. It has not added any-
> thing new to the concept of the church. The char-
> acteristic of the Pentecostal movement, at least in
> Sweden, is that it pushes the congregational idea of
> the independence of the church to the extreme, at
> least in theory. It is clear, therefore, that in some
> respects it has strengthened the free church stream
> of separation during the last forty years. Moreover,
> the movement is in constant flux. In some countries
> this church group has had a good success; in others
> it has made very little progress. In the United States
> there are several groups, but all together they make
> up a comparatively small body alongside the large
> denominations. Pentecostal groups are enjoying rapid
> growth in many parts of the world. [52]

Each free-church group had its struggles during the
years of growth and expansion, but the relatively firm position of the free church in Scandinavia today, even though it
cannot compare to the State Church, is a testimony to the
faith, determination, and optimism of its dedicated leadership
in the pioneer days. Its influence on the State Church is
best seen in Norway, where today, because of the witness
of the free churches, the State Church maintains a strong
evangelical witness. Although the free churches are the

strongest in Sweden, their effectiveness in the cause of organized Christianity in the rest of Scandinavia should not be
minimized. In hymnody their contribution was of great significance as subsequent study will reveal.

NOTES

1. Henry Daquin, Pietism and the Traditional Worship Practices of the Lutheran Church (unpublished Master's
   thesis, Concordia Seminary, St. Louis, 1955), pp.
   6-10.
2. Samuel Macaully Johnson (ed.), The New Schaff-Herzog
   Encyclopedia of Religious Knowledge (Grand Rapids:
   Baker Book House, 1953), IX, p. 57.
3. Ibid., p. 58.
4. Ibid., p. 56.
5. Kenneth Scott Latourette, A History of Christianity (New
   York: Harper and Brothers, 1953), p. 897.
6. Hjalmar Holmquist and Hilding Pleijel (eds.), Svenska
   Kyrkans Historia (Uppsala; 1935) V, pp. 135-137,
   as quoted by Karl A. Olsson, By One Spirit, (Chicago: Covenant Press, 1962), pp. 20-21.
7. Ibid., p. 22.
8. Ibid., p. 23.
9. Ibid., p. 28.
10. Kenneth Scott Latourette, The Nineteenth Century in
    Europe (New York: Harper and Brothers, 1959),
    II, p. 172.
11. Gunnar Westin et al., De frikyrkliga samfunden i Sverige
    (Stockholm: Svenska Missionsförbundets Förlag, 1934),
    p. 29.
12. Ibid., p. 30.
13. Ibid., pp. 31, 32.
14. Latourette, The Nineteenth Century...., II, p. 173.
15. Ibid., p. 133.
16. Latourette, A History...., p. 1140.
17. Latourette, The Nineteenth Century...., II, p. 143.
18. Ibid., p. 144.
19. Ibid., p. 151.
20. Ibid., p. 155.
21. Gunnar Westin, Den kristna friförsamlingen i Norden
    (Stockholm: Westerbergs, 1956), pp. 253, 254.
22. Ibid., p. 255.
23. Ibid., pp. 332-333.

24. Latourette, The Nineteenth Century ..., II, p. 191.
25. Westin et al., De frikyrkliga samfunden ... , p. 7.
26. Ibid.
27. Ibid., p. 56.
28. Ibid., p. 16.
29. Westin, Den kristna friförsamlingen ... , p. 11.
30. Westin et al., De frikyrkliga samfunden ... , p. 13.
31. George M. Stephenson, The Religious Aspect of Swedish
     Immigration (Minneapolis: The University of Minne-
     sota Press, 1932), p. 81.
32. Ibid., pp. 82, 83.
33. Westin, Den kristna friförsamlingen ... , p. 68.
34. Ibid., pp. 69, 70.
35. Stephenson, op. cit., p. 117.
36. Ibid., p. 120.
37. Ibid.
38. Ibid., pp. 86, 92.
39. Olsson, op. cit., p. 120.
40. Gunnar Westin, The Free Church Through the Ages,
     trans. Virgil A. Olson (Nashville: Broadman Press,
     1958), p. 347.
41. Svenska Pingstväckelsen Femtio Ar, ed. Axel Blomqvist
     (Stockholm: Forlaget Filadelfia, 1957), pp. 6, 7.
42. Westin, Den kristna friförsamlingen ..., p. 140.
43. Ibid., p. 258.
44. Johannes Norgaard et al., Baptist Work in Denmark,
     Finland, Norway and Sweden (Stockholm: Wester-
     bergs, 1947), pp. 60-61.
45. Westin, Den Kristna friförsamlingen ... , p. 280.
46. Ibid., p. 290.
47. Ibid., p. 293.
48. Ibid., p. 298.
49. Ibid., p. 320.
50. Ibid., p. 324.
51. Westin, The Free Church ... , p. 279.
52. Ibid., p. 363.

CHAPTER III

THE HYMNODY OF THE PIETIST MOVEMENT
IN SCANDINAVIA

The hymnody of the Reformation in Scandinavia had its roots
in the hymnody of the German Reformation. A similar situation was obtained in the relationship between the hymnody of
Scandinavian Pietism and that of German Pietism. It is alto-
gether appropriate that a brief sketch of the hymnody of
the German pietistic reform precede that of the same movement in the Scandinavian countries.

Church Music Practices of the Pietists

The Pietists instituted many reforms in corporate worship. August Francke had warned them about the danger of
excesses in worship as well as superstitions concerning the
appointments of the sanctuary. Consequently, there was the
tendency toward oversimplification of the liturgy and the
abolishment of anything that was not considered of vital significance to the worship experience.

In reforming the liturgy, Pietists in many cities eliminated the worship services of traditional Lutheranism. Prescribed lessons and texts according to the church year were
not rigidly adhered to, and great stress was laid on the
preaching of practical Christianity as found in the Pauline
Epistles. Spontaneous, impromptu praying was encouraged
as a means of grace rather than prayers prescribed in a service book. The penetential aspect of communion was stressed
as well as the renewal of the baptismal vow and conversion
in connection with confirmation. Personal confession declined
as an ordinance because of the inroads of Pietism.

The Pietists carried on a major part of their reform in

church music and, more particularly, in hymnody. Hymns
became substitutes for various parts of the liturgy; for instance, the creed was often replaced by a hymn. Hymns
gradually degenerated toward a more subjective type com-
mensurate with the subjective, personal emphasis in all of
pietistic worship. Latin chants were abolished and anthems
were no longer used in the service of worship. The chorale,
though not discarded entirely, had a very limited part in the
music of the congregation.

Pietists became increasingly opposed to the use of artistic
music in worship, although the operatic and theatrical style
of singing from Italy made inroads to a certain degree among
them. Controversy developed over the use of instruments
in worship and whether instruments could be used for the
glory of God. Self-display on the part of singers brought
forth considerable criticism from the worshipers.

Hymnody of the German Pietists

The most important and the most interesting contribution
of the German Pietists was their hymns. Pietists of every
rank and walk of life composed hymns, making the pietistic
period the most productive in hymnody since the time of the
Reformation, both in regard to texts and tunes. The following comments are gleaned from Daquin's translation of Nelle's
opening paragraphs on pietistic hymnody:

1. No section in the history of hymnody is as inter-
    esting as that of Pietism.
2. The Pietists considered their poetry as having been
    given by the grace of God.
3. All poetry should brighten every aspect of the
    Christian life, according to the perspective of Piet-
    ism.
4. Never since Luther have hymns been so well re-
    ceived as in the age of Pietism.[1]

From 1675, when the title of "Pietist" was first applied,
to 1697, when the second edition of the first authentic collection was published in Halle, many new and noteworthy hymns
were produced by the German Pietists. Nelle has made an
interesting division in the development of the hymns of this
group:

1. Springtime (1675-1700)--hymns were fresh and direct in their note of joy.
2. Summer (1700-1727)--the period of its highest blossom.
3. Autumn (1727-1750)--a time of "rinsing" and clarification. [2]

As might be expected, not all hymns of this period were of equal merit. What was true of the pietistic hymns in general was equally true of those from pietistic Germany. The Lutheran chorale was replaced by the trite, subjective, sentimental ditty; and the new hymn became a substitute for the polyphonic music of the choir. The following descriptive points regarding pietistic hymnody are selected from various authors mentioned in Daquin's study:

1. Emphasis on the individual.
2. The use of mystical language.
3. The painting of Biblical pictures.
4. Allegorical treatment in texts.
5. Hymns of considerable length (a hymn of Gottlieb Woltersdorff has 263 stanzas!).
6. Need for daily repentence.
7. Need for spiritual fellowship.
8. Very few hymns on the sacraments.
9. The love of Jesus and His atoning death. [3]

Philip Spener was one among the many authors of hymns in the early days of Pietism. He wrote nine texts himself and encouraged others in the writing of religious poetry. Laurentius Laurentii (d. 1722) was one of the best known of the period. Joachim Neander (d. 1680) was the first great poet of the German Reformed church and became known as the "Paul Gerhardt of the Calvinists." His hymns on salvation and the love of Jesus were readily acceptable to the pietists. A later author, Gerhard Tersteegen (d. 1769), is known for his hymns of mystical character which found popular use among the Pietists and those of the Reformed church.

Hymnals of the German Pietists

The center of activity of the Pietists was the city of Halle and the university located there. The first Halle hymnal was published in 1693 and contained several Latin hymns, a

significant inclusion in light of the tenets of Pietism. The
second edition appeared in 1697, which contained many new
and original hymns by Pietists.

Johann A. Freylinghausen (1670-1739), colleague and
son-in-law to Francke, was foremost among pietistic hymnists.
Although he was severely criticized by the Orthodox group
for his hymns of subjective piety, he was still ranked as
the outstanding hymnist not only by the Pietists but also by
his contemporaries in general. In 1704 he published the first
edition of his hymnal Geistreiches Gesangbuch, which contained
683 hymns and 173 melodies. In 1705 a second edition appeared, to be followed by several more in the ensuing years.
This book, which became the standard hymnal of the Pietists,
reached its eighteenth edition. The Neue Geistriches Gesangbuch of 1724 contained eighty-five hymns and 154 melodies.
The two hymnals were combined into one volume in 1741 by
Francke with a total of 1,582 hymns and 600 melodies. Freylinghausen is purported to have been the author of forty-
four hymns and the composer of many of the tunes.

Concomitant to the spread of Pietism was the ever-
increasing interest in its hymns and hymn composition. Centers for hymnody developed in Berlin (from whence came the
"Porst"[4] hymnal, which had great circulation) and in Coethen
where authors stressed the "wounds of the Lamb." Various
aspects of Christian doctrine and instruction were presented
with special warnings against heresy and heretics. Some of
the hymns used extremely sensuous language with the purpose
to arouse the emotions of the singer. Ryden calls attention
to one of the passion hymns of Woltersdorf "which dwells
morbidly on every detail of the physical sufferings of Christ,
and in another he borrows from Scheffler's figure which likens
the soul to a bee deriving its sustenance from the crimson
wounds of Christ."[5]

The Wurtemberg school typifies the best in pietistic
hymnody. Its greatest exponent was Philip F. Hiller. His
hymns bear the imprint of the influence of Johann Albrecht
Bengel, his teacher at Denkendorf. Bengel's sound doctrinal
views led to a healthy type of Pietism which was reflected in
the hymns and other writings of such men as Hiller. His
hymns are churchly in character with a definite, sound Biblical language. A prolific writer, he produced approximately,
1,080 hymns of "scriptural and spiritual depth," many of

which reflected the adversities and trials which he experienced
during his lifetime. They exerted a strong influence on the
Wurtemberg of his day and are still used rather extensively.
Two popular collections of hymns by Hiller were the Little
Paradise and the extremely popular Geistliches Liederkastlein
(Casket of Spiritual Songs). The latter was taken by Ger-
man emigrants to all parts of the world.

Hymns of the Moravian Brethren

Moravian hymnody reached its peak in the hymns of
Count von Zinzendorf, who has to his credit in excess of
2,000 hymns. We have seen in the preceding chapters how
Spener and Francke both exerted strong influence on Zinzendorf. His hymns were extremely subjective and missionary
in character. He wrote his first hymn in Halle at the age of
twelve and his last in Herrnhut in 1760, the year of his death.
His hymns were collected in 1845 in a three-volume work by
Albert Knapp entitled, Geistliche Gedichte des Grafen von
Zinzendorf. This collected work contained 770 of his poems
and, in addition, a biographical sketch of the Count by
Knapp. Several other collections over a period of years contained varied numbers of Zinzendorf's hymns. Zinzendorf's
place in German hymnody is summarized by Julian:

> The key note of Zinzendorf's hymns, and of his re-
> ligious character, was a deep and earnest personal
> devotion to and fellowship with the crucified Saviour.
> This is seen even in his worst pieces, where it is
> his perverted fervour that leads him into objection-
> able familiarity with sacred things both in thought
> and in expression. If his self-restraint had been
> equal to his imaginative and productive powers, he
> would have ranked as one of the greatest German
> hymnwriters. [6]

To Christian Gregor (D. 1801) goes much of the credit for
the continued use of Zinzendorf's hymns because of his constant "pruning" of them. Himself a composer of note among
the Moravians, he saw the worth of many of the hymns of
Zinzendorf and sought earnestly to perpetuate their use by
modifying some of their extravagant expression.

In passing, it is worth noting that the party of Ortho-

doxy produced some hymn writers of distinction. A chief
representative of this more typically Lutheran group was Benjamin Schmolck (1672-1737). Though staying within the fold
of "regular" Lutherans, Schmolck showed much sympathy
toward the pietistic cause. He labored faithfully for thirty-
five years under many restrictions by the Catholic Church
in Silesia. His 1,183 hymns reflect spiritual warmth, praise,
and adoration and have earned him the place next to Paul
Gerhardt in German Protestant hymnody.

Erdmann Neumeister (d. 1756) was one of the strongest
opponents of Pietism. Although August Francke had influenced him greatly as a youth, he could see many dangers in
the Pietist and Moravian teachings and practices and came out
strongly against them. As pastor of St. James Church in
Hamburg for forty-one years, he became famous for his warm
and tender hymns which totaled 650. Besides his well-esteemed
hymns, he is famous as the originator of the Church Cantata.

Ryden evaluates the contribution of these two conservative Lutherans:

> While all the hymn-writers of Germany in the early
> part of the eighteenth century were more or less in-
> fluenced by the pietistic movement, there were some
> who nevertheless refused to be carried away by the
> emotional extravagances of which some of the Halle
> song writers were often guilty. In the hymns of
> these more conservative psalmists we find a happy
> blending of objective teaching and a warm, personal
> faith that reminds us of the earlier hymns of Ger-
> hardt.[7]

Early Pietistic Hymns in Sweden

As with a new movement of any kind, symptoms appear
early which foreshadow the actual breaking forth into an organized activity. This was true in the case of Pietism and
its accompanying hymnody. Mention has already been made
of the hymnody of Jesper Swedberg and of his being accused
of pietistic leanings as reflected in his hymns. Also, Jacob
Arrhenius and Gustaf Ollon have been cited as early exponents
of Pietism by the flavor of their writings. Although he was
professor of history at Uppsala, Arrhenius is remembered

mainly as a song writer. In 1689 he produced his Psalm
Proofs, with a second edition in 1691. He was a substantial
contributor to Swedberg's Psalmbok. Lövgren has remarked
that his paraphrases of David's Psalms contained in the 1695
book have the flavor of "old-Lutheran open confidence." His
collection of "Jesus Songs" and the mysticism and even near-
fanaticism of those of Ollon are an indication of the direction
in which song writers were moving.

Although Swedberg's Book was popular for many years,
it stood out as being too orthodox against the new trends of
expression in Pietism. It was severely criticized even by
the pietists.

The first recognized pietistic song collection was the
one known as Moses och Lamsens Wisor (Songs of Moses and
the Lamb), initiated by George Lybecker (d. 1716), an officer
in the State Mint, and completed in 1717 with sixty-one songs.
It went through several editions until in 1727 it numbered
137 songs. In the 1724 edition a collection of similar size
was added which was known as Osterlings Visor, since Carl
Gustaf Osterling (d. 1732) was the publisher. In it were
several translations from the German as well as some well-
written Swedish originals. This second section bore a rather
lengthy superscription:

> Evangelical and Teaching Songs: or Spiritual Songs
> Covering All Sunday Festivals and Holiday-Evangels,
> Which During the Entire Year are Useable[8]

These "Wisor" were "shot-through" with denunciations
of the religious and social conditions of the era. Immoderate
indulgences in food and drink and showy display were denounced, while sport and dance were completely ruled out.
Songs pointed out the vanity of trusting in baptism and the
communion for eternal salvation.

Conservative Pietism remained fairly tolerant in its attitude toward the State Church, while the radical Pietists
stood firm in their opposition to it. This opposition no doubt
was precipitated by the bigotry of the State Church leaders
exhibited in their tirades against revival meetings and reform
efforts. The radical Pietists produced their own songbook
in Swedish around the year 1732 entitled, Andeliga Wisor om
hwargenanda Materier (Spiritual Songs about Various Things).

(See Appendix C.) It contained translations from Tersteegen
and was a bit more poetic than the earlier collection of "Wisor."
The following is a free translation of one of the songs in the
1732 collection which is a polemic against the State Church.

> The Lamb's virgins long have been quartered in a
>   harlot-house
> Where they have fared most poorly
> And lost their strength and light.
> Long enough has the harlot ruled;
> Long enough her will prevailed;
> Long enough her shame we bore.
> Good and bad were mixed together.[9]

The mystical introversion stands out sharply in many
of the songs in Andeliga Wysor. The shortcoming of "unspiri-
tual" people, the vanity of earthly existence and the longing
for Jesus and heaven are themes which recur often in these
songs.[10] Also included in Andeliga Wysor is a song by John
Bunyan, O Underbare Gud. This is one of the first examples
of a song text of English origin to appear in a Swedish songbook. One can see these songs as a prelude to the revival
songs which appeared in Sweden some years later. This song
collection went through two more editions in 1787 and 1828.

Songs of Swedish Herrnhutism

As a result of the missionary endeavors of Zinzendorf
and his followers, Herrnhutism gained a stronghold; converts
were won over a period of years in Stockholm, Västergötland,
and Skåne. The rich heritage of Moravian hymnody was seen
in the number of people it inspired to write for its cause in
Sweden. Song writers and collections appeared on the scene
in the years which followed the introduction of Herrnhutism
into the north country.

The first collection of Swedish Herrnhutism, Sions Sånger
(Songs of Zion), was published in 1743 and contained 90 songs.
The edition of 1745 contained 130, and subsequently 223 songs
were included in the collection. Lövgren has made a detailed
analysis of the growth of the Sions Sånger including the several authors who contributed to its contents. The edition of
1748 is to be found in the library of Uppsala University. A
list of authors with short biographical notes on each is appended to the 1767 edition.

Concerning the contents, Lövgren points out that while the Lamsens Wisor contained many translations from the German pietists, the Herrnhut book has only thirteen such translations. Zinzendorf wrote six of these included, but his influence is readily noticeable in most of the rest. The most diligent of the contributors was Johan Kahl (1721-1746), who wrote fifty of the songs in the collection. Torsten Nyborg (1720-1792), whose missionary activities included ministries in Pennsylvania, England, and Sweden, contributed a sizable number of hymns as did Olof Kolmodin (1690-1753).

The popularity of Sions Sånger is seen in the printing of 20,000 copies in the 1740's. Westin has cited their effectiveness in the whole Herrnhut movement in Sweden by his comment that "scattered groups of pious people were nourished by Sions Sånger ... " and that in the revival movements in the 1840's, those who separated themselves from the church found great strength in the use of the same.[11] Lector Emil Liedgren in a radio lecture some years ago had this to say concerning the importance of this hymnal:

> In 1743 there appeared the Herrnhut song book "Sions Sånger" which became very important, thanks to its central Christian proclamation, its genuine folksiness and its gladsome straight forwardness. It initiated a quality, which has remained within the Swedish free-church movement and which, above all, has been preserved in the more nationally observed forms of revival religiosity movements of Rosenius' and Waldenström's color.[12]

Another volume of songs that was to captivate the free churches of Sweden was the Zions Nya Sånger issued in the 1780's and promoted by a convert of Herrnshutism, Anders Carl Rutström (1721-1772). Rutström studied at the University of Uppsala but was in poor standing with teachers and fellow students alike. In all probability, the hostility to him was produced by his harsh disposition and undisciplined living. In 1748, after rather extensive contact with the Moravians, he was converted and joined their ranks. He became one of their greatest preachers and was considered by some to be the greatest in Stockholm. Although he was readily accepted as a preacher, in time he incurred the ill will of the pastors by his strange doctrines and his attacks on the State Church. He suffered banishment to Hamburg from 1761 to 1770, when he was permitted to return to Sweden but not allowed to preach. He died in 1772.

According to Lövgren, during the 1740's many Herrnhut songs of a reasonable character were in use, but during the decades following those of the more fanatical kind appeared in great numbers, only to come into disuse later in the period.[13]

The first edition of the New Songs of Zion was printed in Copenhagen in 1778 and smuggled into Sweden. (At this time in Sweden, every manuscript of any kind had to be censored thoroughly before it could be printed.) In the first two editions, the authors' names were not indicated. In the edition of 1821, ninety-two of the songs were credited to Rutström. The book grew in popularity, and the last edition was published in 1923. It became known as the official hymnbook of "Bibeltrogna Vänner" (Bible-True Friends). Oscar Ahnfelt was responsible for the renascence of the hymnal by his including many hymns from it in his own collection. (Ahnfelt and his place in free-church hymnody will be discussed later.)

One of the best-known hymns of Rutström is "lammets folk och Sions fränder" (Chosen Seed and Zion's Children).

> Chosen seed and Zion's children
> Ransomed from eternal wrath,
> Traveling to the heav'nly Canaan
> On a rough and thorny path;
> Church of God, in Christ elected,
> Thou to God art reconciled,
> But on earth Thou art a stranger
> Persecuted and reviled.

A comparison by Liedgren between the two Zions Sänger is here quoted from the Standaret article:

> The first collection of "Zions Sånger" is regarded, as from the viewpoint of lyric and art, to rate higher than the collection of "Zions nya sanger" which was issued in the 1780's. Nevertheless this one was accorded no small significance, perhaps on account of its foremost contributor, A.K. Rutström. This song book was the first of its kind, which commended itself to the public by calling attention to the personal name of an individual. For Rutström's name was given

on the title page. Perhaps its success accounted for
the fact, that when "Andeliga wisjor i hwargehanda
materior" came forth in its new edition it was expressly
stated that it was Tolstadius' song book. Both of
these authors were accorded extraordinary respect
and a high reputation for piety and robust faith.
Rutström's death in prison surely contributed in no
small measure to the distribution of his songs--naturally
in connection with their folksy characteristics. Rutström was a combination of roughness and emotionalism, a trait that admittedly commends itself to a Swede.
He loved the concrete and the drastic:

> "You swim in your blood,
> In anguish you pray:
> You lie on the ground with your face in the dust."

to quote from one of his most well known songs. That
which, however, surely was most prized was the warmth
in Rutström's songs ... His song book was the first
to become of really permanent and evident importance
to the subsequent Free-church song tradition.[14]

Another contributor to Nya Sånger was Magnus B. Mal-
stedt (1724-1798), also a convert to Herrnhutism. He was
educated at Karlstad, Uppsala, and Lund, where he was appointed professor of Latin. He became popular as a teacher
and preacher, but because of his connection with the Herrnhut group he was dismissed from his teaching position and forbidden to do even private teaching. After a series of dis-
missals and reinstatements, his case was settled in his favor,
but with no lifting of previous restrictions concerning his
religious activities. In manuscript form in Uppsala is a collected volume, "Evangelical Songs of Zion," in which are
ninety selections by Malmstedt. He is purported to have written about 600 songs, many of which appeared in Nya Sånger.
His style and content may be seen from a free translation of
a verse he added to a song by Abraham Falk.

> Jesus was now made the world's reconciler,
> He on His heart every sinner did bear,
> When on His cross between heav'n and the earth,
> For our redemption he offered Himself.
> He for our sins doth contend and do battle,
> Pours out His blood in the deepest distress;
> Himself the Judge for the prisoners suffers;
> God would us save, He would not will our death.[15]

An interesting comparison between the Psalmbok and
the collections of the radical Pietists and Herrnhutists has
been made by Lövgren:

> It was said that the Swedish "Psalmbok" of 1695 was
> prompted to a great extent by the Psalms of David,
> while the songbooks published by the radical Pietists
> and Herrnhutists were in no small degree filled with
> sentiments characteristic of Solomon's Song. The
> early collections of songs by the Swedish Pietists in
> spirit reminds one of the Old Testament Prophets. A
> comprehensive Bible knowledge has, however, greatly
> affected the presentation.[16]

Another hymn writer of note who spoke out sharply
against emotionalism and denounced Herrnhutism was Lars
Linderot (1761-1811). He was a revivalist himself and carried
on a ministry on the west coast of Sweden. His songs, for
the most part, are very serious in content and have been
included in many hymnals of the evangelicals in Småland and
Värmland. One of the hymns of Linderot was a favorite of
the legalists.

> No one attains to the heavenly rest
> Who does not press for the guerdon;
> The soul must fight for the faith of the blest
> Bearing the warrior's burden.
> That way is narrow and the door is strait,
> Only sober faith can open heaven's gate.
> Hence we must press, yea press for the prize
> Or Heaven is lost forever.[17]

Psalmbooks of the Late Eighteenth
Century in Sweden

By the middle of the eighteenth century, there arose
considerable criticism against the Gamla Psalmboken (Swedberg's) because of its faulty language, poor poetry, lack of
categories, trite melodies, etc. In the year 1765 a Prof-
Psalmboken was published in Stockholm on the command of
"His Majesty the King." (See Appendix D.) In the foreword
to the hymnal, it is mentioned that the committee was intent
that the hymns contained therein should be to the edification
of those who use them and in the best intersts of Orthodoxy.
Purity of the Swedish language was diligently striven after in

proper and decent expression. The following quotation from
the introductory statement explains the contents and declares
the purpose of the book:

> In this collection certain Psalms under certain topics
> are still missing as for instance certain virtues and
> certain vices; which should have been included in the
> first main division: concerning especially Evil Angels,
> and the war against them which is required. Regard-
> ing the temptations of Christ; His miracles, in common
> and their usefulness; His intercessory work, etc.,
> which ought to have been dealt with in the second
> main division. But if such failures be remedied in
> the future by more efficient pens, the Committee
> promises that whatever comes in, will be added as an
> appendix when the next collection is published.
>
> Finally, and since the purpose of this project, next
> to the glory of the great God, is that our Swedish
> Church may have a comprehensive, more suitable and
> for the future more serviceable Psalm Book, those of
> the Committee, with due consideration, will take up
> the well grounded reminders on matters that can be
> submitted, by which their attempts can be helped all
> the more and be improved. And they will especially
> appreciate, if, besides the remarks about the items
> that need correction, specific suggestions for a happy
> change be communicated. Stockholm, the 23rd April,
> 1765.[18]

A second edition was published in 1767, which added
308 hymns to the 177 in the first edition. The aim of this
second edition was to please both the orthodox churchman as
well as the pietist. Its foreword states the purpose for the
inclusion of certain types of songs:

> Psalms which only under peculiar circumstances could
> be sung publicly in church are placed under the cap-
> tion HUSTAFLAN; which has afforded the committee
> occasion to find room under the same title for some
> psalms which otherwise pertain only to use by indi-
> viduals, certain classes, or particular persons in dif-
> ferent spiritual or physical circumstances. For the
> committee has purposed thus to promote in part godly
> family devotions, and in part see it that there were

psalms suitable for those who prepare to take in the
Lord's Holy Supper and examine the condition of their
own soul for the occasion.[19]

A detailed listing of the contents of this hymnbook appears
in Appendix B.

Several private "Psalmbooks" were published because
of the slowness of a central committee to initiate further revisions in the hymnody of the Church. In 1796 two such
collections were published: Psalmer by Kristoffer Dahl and
Samuel Odman's Försök till Kyrkosånger. An attempt to im-
prove existing psalmody was made with the publication of
Omarbetning af svenska psalmer, försökt by Michael Choreus
and Johan Olof Wallin in 1807. It is generally believed that
the hymns in this collection did not represent any great improvement.

The Psalmbok of 1819

        Next to the Swedberg hymnal of 1695, the book revised
and edited for the whole of Sweden by J.O. Wallin stands as
the most influential of all the publications of the nineteenth
century. Wallin was born in Stora Tuna in 1779 and early
in his life displayed his unusual endowment as a poet. In
1805 and 1809 he was awarded the prize for poetry at the
University of Uppsala. His popularity as a preacher and
pastor led him to Stockholm and ultimately to the archbishopric
of Uppsala.

        In 1811 Archbishop Lindblom appointed a committee to
undertake the preparation of a new hymnal. The Uppsala
"Professors' Hymnal" had appeared in 1793 but was rationalistic in tone and reflected the neology of the day. The new
book was issued in 1816 and, after some degree of alteration,
was published officially in 1819. Known as Den Svenska
Psalmboken, af Konungen gillad och stadfästed (The Swedish
hymn-book approved and confirmed by the king), it was
mainly the work of Wallin, who had dreamed of a new hymnal
years before. Among the 500 selections, the book contains
130 hymns in addition to 150 translations by Wallin.

        Even though Wallin himself was strictly a state church-
man, his hymns have found their place among the free-church

group. In the foreword to the 1816 proposal of the book, Wallin expressed his own ideas as to the purpose and use of a hymnal: "A well arranged psalmbook ought, according to my understanding, to be in all respects, everybody's possession and everybody's refuse."[20] The book is still held in high esteem by the Swedish people, and many of Wallin's hymns found their way into the free-church hymnals. The use of the hymnal eventually was made compulsory in the Church of Sweden.[21] The hymnal went through several revisions until 1921, when a section entitled Nya Psalmer was added, making a total of 673 hymns. A more complete analysis of Wallin's hymnal is to be found in Appendix E; suffice it to say here that hymns covering every aspect of Christian life and doctrine are to be found within its covers.

Concerning the influence of the 1819 Psalmbok, Ryden has this to say:

> The profound influence which Wallin's hymns have exerted over the Swedish language and its literature for more than a century is eloquent testimony not only to his poetic genius, but also to the faithfulness with which he adhered to the high standards he had imposed on himself.[22]

Although Wallin had the greatest share in the preparation of the new Psalmbok, he had several other Swedish poets who collaborated with him. Foremost were F.M. Franzen (1772-1847), Johan Åström (1767-1844), L. Ödman (1750-1829), S.J. Hedbörn (1783-1849), and G.J. Adlerbeth (d. 1818). Franzen worked the closest to Wallin in the selection and compilation of the large number of the compositions which make up this memorable volume. Born in Finland of Swedish parents, he became professor at the University of Abo and later accepted the call to a pastorate in Sweden. It was during this time when he served the Church at Kumla that he wrote most of his finest hymns. He became a famous preacher and, subsequently, assumed the pulpit in St. Clara church in Stockholm. This appointment was a stepping stone to his becoming Bishop of Harnösland when he was sixty-two years of age. In 1812 at the outset of his ministry in Sweden, he became closely associated with Wallin in the preparation of the hymnal. The collection contained twenty-nine hymns from his pen on a variety of subjects including immortality, philosophy, advent, evening, communion, children's hymns, and missions.

He ranks among the great hymnists of the north country and
has continued to be a favorite of Christians in several groups.

Hedborn is represented in the 1819 "Book" with hymns
of devotion, Epiphany, and communion. Åström, a parish
priest and poet of unusual ability, contributed no less than
eighteen songs, some of which have a tinge of rationalism in
them. His hymn for All Saints Day is a revision of Laurentii
Laurinus' written in 1620.

As has been previously indicated, Den Nya Svenska
Psalmboken became very popular, however, in areas like Norrland and Småland, opposition developed because of the preva-
lence of neologian religious thought. A revision undertaken
by Johan Henrik Thomander (1789-1865) and Peter Wieselgren
(1800-1877) was completed in 1849. The intention of these
two men was to make the tests more acceptable to the Orthodox group, which necessitated the elimination of some of the
early hymns by Wallin himself. Further revision was discussed
in 1868; in 1889 a new proposal was rejected, and a later revision of 1896 was turned down by the Kyrkämötet. Several
proposals were then made by private individuals until the
1921 revision, when the king decreed that it be continued as
the official hymnal for the State Church of Sweden.

Peter H. Syreen (1776-1838) pursued a rather varied
career both in his educational and vocational experience. He
received his formal education of Vaxjo and Uppsala and served
as teacher, preacher, writer, and bookstore proprietor in
his early years. He issued many books but is best known
for his collection of 500 songs, Christelige Sångbok till bruk
vid Enskil husandakt (Christian Songbook for use in Separate
House Worship) published completely in 1826. This hymnal
was the result of promptings by Syreen's friends and close
associates for a new means of expression of their faith. The
first part was issued in 1823 as a trial venture; its success
brought about the completion of the entire collection.

The songs in the Syreen book were taken mainly from
old Herrnhut and pietistic songbooks; in addition, Syreen
included several of his own authorship. Popular songs from
Moses och Lamsens Wisor, Sions Sånger, and several by Lars
Linderot were among those selected. Because the book had
a pietistic flavor it became popular among the pietists, especially in southern Sweden. It is represented by three songs
in the Nya Psalmer supplement of the 1921 Wallin book.

The following topical headings in this hymnal give an indication of the scope of its contents:

> Our Present Christendom
> The Awakened Sinner's Complaint and Hope
> Loving Warning, Advise and Encouragement for God's
>   Children
> Some Christian Duties
> During Spiritual Distress, Temptations and Troubles
> The Plaint of the Saints, Encouragements and Hope
> Privileges and Benefits for True Christians
> Songs for Festive Occasions
> Seasonal Songs and Special Times of Day
> On Evangelical Texts
> The Vanity of the World and Times, Concern for a
>   Correct Preparation for the Incorruptible Life of
>   Eternity
> The Victory of Zion, the Fall of Babylon

The following stanzas selected from one of the hymns are a sample of the general style of the hymnal:

> Our life is very brief, Our lifetime runs away
> Before we comprehend it. We hardly start our life
> Until in death it's ended. No plaint will help us here;
> Our life is very brief. Our lifetime runs away.
>
> Behold, eternity, There stands with certainty
> At ends of time before us, Where doom and wage we
>   get
> For all we here are doing. My soul, give heed to
>   this:
> For us eternity, is certainly a-coming.

C.O. Rosenius and the
Hymns in Pietisten

Carl Olav Rosenius is considered today to have been the foremost lay-preacher in Sweden. He was the son of a pastor of Upper Norrland who was a friend of the läsare (readers). From the time of his birth on February 3, 1816, he was dedicated by his parents to the ministry of the church, and they lived to see this desire fulfilled. Early in life he showed a bent toward the preaching ministry by gathering a

few of his "awakened" friends around him and preaching to
them. Permission for such gatherings was granted by Franzen, who was presiding bishop at the time. This was his
first field of activity in the city of Pitea.

    Rosenius pursued studies for a time at Uppsala, but
ill health, the low moral standards at the university, poverty,
disgust, and university life in general were cause for inter-
rupting his term of study. For a time his own religious beliefs were severely shaken. Just at this time he met the
Methodist preacher, George Scott, with whom he eventually
became associated as has already been mentioned in Chapter
II. This association led to his assuming the editorship of
Pietisten, which journal did much for the cause of Pietism
in all of Scandinavia. In his relatively brief life which ended
in 1868, he engaged in many, varied labors within the church
which resulted in the strengthening of the free church in
the entire north country.

    Our interest in Rosenius centers in one aspect of his
church activities, his prose, and poetic writings. In both
Rosenius and his wife, Agatha, there was a poetic vein. In
Carl Olav this appeared quite early, although for him his
greatest ability lay in his writing of prose. During the course
of the years, however, he contributed many hymns through
the Christian monthly, Pietisten, some of which were translations and revisions. He has even been accused of plagiar-
ism in some instances. His poetry does not always flow easily
but its intensive gospel proclamation caused it to become extremely popular and widely used among the Pietists in all of
Scandinavia.

    Although not a separatist himself, Rosenius was sig-
nificantly influenced by Moravianism. He was an ardent admirer of Rutström and tried in the pages of Pietisten "to
nourish the Rutström tradition: by frequently including many
of Rutström's hymns for the spiritual enrichment of his readers."[23] Olsson sheds further light on this aspect of his relationship to the Moravians:

        The Rosenian conventicle also contributed to the de-
        velopment of a revival hymnody. The impact of Mora-
        vian piety on the Rosenian revival appears nowhere
        more clearly than in the hymns which were sung and
        created by the circle around Rosenius. In addition

to the hymns from the Psalmbok, the Rosenius conventicles used hymns from the Songs of Zion and the
New Songs of Zion. Because many of the hymns in
the latter book were by Rutström, or were attributed
to him, it became common practice to speak of the
collection as "Rutström's songs."[24]

During the Rosenian revival, interest in the foreign
missionary program was high. This, coupled with revival
enthusiasm, resulted in a growing dissatisfaction with the
Wallin Psalmbok. The läsare in Norrland refused to use it
almost entirely. Rosenius tried to show himself sympathetic
toward their aversion to the Psalmbok. In his correspondence
with them, he called to their attention the revised book of
Thomander and Wieselgren which was soon to be published.
Rosenius' evaluation of the new book is explained further
by Lövgren:

> Those of our most noted Doctors of Theology have
> therefore undertaken a cleansing in the New "Psalm-
> bok" by eliminating what is most offensive to evange-
> lical truth. Their new "psalmbok" is soon to be pub-
> lished. It is thus from high church sources publicly
> admitted that things are not well with the New "Psalm-
> bok." [Wallin's evidently is meant.] And how could
> it be, when to a great extent it is authored by un-
> regenerated teachers and geniuses? She is an off-
> spring of the outwardly mixed church and resembles
> her as any daughter is like her mother.[25]

When the new book was published in 1849, it was substituted for Wallin's in many circles. In the Fosterlandsstiftelsen report of 1875, it was mentioned that already 9,000 copies
had been printed. Wallin's Psalmbok was still held in high regard by many while they still admitted that it contained all
too many controversial expressions and did not furnish enough
hymns of missionary emphasis. Even the revision, it was felt,
did not contribute enough to the revivalistic spirit which was
abroad in those days. Soon a whole chain of songbooks of
the revival type began to be produced "more in line with the
spirit and needs incident to revival."[26]

The hymns of Rosenius cover a wide variety of subjects.
This is also true of his revisions, translations, and those
which were more or less "plagiarized." In many cases no

credit is given. The sample lines of Rosenius' poetry have
been gleaned from issues of Pietisten, Lövgren and the Standaret.

One of the most widely known and used of the Rosenius
hymns is the one on Christian brotherhood with the beginning
line "Med Gud och hans vänskap hans Ande och ord" (With
God and His Friendship, His Spirit and Word). It has appeared
in many of the hymnals of Scandinavia, in particular the second section of Nya Psalmer, (No. 594) of the Wallin collection.
The following is a translation by C.R. Osbeck of the first
and last stanzas as they appear in most English hymnals.

> With God and His Friendship, His Spirit and Word,
> With brethren partaking the bread of our Lord,
> With courage and joy we will meet coming days;
> The Shepherd is with us, the Shepherd is with us,
> The dear, loving Shepherd, He guides all our ways.
>
> O Jesus! be with us, abide with us still,
> And care for us, bear us, and teach us Thy Will.
> Thy glory, O Jesus, Thou'lt soon let us see:
> Praise, glory and honour, Praise, glory and honour,
> Praise, glory and honour, our Saviour, to Thee.[27]

Lövgren maintains that this hymn by Rosenius is built on the
Moravian hymn "O selige Stunden," which he assumes also
inspired Clara Ahnfelt's "Ack saliga Stunder."[28] He also
points out that in another hymn ascribed to Rosenius, the
first two stanzas are his but the last three are from a collection of Moravian hymns of 1806.

A common practice of Rosenius was to make drastic
changes in the poems he used in Pietisten, for instance, in
the addition of stanzas as would suit his purpose. A case
in point concerns a hymn, originally by the Baptist Gustaf
Palmquist, "Jag har en vän, sa huld, så mild, så tålig" (I
Have a Friend, So Helpful, Mild and Patient). Lövgren con-
tends that Rosenius altered the song, but to what extent it
is not known. It appears in many books with credit given
only to Rosenius. Such is the case with "En Vän Framför
andra, min Frälsare huld" (A Friend Above Others, My Savior and Lord).

In 1849 a thirty-four stanza composition by a government official was printed in Pietisten. Revised and abbreviated from a longer composition, it speaks of the blessedness and election of the Christian. A translated excerpt from the song gives an idea of the general thought throughout:

> Deep was its fall to unspeakable fate
> Which scarred the whole gamut of nature;
> Dire was its curse, everlasting its death,
> Our wretched and lost generation!
> God's judgment was changeless--
>   despairing we lay
> in bondage eternal; we only could hear
> The taunts of the damned in their prison.

The pietistic flavor, which is found in so many of the hymns with which Rosenius had to do, is seen in these few lines which appeared in Pietisten in 1854.

> Dare thyself without fear,
> Trust that Jesus did all for thee,
> He for thee hath victory won,
> Crushed the serpent who was mighty,
> Opened us heaven's gate
> Dare thyself, without fear.

A hymn which is found in many of the Swedish hymnals presents the figure of the "Good Shepherd." It appeared in Pietisten in June of 1847 with no indication of its authorship. In the hymnals stanzas from Herrnhutian, sources are indicated as well as those contributed by Rosenius. This couplet gives us an idea of the thrust of its message.

> As I go in forest, mount or valley,
> Follows me a Friend, I hear his voice.

Although the songs of Rosenius, exemplified by those appearing in Pietisten, did not reach the literary level of those found in Wallin's hymnal of 1819, they did have a strong appeal to those of pietistic leanings. The writer has continually read of Rosenius' songs which became favorites among the evangelicals of his day and succeeding generations.

Other Contributors to Pietistic Song

The nineteenth-century revival period witnessed

the rise of many women hymnists. Charlotte Elliot and Frances
Ridley Havergal were popular in England: American hymnody
was enriched by the poems of Fanny Crosby and Sweden received many songs from Lina Sandell.[29]

Lina Sandell became prominent as a song writer in the
midst of the extensive ministry of C.O. Rosenius. Born into
a Lutheran pastor's home in 1832, she was the typical frail
child who preferred to stay within the shelter of the home
rather than engage in childhood play activities. Tragedy
came into her life in the drowning of her father, which she
witnessed from the deck of the boat on a journey to Gothenburg. Tradition has it that one of her earliest hymns "Herre
ferdöljej ditt anskte för mig" (Hide not Thy face for me dear
Lord and Saviour) was written during her sorrow in the loss
of her father, "a song that was to be immortalized, together
with its plaintive Finnish melody, in Dr. F.M. Christiansen's
'Lost in the Night.'"[30] Oscar Lövgren maintains that this
hymn was written sometime before her father's death. In the
year of her father's death, 1868, she contributed fourteen of
her poems anonymously in a Christian journal published by
Fosterlandsstiftelsen, Budbärarer. These early hymns have
remained among the favorites of the Swedish people even though
she wrote some 650 more in the coming years. The following
is a translation of what is perhaps the favorite among all of
her songs, "Trygare kan ingen vara."

> Children of the heavenly Father
> Safely in His bosom gather;
> Nestling bird nor star in heaven,
> Such a refuge e'er was given.
>
> God His own doth tend and nourish,
> In His holy courts they flourish,
> From all evil things he spares them,
> In His mighty arms He bears them.
>
> Neither life nor death shall ever
> From the Lord His children sever;
> Unto them His grace He showeth,
> And their sorrows all He knoweth.
>
> Though He giveth or He taketh,
> God His children ne'er forsaketh,
> His the loving purpose solely
> To preserve them pure and holy.

Lina Sandell's hymns will be discussed in a later chapter in their relationship to the entire field of Christian hymnody; in passing it is worth noting that as a hymn writer she
ranks among the highest in the percentage of her hymns to
be found in the major Swedish free-church hymnals. The
hymn quoted above has been included in hymnals of many
American denominations of non-Swedish background.

Another woman hymn writer of note is Elizabeth Ehrenborg-
Posse, who also lived during the time of the Rosenius revivals.
Born into Swedish aristocracy in 1818, she came under the
influence of Rosenius and the Pietists. She had a particular
interest in working with young children, and from the small
group of youngsters which she invited into her home on Sunday in 1851, the work progressed to the point where larger
quarters were necessary. This activity earned for "Betty"
Ehrenborg the credit of having started the Sunday school
movement in Sweden. After a sojourn in England where she
studied the Sunday school movement, she returned to Stockholm and began Sunday school work in the Kungsholm district.
New teachers were recruited and trained, and the work progressed. She wrote hymns and translated many English hymns
into Swedish for use in this school. In 1856 she was married
to Baron J.A. Posse, who was himself an enthusiastic supporter of Sunday school work.

While in England, Mrs. Posse became interested in the
numerous children's hymns, some of which she translated into
her native tongue. Upon her return to Sweden, she became
involved further in translation work. Then Per Palmquist
sought her help in translating hymns for use in his Sunday
school in Stockholm. When he was in London, he purchased
a large hymnbook from George Scott entitled, Training School
Songbook from which Mrs. Posse translated hymns for use in
his school. In 1852 Palmquist published a booklet, Andeliga
Sånger för Barn, which contained many of Mrs. Posse's translations.[31] Several of her translations also appeared in Palmquist's Pilgrims Sånger. William Cowper's "There Is a Fountain" was translated and adapted for children's use by her.
Her most famous hymn is a well-loved Swedish Christmas carol,
"När juldag's morgon glimmar" (When Christmas Morn Is Dawn-
ing). This hymn was examined in two different hymnals where
she is listed as a co-author and arranger, respectively. Ryden suggests that that there may have been a "German ante-
cedent" but seems to be willing to give her full credit for the

authorship. Among her many translations are two well-known
hymns from the English, "Just As I Am" by Charlotte Elliott
and "Rock of Ages" by Augustus Toplady, both of whom were
British hymnists. These hymns are representative of many
which were translated by her and which appeared in subsequent editions of Palmquist's booklet in 1854 and 1832.[32] Mrs.
Posse is well represented in modern hymnals of Scandinavia
by many of her translations and original lyrics. She died in
1880.

One person, above all others, who helped to get the
songs of Swedish pietism into the religious circles of Scandinavia was Oscar Ahnfelt (1813-1882). Born into a moderately
pietistic family, he intended to enter the ministry of the State
Church. After some time in study at the University of Lund,
he returned home to devote himself to his musical interests.
He had come to Stockholm to begin serious study in music
and while there he came under the preaching of a pietistic
minister. Additional contact with Rosenius resulted in a
spiritual crisis for Ahnfelt, after which the two became close
friends and coworkers.

Ahnfelt's initial ministry was in the field of music, but
Rosenius was desirous of using him as a lay preacher. His
combination of talents in music, composing, and preaching put
him in great demand throughout Sweden. His greatest contribution was in musical composition in supplying new songs for
the conventicles. Until now, mostly Moravian hymns had been
used. He set his own lyrics to music, even though many of
them were substandard, and also provided musical settings
for the poems of other authors.

At first his songs were transmitted orally. The great
Swedish singer, Jenny Lind, not only sang them, but, by a
generous monetary contribution, she also helped Ahnfelt begin
publication. The first book, published in 1850, contained
twelve selections. It was titled Andeliga Sånger / med ac-
compagnement af / Pianoforte eller Guitarre / componerade /
samt / damaissle / Jenny Linde / . Up until 1877, eleven
similar pamphlets were published with a total of approximately
200 compositions. No lyrics were by Ahnfelt (probably only
some revision), and his melodies were mostly adaptations of
folk tunes. The book contained hymns by Lina Sandell,
Rosenius, and others which earlier had been published in
Pietisten. Ahnfelt himself is well represented in scores of

hymnals by his melodies which have become favorites among Scandinavians.

It is of interest to note that Jenny Lind thought of herself as a pietist and frequently visited the conventicles. Rosenius considered her to be one of the Läsare. She is supposed to have gained great spiritual enjoyment from the preaching of Rosenius and the music of Ahnfelt.

Lina Sandell gives Ahnfelt the credit for her success as a hymn writer. Not only did he provide many melodies for her songs, but he also sang them as he traveled throughout Scandinavia. Said Mrs. Sandell-Berg, "Ahnfelt has sung my songs into the hearts of the people."[33] He is represented in the latest Baptist hymnal of Sweden by thirteen entries of his melodies.

Among the circle of the "awakened" in Stockholm in which he moved, Ahnfelt met Clara Stromberg. She had received spiritual release through the preaching of Rosenius and became active within the company of his followers. In the summer of 1851, she and Ahnfelt were married. Clara Ahnfelt wrote several songs, some of which are still to be found in recent compilations particularly in Sweden.

Pietistic Song in Denmark

Just as the hymns of Swedish Pietism had their roots (to some degree at least) in the hymns of Swedberg, Arrhenius and Ollon, so the hymns of Denmark in this period were foreshadowed in the hymns of Thomas Kingo (1643-1703), the first of the great Danish hymnwriters. He was born at a time of spiritual and cultural lag in the history of Denmark and was destined to contribute spiritually and culturally to the life of his native land.

A depression which followed the Thirty Years' War threatened the very life of Denmark. Kingo's home felt the trying period in full measure. Aaberg describes the conditions:

> The country's unsuccessful participation in the Thirty Years' War had brought on a depression that threatened its very existence as a nation; and a terrible

pestilence followed by new wars increased and pro-
longed the general misery, making the years of Kingo's
childhood and youth one of the darkest periods in
Danish history.

But although these conditions brought sorrow and
ruin to thousands, even among the wealthy, the humble
home of the Kingo's somehow managed to survive.
Beneath its roof industry and frugality worked hand
in hand with piety and mutual love to brave the storms
that wrecked so many and apparently far stronger
establishments. Kingo always speaks with the greatest respect and gratitude of his "poor but honest
parents." In a poetic description of his childhood
years he vividly recalls their indulgent kindness to
him.

"I took my pilgrim staff in hand
Ere I attempted talking;
I had scarce left my swaddling-band
Before they set me walking.
They coached me onward with a smile
And suited me when tearful.
One step was farther than a mile,
For I was small and fearful."[34]

Kingo's education included study in the city of Hiller,
where he began his study of Danish literature, and the University of Copenhagen where he delved into theology. Through
his preceptor at the University, Professor Bartholin, Kingo
came under the influence of the pietistic movement in a rather
secondhand way, but it was effective. Years before, Bartholin had come under the tutelage of Holger Rosenkrans, a
close friend of John Arndt, the German Pietist. The result
for Kingo was that he strongly favored the "Arndt-Rosenkrans
view of Christianity."

Following the years of struggle between Denmark and
Sweden, Kingo was ordained in the Church of Our Lady in
Copenhagen in September 1661. His next pastorate after seven
years was in his home city and church in Slangemp. About
this time he really began to attract attention by his poetry.
He had already begun to re-edit the Danish Psalmbog, which,
as has been mentioned, had gone through three editions. His
own small volume Spiritual Songs, Part One appeared in 1673,

containing fifteen morning and evening hymns. The book was
received with great enthusiasm, and the hymns were sung
throughout Denmark. In the following years, they were
translated into several languages. His elevation to the archbishopric of Fyen in 1677 is credited to the impression his
hymns made on the Danish church and nation.

The first volume of Spiritual Songs was dedicated and
addressed to King Christian V; the second part, published
in 1684, was dedicated to the Danish queen, Charlotee Amalia.
It contained twenty hymns and seventeen "sighs." The themes
presented in the second volume are penitence, repentance,
and faith and seem to reflect the poet's own spiritual struggles
and victories.

By this time Kingo was at the pinnacle of his fame as
the Danish people realized that a man of great stature and
ability was in their midst. In 1679 he was honored by being
made a member of the nobility, and in 1682 he was awarded
the honorary degree, Doctor of Theology. In 1683 came the
appointment to edit a new hymnal for the people of Denmark
and Norway. Thomisson's hymnal of 1569 had served the
Church for well over 100 years but changing language and
literary taste necessitated something new. Thus the king
honored Kingo by assigning him to this task of great magnitude. The instructions concerning the preparation of the
hymnal are summarized by Aaberg:

> The carefully prepared instructions of his commission
> directed him to eliminate undesirable hymns; to revise
> antiquated rhymes and expressions; to adopt at least
> two new hymns by himself or another for every peri-
> cope and epistle of the church year, but under no
> circumstances to make any changes in Luther's hymns
> that would alter their meaning. [35]

When the first draft of the new hymnal reached the king
six years later, it was obvious that Kingo had completely
ignored the instructions. Included were 267 hymns of which
137 were his own. His treatment of the "old" hymns aroused
a storm of protest, in that some of them were hardly recog-
nizable. Although the king had already approved the proposed
hymnbook, he revoked his action and appointed a commission
to supervise continued work. Kingo was humiliated, crushed,
and financially disabled by the king's action. In addition to

his work on the hymnal, he had personally invested his funds
in a printing press and materials for its publication.

Soren Janasson, provost at the Cathedral of Roskilde,
was appointed by the king to undertake the work from which
Kingo had been dismissed, and in 1693 the book was finished.
It did not contain one of Kingo's hymns! Although the hymnal
was of high calibre, the king realized that the omission of
Kingo's hymns was the work of his enemies, and such an act
of contempt on their part would never pass unnoticed by the
Danish people. Again a committee was appointed to prepare
a hymnal that would duly recognize the work of Kingo. He
was consulted by the committee on the many aspects of publication and was asked to write new hymns to complete the desired numbers. The new hymnal was ready in 1699. It contained 297 hymns, including eighty-five by Kingo, and was
well received by the church. Although he did not fully recover from the indignity which he had suffered, he did live
to see his efforts finally crowned with success. The title
page of the hymnal is a tribute to the labor of Denmark's
great poet:

> The authorized new Church hymn-book, suitably
> adapted from old spiritual songs and carefully revised,
> and enriched with many new hymns, according to his
> Majesty's most gracious command, by the principal
> clergy in Copenhagen, for the service of God on Sun-
> days, festivals, prayer-days, and for other godly
> uses in the Church in Denmark and Norway, and in
> like manner according to the royal command prepared
> for the press by Thomas Kingo, Bishop in the Diocese
> of Funen.[36]

The hymns of Kingo cover a variety of subjects. Aa-
berg has divided them into the following categories: Festival
Hymns, Sacramental Hymns, Historical Hymns, and Hymns on
the Gospels and Epistles. He is known as the Easter Poet of
Denmark, mainly because of one Easter hymn, although the
Easter theme is the subject for many hymns written by him.
Two stanzas are included here, which are typical of the entire
five-stanza hymn.

> Like the golden sun ascending
> In the darkly clouded sky
> And on earth its glory spending

Until clouds and darkness fly,
So my Jesus from the grave,
From death's dark, abysmal cave,
Rose triumphant Easter morning,
Brighter than the sun returning.

Thou wilt hence to life awake me
By thy resurrection power;
Death may wound and overtake me,
Worms my flesh and bones devour,
But I face the threat of death
With the sure and joyful faith
That its fearful reign was ended
When Thy might its portal rended.

Kingo's place in Danish hymnology is enunciated clearly
by Aaberg. On the strength of his remarks and because of
the pietistic influence of Bartholion on Kingo, the writer has
felt justified in including Kingo at least as a forerunner of
the pietistic hymnists of Denmark. Aaberg comments as follows concerning the thrust of Kingo's hymns:

> Kingo is often called the singer of orthodoxy. His
> hymns faithfully present the accepted doctrines of
> his church. No hymnwriter is more staunchly Lu-
> theran than he. But he was too vital to become a
> mere doctrinaire. With him orthodoxy was only a
> means to an end, a more vigorous Christian life.
> Many of his hymns present a forceful and straight-
> forward appeal for a real personal life with God.
> The following hymn may be called an orthodox revival
> hymn. It was a favorite with the great Norwegian
> lay preacher, Hans Nielsen Hauge.

The power of sin no longer
Within my heart shall reign;
Faith must grow ever stronger
And carnal lust be slain;
For when I was baptized,
The bonds of sin were severed
And I by grace delivered
To live for Jesus Christ.

Would I accept the merit
Of my baptismal grace

And with my faith and spirit
The Savior's cross embrace,
How great would be my blame
Should I abide in evil
And not renounce the devil
In Christ my Savior's name.

It can bestow no treasure
On me that Christ arose.
If I will not with pleasure
The power of death oppose,
And with my heart embrace
The Savior, who is risen
And has from error's prison
Redeemed me by His grace.

Lord Jesus, help me ever
To fight "the old man" so
That he shall not deliver
Me to eternal woe,
But that I here may die
From sin and all offences
And, by the blood that cleanses,
Attain my home on high.[37]

The warmth and earnest Christian spirit in Kingo's
hymns have earned for them a place of permanent value in
the hymnody of the Christian congregation. Ryden concludes
his chapter on the great poet with the tribute by Grundtvig:

"He effected a combination of sublimity and
simplicity, a union of splendor and fervent
devotion, a powerful and musical play of words and
imagery that reminds one of Shakespeare."
And on Kingo's monument at Odense is this beautiful
epitaph, also written by Grundtvig:

Thomas Kingo is the psalmist
    Of the Danish temple choir.
This his people will remember
    As long as song their hearts inspire.[38]

The book of 1699 continued to be used quite extensively
throughout Denmark as various attempts were made to reform
it. One of the first to exert effort in this direction was Hans

Adolph Brorson (1694-1764), known as the Christmas Poet of
Denmark. Brorson was born into a Lutheran pastor's home
in Ranrup in the border province of Schleswig. Early he
came under the influence of the pietistic revival which was
sweeping the Lutheran church. Aaberg comments on the pietist movement in Denmark:

> The strong revival movement that was sweeping the
> country and displacing the old orthodoxy, was en-
> gendered by the German Pietist movement, entering
> Denmark through Slesvig. The two conceptions of
> Christianity differed, it has been said, only in their
> emphasis. Orthodoxy emphasized doctrine and Pietism,
> life. Both conceptions were one-sided. If Orthodoxy
> had resulted in a lifeless formalism, Pietism soon lost
> its effectiveness in a sentimental subjectivism. Its
> neglect of sound doctrine eventually gave birth to
> Rationalism. But for the moment Pietism appeared to
> supply what orthodoxy lacked: an urgent call to
> Christians to live what they professed to believe. [39]

Brorson joined the pietist group, and, along with his
two brothers, worked diligently in the renewal of the Lutheran
church in Denmark. Aaberg elaborates further on their activities:

> And they did not spare themselves. Both separately
> [and] cooperatively, they labored zealously to in-
> crease church attendance, revive family devotions,
> encourage Bible reading and hymn singing, and mini-
> mize the many worldly and doubtful amusements that,
> then as now, caused many Christians to fall. They
> also began to hold private assemblies in the homes,
> a work for which they were bitterly condemned by
> many and severely reprimanded by the authorities.
> It could not be expected, of course, that a work so
> devoted to the furtherance of a new conception of
> the Christian life would be tolerated without opposi-
> tion. But their work, nevertheless, was blest with
> abundant fruit, both in their own parishes and through-
> out neighboring districts. Churches were refilled with
> worshippers, family altars rebuilt, and a new song
> was born in thousands of homes. People expressed
> their love for the three brothers by naming them "The
> Rare Three-Leafed Clover from Randrup." It is said

that the revival inspired by the Brorsons even now,
more than two hundred years later, is plainly evident
in the spiritual life of the district.[40]

After study at the University of Copenhagen, Brorson
became pastor in his own town of Randrup, where he spent
eight successful years. His first hymns were written during
this time. From Randrup he removed to Tønden and became
associated with Rev. Johan Herman Schroeder, a German
preaching pastor from Hamburg, himself an ardent pietist
and hymn enthusiast. It is said that singing was a major
activity of the services in this particular church. Schroeder
himself was a hymnist, and shortly after Brorson joined the
staff, the former produced a German hymnal containing 1,157
hymns.

There was evidently a friendly conflict between the use
of Danish and German in the Tønden congregation which produced its problems, particularly to the Danish-speaking preacher. To insure singing in the one language for the Christmas
festival of 1732, he published a small booklet of Christmas
hymns for the use of the congregations. This established him
at once as one of the great hymn writers of the church. The
collection consisted of ten hymns in all, several of them on the
Christmas theme. They were of the highest literary quality
and considered by literary critics to be some of the finest
in the Danish language. The second hymn in this hymnal
is considered the best in the collection. Aaberg has given
a complete translation of it, from which is quoted the first
stanza:

> This blessed Christmastide we will
> With heart and mind rejoicing,
> Employ our every thought and skill,
> God's grace and honor voicing.
> In Him that in the manger lay
> We will with all our might today
> Exult in heart and spirit,
> And hail Him as our Lord and King
> Till earth's remotest bounds shall ring
> With praises of His merit.[41]

The success of his Christmas hymns prompted him to
publish five collections within the next year. In 1739 they
were collected into one volume, Troens rare Klenodie (The

Faith's Rare Jewel). Its contents include sixty-seven originals and 216 translations. (Julian estimates that his translations make up three-fourths of his contributions to Danish
hymnody.) The pietistic flavor is strong in his poems, and
there are many instances of extreme Pietism with its emphasis
on the wounds and blood of Christ. In spite of this, it was
well received and many of the hymns remain in popular use.
Before Brorson died, the book passed through six editions.
The edition of 1823 was edited by his grandnephew, A. Winding Brorson. In his rather lengthy introduction, he has this
to say concerning his uncle's psalms:

> "Troens Rare Klenodie" comprises 233 numbers, where-
> of the greater part are translations or revisions from
> the German. The most of those I have singled out
> are originals, of which Christmas and New Year Psalms
> are according to my opinion outstandingly beautiful.
> Fifty to sixty years ago these Psalms were known and
> treasured, not only in Denmark but as a friend and
> acquaintance had assured me, also in Norway. For
> anyone who has discernment for soulful religious poetry
> here will be found a rich overflow of edifying songs,
> out of which I have chosen those which I considered
> most fitting both for the present and the future. For
> it cannot be denied that such a choosing was called
> for, and it will be for others to pass judgment as to
> whether or not I have been circumspect in my select-
> ing. [42]

One of the great contributions of Brorson was his revival hymns, which, according to Aaberg, were sadly lacking
in the Lutheran communion. The Pietist clarion call to spiritual revival is found throughout these poems. The following
excerpt is a sample of this type of hymn:

> Awaken from you idle dreaming!
> Ye lukewarm Christians, now arise.
> Behold, the light from heaven streaming
> Proclaims the day of mercy flies.
> Throw off that sinful sleep before
> To you is closed the open door.

Strongly allied to this theme is the warning of impending judgment:

O heart, prepare to give account
Of all thy sore transgression.
To God, of grace and love the Fount,
Make thou a full confession.
What hast thou done these many years
The Lord hath thee afforded.
Nothing but sin and earthly cares
Is in God's book recorded.

Pietism emphasized a virile and active faith in contrast
to the more formal faith of Orthodoxy. This first stanza by
Brorson is typical of the entire hymn.

The faith that Christ embraces
And purifies the hearts
The faith that boldly faces
The devil's fiery darts,
That faith is strong and must
Withstand the world's temptation
And in all tribulation,
In Christ, the Saviour, trust.

Significantly Brorson wrote no noteworthy hymns on
the sacraments as did Grundtvig and Kingo. This is to be
expected since the sacramental aspect of communion and baptism was de-emphasized by the pietists.

The revision of the Psalmebog of 1699, originally pro-
jected by Brorson, was completed by Eric Pontoppidan in 1740.
It bore the title Den ny Salmebog. Although Brorson did not
officially oversee this revision, he contributed a sizable number of hymns and translations. Kingo's hymns for the most
part were changed very little, and most of the new material
was from Brorson. Winding Brorson has commented concerning the compilation and editing of this hymnal:

The Pontoppidan Collection which first came out in
1740, next in 1745 and finally in 1775 (if there were
later ones I don't know) was a selection of all the different authors known, but without putting the author's name under each composition. Brorson's Psalms
were for a long time both before and after the first
publication of Pontoppidan's Psalm Book, so popular
that they were often sung from memory by the common people in Julland, as was practiced in those times

for usable godly encouragement. But never in my
youth were they ascribed to Brorson by name, but
were simply said to be of Pontoppidan's Psalms. In-
deed it may never have occurred to anyone that the
Christmas Psalm, so admired by our foremost poets,
was of Brorson, had not Prof. Rahbek set him in his
proper light.[43]

Among the many fine memorials to Brorson is the volume
entitled Hans Adolph Brorson's Swan Song, which is a collection of unpublished songs compiled by his son, Sal. Biskop
Brorson. They reflect his own assurance and hope during
the trying experiences of his later life. The collection has
been immortalized by the hymn "Behold a Host" which became
famous by its association with Edvard Grieg's musical setting.
Ryden has called it the most popular Scandinavian hymn in
the English language. The translation of a stanza from the
hymnal of the Danish Lutheran Church in America is given:

Behold the mighty whiten robed band
Like thousand snowclad mountains stand
        with waving palms
        And swelling psalms
Above at God's right hand.
These are the heroes brave that came
Through tribulation, war, and flame
        And in the flood
        Of Jesus' blood
Were cleansed from sin and shame.
Now with the ransomed, heavenly Throng
They praise the Lord in every tongue,
        And anthems swell
        Where God doth dwell
Amidst the angels' song.

Concerning the publication of this collected volume, these
comments are from Brorson's grandnephew:

The song is written during the last year of his life,
mainly for himself and those nearest to him, as stimu-
lation to inner godly encouragement during his frequent sufferings to body and mind, without any idea
at the time that the song would ever be published.
But when some copies thereof, some with and some
without his knowledge (among which were found some

material not composed by himself) were passed around,
inside and outside his diocese and were re-written,
it happened as one often has seen proved, that word
and meaning could be altered. After the passing of
Sal. Brorson to the father, many have made known
their longing to see the manuscript in print. In consideration of reasons named in the foregoing so much
the less has anyone proposed to publish a collection
of songs purely his own before this. But when it is
general knowledge that his many years ago published
songs and later added Psalms, which are so hearty
and edifying have been much sought for and put to
use in many in our Danish and Norwegian Zion, this
is sent forth.[44]

The movement of rationalism which swept Europe in the
latter part of the eighteenth century produced a new and
mutilated hymnal. The Evangelical Christian Hymnal published
at this time eliminated many of the hymns of the type of Brorson's and drastically revised others. However, Brorson's message was kept alive in the hearts of the Scandinavian people.
Small groups of laymen met in homes for periods of devotion
at which time they nurtured themselves on Luther's sermons
and Brorson's hymns. During the evangelical awakening in
the nineteenth century, the hymns of Brorson were restored
to their rightful place in public worship.

Brorson's relationship to the Lutheran church and Pietism is summed up by Aaberg:

Although Brorson remained a loyal son of the established church, he wrote his finest hymns on those
phases of Christianity most earnestly emphasized by
the movement to which he belonged. While this is
only what could be expected, it indicates both his
strength and limitation as a hymnwriter. He was above
all the sweet singer of Pietism.[45]

At this time of despair and spiritual decline, which began with the death of King Christian VI, Nicholas Grundtvig
entered the scene of the religious life of Denmark. He was
born in 1783 at Odby into the family of Johann and Catherine
Marie Grundtvig. Johann was pastor of the parish church
and a strong evangelical Lutheran. Nicholas' education began
at nine years of age under a pastor-tutor, L. Feld. At fifteen

he enrolled in the Latin school at Aarhus from which he
emerged quite cynical in his attitude toward religion and his
spiritual heritage. From 1800 to 1805 he studied at the University of Copenhagen. As he looked back on his university
experience, he described himself as a "narrow-minded Pharisee,"
quite satisfied with his moral and spiritual attainments. Grundtvig accepted a position as tutor in a wealthy family. He read
extensively, including his much-neglected Bible, and became
interested in poetry and literature.

In the midst of continuing uncertainties concerning
Christianity and his personal faith and the desire to continue
writing, in which field he had seen a measure of success, he
reluctantly accepted his father's invitation to become his assistant. He prepared what later became his famous ordination
sermon in which he attacked the rationalism of the Danish
clergy. The sermon was the beginning of a long controversy
within the church of Denmark, which lasted during the remaining years of Grundtvig's life. The clergy were insulted at
his insinuations concerning their message and demanded an
apology from the young cleric. The whole affair was a turning point in his life, and from now on he appealed in his messages to the Bible and the message of history in his defense
of evangelical Christianity, which he now embraced. After
this experience, and with his feet on firm theological ground,
he willingly entered into the work as his father's assistant
following his ordination in 1811.

Grundtvig endeared himself to the people of the parish
in Udby. Besides his duties as parish priest, he again turned
his attention to writing; during his brief ministry at Udby,
he produced three rather sizable works. He sought to raise
the spiritual level of his people to restore historical Christianity to its proper place in his native Denmark by numerous
prose and poetic works. Upon his father's death in 1813, he
removed to Copenhagen where he occupied himself almost ex-
clusively in writing both secular and religious works. So
fruitful were the results of this labor that a friend remarked,
"Kingo's harp has been strung afresh."[46]

In 1821 King Frederik VI appointed Grundtvig to the
pastorate in the parish of Prastø, but after one year he returned to Copenhagen as chaplain of St. Savior's Church in
Christianshavn. His long desire for a pastorate in the capital had been fulfilled. Although his ministry was conducted

on a grand scale and people thronged to hear him preach,
Grundtvig was much dissatisfied with their preoccupation with
rationalism and their apathy toward the evangelical faith. He
was entirely in sympathy with the evangelicals and Pietists
and encouraged by their support of his preaching; nevertheless, he did not approve of their private assemblies. Quite
openly he put the blame on the pastors of the State Church
for the severance of such groups from the establishment.
His writings were concerned with the problem but seemingly
brought little results. Only the future proved that, as a
result of his ministry, rationalism had been dealt a crushing
blow by his efforts.

When Grundtvig was told that only hymns from the
authorized hymnal would be used in the great anniversary in
1826 celebrating a thousand years of Christianity in Denmark,
he realized this decision was against him personally. Grundtvig resigned from his pastorate. Mixed reactions followed
his resignation.

After an absence of six years, he once again entered
the pulpit. Against his better judgment he became pastor of
an independent congregation. After much deliberation and
discussion with the authorities, the church was granted the
use of the abandoned building of the Frederik Church and
permitted to hold a vesper service each Sunday. He was
limited in his privileges, not being allowed to administer the
sacraments or to instruct the young people. He could not
even confirm his own sons. At the time he was contemplat-
ing resigning from the Frederik Church, he was offered the
position of pastor of Vartov, an institution for the aged.

From the time he assumed this position in 1839 until
his death, the chapel at Vartov became the center for the
ever-growing Grundtvig movement. Even the queen attended
the meetings in the chapel to enjoy the preaching of Grundtvig
and the enthusiastic singing of the congregation. Some of his
own hymns which were introduced at Vastov found their way
into the assemblies over the whole of Denmark. It is believed
that the traditional singing of this congregation set the pattern for the entire Church of Denmark.

Mention should be made at this point of his contribution
in another area of Danish life, that of Danish folk school.
The first of these "Grundtvigion" schools opened in Rodding

in 1844 and marked the beginning of the public school movement in Denmark. The movement eventually spread to include
all of Scandinavia and earned for Grundtvig the title of "father
of the public school in Scandinavia."[47]

Brief mention has already been made in Chapter I to
Grundtvig's recasting of old Danish hymns. In addition to
revision and some translation, he has left a rich legacy of
hymns which are still being used even outside of Scandinavia.
Some of the earliest hymns came out of that period of his life,
around 1810, when he was experiencing the inner spiritual
and mental struggles. One poem was on the theme of the
visit of the Magi. This remained his sole contribution for a
considerable length of time. Aaberg has listed his additional
contributions from 1810 to 1825:

> During his years of intense work with the sagas he
> only occasionally broke his "engagement" with the
> dead to strike the lyre for the living. In 1815 he
> translated "In Death's Strong Bonds Our Savior Lay"
> from Luther, and "Christ Is Risen from the Dead"
> from the Latin. The three hundredth anniversary of
> the Reformation brought his adaptation of Kingo's
> "Like the Golden Sun Ascending" and translations of
> Luther's "A Mighty Fortress Is Our God" and "The
> Bells Ring in the Christmastime." In 1820 he pub-
> lished his now popular "A Babe Is Born at Bethlehem"
> from an old Latin-Danish text, and 1824 saw his splen-
> did rendering of "The Old Day Song," "With Gladness
> We Hail the Blessed Day," and his original "On Its
> Rock the Church of Jesus Stood Mongst Us a Thou-
> sand Years."[48]

As dissatisfaction mounted toward the rationalistic Evangelical Christian Hymnal, Grundtvig was urged from all sides
to produce more hymns. Since he was occupied with prose
writings, he had set aside his activity in hymnody; but in
the pressure from his friends in the church, he resumed the
writing of hymns around the year 1835. A pastor friend,
Gunni Busck, was so overjoyed at Grundtvig's renewed interest in this field that he sent him a sizable contribution to
finance the work. Funds were coming from other sources as
well. Within the space of a year, he had studied rather completely the history of Christian hymnody and produced his
first volume Songs of the Danish Church. It numbered 401

hymns, originals and translations from ancient sources. Although it was not officially adopted or well received outside the circle of his own followers, many of the hymns in this hymnal have been used in later collections.

Meanwhile, agitation for a revision of the old Danish hymnal continued. The natural one to head up such a task was Grundtvig, but because of a political situation in the church he had no part in the first attempt. The appointed committee produced the supplement to the hymnal which came from the press in 1843. Hymns by Kingo, Brorson, and Grundtvig were included, and the supplement was widely circulated. Because the church, in general, still was not satisfied with the new supplement, a new committee for further revision was appointed, headed by Grundtvig himself. The supplement was submitted in 1845; in spite of well-balanced contents, the conference rejected it on the basis that the hymnal bore the imprint of Grundtvig--again a biased political opinion.

Realizing that he could expect no better treatment in the future, Grundtvig set about to provide more material for his friends in the private assemblies. In 1845 he produced a small book of Christmas hymns and sometime later a similar one for Easter. Several collections for various seasons followed until all were collected into a single volume for use at Vartov. Many of the hymns were introduced into the Lutheran congregations in spite of official edicts against their use. According to Ryden, the greatest of Grundtvig's hymns deal with the church and its sacraments.

Although Grundtvig was concerned with the low condition of the church of his day, he did not despair but continually expressed hope in its ultimate triumph. One of the best known of such hymns is in "Built on the Rock." The first stanza, quoted below, is indicative of the spirit and message of the entire hymn.

> Built on a Rock the Church doth stand,
>   Even when steeples are falling;
> Crumbled have spires in every land,
>   Bells still are chiming and calling;
>   Calling the young and old to rest,
>   Calling the souls of men distressed,
>   Longing for life everlasting.

While Kingo is the poet of Christmas and Brorson the poet of Easter, Grundtvig has become known as the poet of Pentecost. Almost equal to his hymns on the Church are those on the work of the Spirit in the life of the believer. Because of his treatment of the text, it is difficult to discern whether a certain hymn is an original or an adaptation. His version of the Pentecost hymn "Veni Sancte Spiritus" illustrates this point.

> Holy Spirit, come with light,
> Break the dark and gloomy night
> With Thy day unending.
> Help us with a joyful lay
> Greet the Lord's triumphant day
> Now with might ascending.

The concept of Pentecost as coming at the beginning of the summer is purely Danish and is expressed in a novel way in another of his hymns for this season.

> The sun now shines in all its splendor,
> The fount of life and mercy tender;
> Now bright Whitsunday lilies grow
> And summer sparkles high and low;
> Sweet songsters sing of harvest gold
> In Jesus' name a thousand fold.

Space does not permit extensive quoting of Grundtvig's poetry. It is worth noting, however, the various themes on which he has written: the Kingdom of God, the sacraments, opening and closing hymns, psalm texts, personal Christian living, and the Word of God.

Before concluding our study of Grundtvig, a word is in order concerning his style. Although he was a prolific writer and produced many volumes of poetry, he had no peer as a writer. Aaberg has described his poetry as "rough but expressive" and abounding in "rich imagery." One finds a deep warmth of personal experience and commitment in his poems, although some of his devotional hymns are quite objective in nature. Many of his great hymns are those in praise of Christ as Redeemer. Aaberg mentions that Grundtvig considered himself a "skjald," endowed with the gift of intuition and insight into deep spiritual things, thus being able to defend himself against the criticism of his sometimes "jumbled style."

The fiftieth anniversary of his ordination was an occasion for great celebration. The details are described by
Aaberg:

> Grundtvig's fiftieth anniversary as a pastor was cele-
> brated with impressive festivities on May 29, 1861.
> The celebration was attended by representatives from
> all departments of government and the church as well
> as by a host of people from all parts of Scandinavia;
> and the celebrant was showered with gifts and honors.
> The king conferred upon him the title of bishop; the
> former queen, Carolina Amalia, presented him with a
> seven armed candlestick of gold from women in Norway,
> Sweden and Denmark; his friend, Pastor P.A. Fenger,
> handed him a gift of three thousand dollars from
> friends in Denmark and Norway to finance a popular
> edition of his Hymns and Songs for the Danish Church;
> and another friend, Gunni Busck, presented him with
> a plaque of gold engraved with his likeness and a line
> from his hymns, a gift from the congregation of Var-
> tov.[49]

An additional tribute is paid Grundtvig by Aaberg:

> Grundtvig found the spiritual in many things, in the
> myth of the North, in history, literature and, in fact,
> in all things through which man has to express his
> God-given nature. He had no patience with the piet-
> ists who looked upon all things not directly religious
> as evils with which a Christian could have nothing
> to do. Yet he believed above all in the Holy Spirit
> as the "Spirit of spirits," the true agent of God in
> the world.[50]

Ryden closes his chapter on Grundtvig by his mention
of the poet's last day on earth. He also pays tribute to the
life and work of this remarkable man:

> On Sept. 1, 1872, when nearly 89 years old, he con-
> ducted services in his church at Vartov as usual,
> preaching a sermon full of warmth and feeling. On
> the following day he passed away while sitting in his
> chair and listening to his son as the latter read to
> him. Thus ended the remarkable career of the saga
> of Denmark who once was the loneliest man in all the

land, but who always will be remembered as the greatest historian, poet, educator, religious philosopher,
hymnwriter and folk leader that nation has produced.[51]

Additional Hymn Writers of Nineteenth-Century Denmark

The Danish Lutheran hymnal contains hymns from nearly
sixty native writers. Because of the stature of Kingo, Brorson, and Grundtvig, it would have been easy to overlook
others who also made a substantial contribution to the evangelical cause through their hymns. Among these hymnists one
finds the name of Ambrosius Stub (1705-1758) who was considered the greatest of eighteenth-century Danish poets. A
woman hymnist, Birgitte Boye, was the author of a sizable
number of hymns. In the hymnal of 1870, there are approximately 150 of her hymns. The Guldberg Hymnal of 1778 contained 124 originals by her as well as twenty-four translations.
These comprise approximately a third of the contents of this
volume by H. Guldberg.

The evangelical revival of the mid-nineteenth century
produced several hymn writers of note among whom was Casper J. Boye, a gifted writer and the author of the Spiritual
Songs collection.

Another volume by the same title was produced by
Boye's contemporary, Herman Andreas Timm. A prominent
member of this group was Theodore Vilhelm Oldenburg, whose
hymns appeared in various religious periodicals to which he
contributed regularly. Although not definitely aligned with
the pietistic movement, the hymns of these writers show a
close affinity to the cause.

Foremost among the writers of this period is Grundtvig's
close friend Bernhard S. Ingemann (1789-1862). Like the
former, he was born into a pastor's house and went through
a series of spiritual crises as well, from which he emerged
triumphantly as did Grundtvig. Through Grundtvig's influence he became interested in writing; and after study which
included visits to France, Switzerland, Italy, and Germany,
he embarked on his literary career. His writings did much to
foster the revival of the national spirit both in Denmark and
Norway.

Ingemann, in spite of his popularity as a secular writer,
is now best known through his hymns. He brought out his
first volume of morning and evening hymns in 1822. This
was followed by a volume of church hymns in 1825, a reprint
of which was made in 1843.

Because of the popularity of these hymns, Ingemann was
commissioned in 1855 by the clerical synod of Roskilde to
produce a new Salmebog. It was based on Kingo's book and
contained new hymns by Brorson, Grundtvig, Ingemann, and
C.J. Boye.[52]

Two of the most popular of Ingemann's poems are "Through
the Night of Doubt and Sorrow," in a translation by Sabine
Baring-Gould, first published in 1867 in the People's Hymn
Book in England; and the favorite of his lyrics, "Dejlig er
Jorden" (Pilgrim Song), which is sung to the melody of "Beautiful Savior." Aaberg's translation of the first stanza gives
a general idea of the spirit of the hymn.

> Fair is creation,
> Fairer God's heaven,
> Blest is the marching pilgrim throng.
> Onward through lovely
> Regions of beauty
> Go we to Paradise with song.

Norwegian Hymnists of the Pietistic Period

The Norwegians followed the lead of Denmark in the
choosing and use of their hymns. Kingo's hymnal was the
authorized book for their use, followed by the revisions of
Pontoppidan, Guldberg, and Hauge. Pietism produced few
young hymnists of note in Norway, that is hymnists who were
definitely identified with the movement such as Brorson was
in Denmark. Grundtvig did not consider himself a Pietist;
however, as has already been noted, Pietists readily accepted
his hymns, and his preaching satisfied their demands. In
Norway more than in Denmark, there were hymnists who perhaps were even more openly denunciatory of Pietism, with
the Pietists in a reciprocal relationship; on the other hand,
as one examines the hymns from both countries, one senses
the pietistic emphasis on deep spirituality and the opposition

to rationalism. For this reason the following several composers
from Norway are included at this juncture.

The latter part of the nineteenth century produced much
Norwegian hymnody. The Napoleonic wars effected a break
in political ties with Denmark, and in this new spirit of na-
tionalism, a hymnody was born in Norway.

One of the first to feel the need of hymns distinctly
from his native land was Wilhelm A. Wexels (1797-1866). He
was a minister of the Norwegian State Church and served
one parish, Our Savior's Church in Oslo, during his entire
ministry. Wexels was a controversial figure, denounced by
the liberals and conservatives alike, but many felt he was
God's prophet to lead Norway away from rationalism and back
to the historic Christian faith. Because he was influenced
by Grundtvig in his concept of the Church, the Pietists were
skeptical of him and he of them, although both were concerned
about a real renewal in the Church. Upon the death of his
wife, his thoughts and preaching centered on the life beyond
the grave, and at times he expressed belief in a "second
chance" after death for one never committed to the Christian
faith.

In spite of the controversy which he engendered, his
congregations increased until great throngs came to hear him
preach in Our Savior's Church. The strong evangelical witness of the Norwegian Church referred to in Chapter II is
traceable to the ministry of Wexels a century ago. Ryden
makes this claim for him:

> Church historians claim that Wexels' ministry proved
> to be a turning point in the Church of Norway, mak-
> ing a return to conservative Lutheran teaching.
> Eventually he had as many friends as once he had had
> enemies. He was even offered the bishopric of Ber-
> gen, but refused to accept the honor, preferring to
> remain with his beloved congregation in the nation's
> capital. [53]

Besides his popularity as a preacher, Wexels was also
popular as an author and poet. Besides his editorial duties,
he published a New Testament Commentary, a Bible history,
and a book of devotions. In 1834 he published an official
hymnal for the Norwegian church, <u>Hymn Verses Selected from</u>

Old Hymns for Use in the Home and the School. The contents
as listed by Ryden are most interesting. It contained 714
hymns, including originals and translations by Wexels, fifty
translations of the Wallin Psalmbok and several from the German.[54] This book was published in revision in 1844 followed
by two other collections, the last of which he desired to be
accepted as a proposed official hymnal. This proposal was
rejected as were two other attempts at such a book. It was
to be Lanstad's task to furnish such a hymnal.

Although Wexels failed to be recognized for a "great"
and monumental work in hymnody, his individual hymns found
their way into the hearts of the Norwegian people. He is well
represented in the hymnals of both the State Church and the
free-church denominations.

The general spirit of his hymns can be sensed in what
was perhaps the favorite of the Norwegian people, "O Happy
Day," written for the Norwegian Mission Society in 1846. The
translation by George A.T. Raygh is quoted below:

> O happy day, when we shall stand
> **Amid** the heavenly throng,
> And sing with hosts from every land
> The new celestial song.
>
> O blessed day! From far and near
> The servants of the Lord
> Shall meet His ransomed children there
> Who heard God's saving Word.
>
> O what a mighty, rushing flood
> Of love without surcease
> Shall surge about the throne of God,
> In joy and endless peace!
>
> Lord, may Thy bounteous grace inspire
> Our hearts to watch and pray,
> That we may join the heavenly choir
> Upon that glorious day.

It remained for Magnus B. Landstad (1802-1880) to edit
the revised hymnbook of the Norwegian State Church in 1869,
which book has remained long in the service of the Church.
Lanstad was born in 1802, and like so many others grew up

in the home of a Lutheran pastor. The third of a family of
ten children, he knew the hardships of war and poverty.
His father recognized unusual talent in the boy, and at the
age of twenty he was influenced greatly by the writings of
Philipp Nicolai and Bishop Arrebo of Denmark. Reading their
hymns gave him the insight into the old hymns of the church
and inspired him in the direction of becoming a writer himself. Lanstad's translation of "Wachet Auf" of Nicolai eventually found its place in the Norwegian Lutheran hymnal.

In 1828 he was appointed vicar of the church at Gaus-
dal; during this pastorate his first hymn was written. In his
next pastorate he continued to write hymns. When he succeeded his father in the church in Seljark, he published his
first book of devotional poetry. Successive pastorates in
Fredrikshold and Sandeherred allowed him more time for the
writing of hymns.

Lanstad's early interest in folklore was seen in his col-
lecting and publishing of old Norwegian folksongs. His long
association with this aspect of Norwegian life is revealed in
the "folksy" character of his "psalms."[55] The Pietists denounced him for his interest in anything so "secular" as
folksongs, and his own congregation in Telemark, which was
dominated by a Pietist group, refused to let him use his own
hymnbook in worship.

Because of the pressures of the situation in Telemark
he removed to Fredrikshold where three of his children died.
During these trying days, Lanstad wrote some of his most
meaningful hymns, among them, the ressurection hymn "Jeg
vet mig en søvn i Jesu namn" (I know of a sleep in Jesus'
name).

His interest in and emphasis on the second advent of
Christ are to be seen in the hymn which begins "Jeg løfter
op til Gud min sang" (I raise to God my praise in song).
Lövgren describes the hymn as being "full of sanctified inspiration and Christ-loving longing for the Bridegroom."[56]

The hymns of Martin Luther and his successors in
Germany were of particular interest to Lanstad, so much so
that he studied them extensively. He wrote a penitential
hymn much in the style of Luther's "Aus tiefer Not."

To Thee, O Lord, the God of all,
With contrite heart I humbly call,
And view my sins against Thee, Lord,
The sins of thought and deed and word;
In my distress I cry to Thee,
O God, be merciful to me.

In the revised Kirkesalmebog of Landstad, which has
been reprinted as late as 1956, are some of his originals and
translations, among them several of Luther's hymns. Hymns
of Kingo, Brorson, and Grundtvig are also included in this
volume of nearly 900 selections.

The popularity of Landstad's hymns can best be seen in
their extensive use of the hymnals of the State Church as
well as in those of the free-church groups. His hymns were
made popular by the musical settings of Ludwig Lindeman,
about whom more will be said in Chapter V.

Summary

The study of the hymns of the pietistic period substantiates Nelle's claim that no period in the history of hymnody
is as interesting or as productive as that of Pietism. The
emphases of the hymns on the mystical, personal religious experiences, and the person and ministry of Christ had their
appeal to those who reacted to the formal, objective worship
of the State Church. Hymns provided a framework and basis
for the private, as well as corporate, worship of the Pietists.
The simplicity of their hymns complemented their desire for
simplicity in worship.

Poets and authors within the pietistic fold were inspired
to express their faith in sacred verse. From the writings of
Spener and Zinzendorf, to the poems of the Pietists in Scandinavia, those who use them found in them vital expressions
of Christian faith as they had experienced it. In addition to
these expressions, the hymns dealt with evils in the church
and vices in the world, and warned the Pietists against these
existing conditions. Believers were admonished in many hymns
to wear the "warrior's armor" in the fight against sin and
wickedness.

Not only were private collections of hymns produced in

great number by the Pietists, but pietistic hymns found their
way into authorized hymnals of the established Church. The
hymnals of Swedberg and Wallin, as well as less important publications, are cases in point. Many of these hymns were
gleaned from official publications such as Pietisten and other
religious journals which were widely read by the Pietists.

The hymns of the free-church groups in Scandinavia
had their origin and inspiration in the hymns of Pietism. The
study of free-church hymnody verifies this assertion. While
much of pietistic hymnody is inferior in content and expression, scores of hymns of the Pietists have found a recognized
place among the great hymns of Christendom.

NOTES

1. Wilhelm, Nelle Geschicte des deutschen evangelischen
   Kirchenlieds (Hamburg: Gustav Schloessmans Verlags-
   buchhandlung, 1904), p. 150 ff., quoted by Daquin,
   p. 134.
2. Ibid., p. 152.
3. Ibid., pp. 135-139.
4. Ibid., pp. 151, 152. (A pietistic hymnal named for its
   publisher, Johann Porst, cited by Nelle, p. 166 ff.)
5. E.E. Ryden, The Story of Christian Hymnody (Rock
   Island: Augustana Press, 1959), p. 125.
6. John Julian, A Dictionary of Hymnology (London: John
   Murray, 1925), p. 1302.
7. Ryden, op. cit., p. 129.
8. Lövgren, op. cit., I, p. 178.
9. Ibid.
10. Ibid.
11. Westin et al., De Frikyrkliga samfunden ... , pp. 23,
    25.
12. Translated from the Standaret of June 26, 1934.
13. op. cit., I, p. 204.
14. Standaret, June 26, 1934.
15. Lövgren, op. cit., I, p. 235.
16. Ibid., p. 171.
17. Olsson, By One Spirit, p. 66.
18. Then Svenska Prof-Psalmboken (Stockholm: Lorens Lud-
    wig Grefing), foreword to the first edition, 1765.
19. Ibid., foreword to the second edition, 1767.
20. Olson, op. cit., p. 55.

21. Latourette, Nineteenth Century ... , p. 169.
22. Ryden, op. cit., p. 176.
23. Standaret, June 26, 1934.
24. Olsson, By One Light, pp. 55, 56.
25. Lövgren, op. cit., II, p. 337.
26. Ibid.
27. The Gospel Hymnal (Chicago: Baptist Conference Press, 1950), No. 5.
28. Lövgren, op. cit., II, p. 349.
29. Ryden, op. cit., p. 176.
30. James P. Davies, Sing with Understanding (Chicago: Covenant Press, 1966), p. 80.
31. Sven-Åke Selander, Den Nya Sången (Lund, Sweden: Gleerup Bokforlag, 1973), p. 249-250.
32. Ibid., p. 250.
33. Ryden, op. cit., p. 190.
34. Aaberg, op. cit., p. 23.
35. Ibid., p. 41.
36. Julian, op. cit., p. 1001.
37. Aaberg, op. cit., pp. 49, 50.
38. Ryden, op. cit., p. 207.
39. Aaberg, op. cit., p. 62.
40. Ibid., p. 64.
41. Ibid., pp. 68, 69.
42. A. Winding Brorson, Nogle af salig Biskop Hans Adolph Brorsons Psalmer (Kjobenhann: Andreas Seidelin, 1823), pp. 8, 9.
43. Ibid., pp. 18, 19.
44. Ibid., p. 30.
45. Aaberg, op. cit., p. 84.
46. Julian, op. cit., p. 1001.
47. Ryden, op. cit., p. 216.
48. Aaberg, op. cit., p. 122.
49. Ibid., pp. 155.
50. Ibid., pp. 157, 158.
51. Ryden, op. cit., p. 219.
52. Julian, op. cit., p. 1002.
53. Ryden, op. cit., p. 234.
54. Ibid., p. 235.
55. Lovgren, op. cit., II, p. 386.
56. Ibid., p. 387.

CHAPTER IV

THE HYMNODY OF THE FREE CHURCHES
OF SCANDINAVIA

Hymnody of the Swedish Baptists

In the way of a recapitulation, it is pertinent to re-emphasize that the first free church of Sweden which continues to the present day is the Baptist Church. The first congregation was organized in the Holland district in 1848 under the leadership of F.O. Nilsson, who, as had been noted, was expelled from his native country of Sweden in 1850. The quickening of the spiritual life in Sweden during the latter part of the nineteenth century can be credited in great measure to the influence of the Baptists.

With the religious awakening at this time, there appeared many new hymns of praise written for the use of the Baptist assemblies. In 1843 F.O. Nilsson produced in Göteborg a booklet of hymns of poor quality for use among the Swedish Baptist converts. Samlinga af några Andeliga Sånger contained 31 songs, mostly translations of English hymns, many of them by Charles Wesley. (See Appendix F.) Selander's book seems to be the only source of information concerning the collection. In it he makes this comment:

> It is especially noteworthy that Nilsson presents so many songs of the Wesley brothers in spite of the evident fear for the 'methodical' in the Swedish revival. Some of the translations later passed into other collections. This is a good sign that the songs kept the same inter-confessional character, that they got in their homeland. [1]

In spite of the inferior quality of the booklet as a whole,
Selander asserts:

> It is of great importance in this context since it was
> the first serious attempt to make use of English hymn
> material in the Swedish revivalist movement. In his
> work Nilsson was in contact with Scott in Stockholm;
> it is known that he witnessed at least one of his meet-
> ings, and he spread the tracts published by Scott.
> The source of his collection of hymns was probably a
> hymn book published by the Seamen's Friend Society
> in New York.... The collection was called Seamen's
> Hymns.[2]

While the hymns of the Established Church, such as
those by Spegel, Franzen, and Wallin, took on new meaning
and those of the Pietist-Moravian tradition remained ever
popular, hymns by Baptist converts were a natural consequence of the new movement. Among the early accessions to
the Baptist cause were the Palmquist brothers, Johannes, Per,
and Gustaf. The latter two became famous by their literary
contributions not only with respect to the Baptist group but
in the general religious awakening in Sweden.

Considered to be the first Baptist hymn writer of
Sweden, Gustaf claims major interest because of his influence
on the hymnody of the Baptist movement in the early days.
He was born in 1812 in the Jönköping district. When he was
six years old, his father died leaving the widow and seven
children to dire circumstances.

Gustaf's early education was acquired in his own home.
At the invitation of his brother Johannes, who was a teacher
in the Narke district, he attended the same school and received further education which was to prepare him for his
future occupation in the field of music. In the fall of 1837,
he enrolled in the music school in Stockholm and the following
year qualified for the positions of both teacher and "Kantor."
In the time immediately following, he taught in Stockholm and
Värmland.

While in Stockholm both he and his brother Per were
influenced by the evangelical revival, and following a spiritual
crisis, each entered at once into the evangelistic effort. Gustaf went to America in 1851 to do missionary work among the

Swedes and shortly after that joined the Baptists and their
cause. As has been mentioned in the previous chapter, he
founded the first Swedish Baptist Church in America at Rock
Island, Illinois, and for a time served as its pastor. Following his pastorate in Rock Island, he served in a similar capacity in a church in Chicago and engaged in the training of
young ministers to serve the Swedish denomination in America
He returned to Sweden in 1857 to aid the Baptist cause there
and was instrumental in establishing the training school for
colporteurs in the same year. He became popular in his home
country as an accomplished preacher and teacher. He died
in 1867 in the midst of a brilliant and promising career among
the Swedish Baptists.

Chief among his many contributions to the evangelical
cause in Sweden are his hymns and hymn publications. In
America, Gustaf came to know many hymns in the English
language. Upon his return to Sweden, he translated many
of these hymns into Swedish and wrote many originals. Inspired and encouraged by his brother Per's publication Spiritual Songs for Children, Gustaf published in 1859 a volume
called Pilgrim Songs on the Way to the Heavenly Zion, (Pilgrims-
Sånger). The first edition contained 221 selections; about
100 were translations from the English with musical settings.
Nearly fifty songs were written by Swedish authors, and
many were taken from Per's book of songs for children. In
the same year, a second edition was printed with the addition
of five more songs. Although the title of this book appears
over the names of both brothers, it was Gustaf who was the
main editor and compiler. Only four in this collection are
originals of Gustaf. Pilgrims-Sånger went through about forty
editions, including the musical edition of 1860 and a supplement of eighty-eight new songs in the edition of 1862, which
reached the publication figure of 400,000 copies. The 1862
supplement contains a number of originals by Gustaf Palmquist
as well as selected verses and songs from the Swedish Psalm
Book (see Chapter V). The foreword indicates that many of
the translations had been used in English revival meetings
and eventually made their way to Sweden. Mention has already been made in Chapter III of the translations of children's hymns by Mrs. Posse for the Palmquist's songbooks.
Their popularity and enthusiastic reception resulted in their
being translated and published for use by many of the free-
church congregations. Further comment by Palmquist includes
an apologetic in which he explains that these songs were not

Concurrent

meant for the "musically elite" but for the more "simple minded and less educated" among the people. Their purpose was mainly to bring comfort where needed and to aid in evangelistic efforts in the church. Pilgrims Sånger was used mainly in Baptist circles but was also popular in other "revival" groups of Sweden.[3]

In 1878, nearly twenty years after the publication of Pilgrims-Sånger, Dr. Erik Nystrom, at the behest of Per Palmquist, produced a new hymnal, Församlings-Sångbok. Earlier, Nystrom had published a collection of Sankey's songs in translation, but since he did not have legal authority to include them in this new book, he set about to translate additional songs of Sankey for this purpose. Included in the 1878 book were over 100 translations from English as well as a number of originals. Many of the texts were based on Biblical psalms.

Palmquist had hoped that this new hymnal should become popular and be used not only in Baptist circles but in many free congregations in Sweden. Although the contents of this book included hymns on practically every aspect of Christian doctrine, worship, and experience, it did not become popular among the Baptists. Also in Missionsförbundet it was used only sparingly. As far as the Baptists were concerned, no doubt their indifference to the Församlings Sångbok grew out of their desire to have a hymnal of their very own. In the meantime, Pilgrim-Sånger remained popular among the free-church congregations. It is estimated that about one third of the songs in Pilgrims-Sånger are in use in Sweden today.

Concurrent with the issuing and rejection of the 1878 volume came the appointment of a committee among the Baptists to explore the possibility of producing a decidedly Baptistic hymnal to meet the existing need. While Pilgrims-Sånger satisfied the layman, pastors felt the need for a hymnal with a wider variety of contents than was present in either of the books. In 1880 the new hymnal Psalmisten came from the press. While it was principally for the Baptist groups, it was so designed that other free-church groups could use it with great benefit. Concerning the contents, Anders Wiberg makes these comments in the preface to the first edition:

> In the entire collection there are 168 selections partly unchanged and partly revised more or less as to form, taken from Swedish Psalmbook, Rütstrom's Hymns,

Finnish Psalmbook Proposal, Church of Brethren's
Hymnal, T. Truve's Songs, A Palm's Collection etc.
The other 362 are in part translations of favorite
hymns from other countries, and in part original
Swedish hymns. For those who love the old well-
known "Pilgrim Hymns" it will be pleasing to know
that Herr Per Palmquist has granted permission for
twenty of these hymns to be included in "Psalmisten."[4]

Also included in Psalmisten are forty-nine metrical versions of
the psalms of David based on the Biblical psalter, which appear at the beginning of the book. The rest of the hymns
are divided according to the following categories:

God and the Life of Christ
The Work of Grace in General
The Christian Life
The Word of God
God's Church
Hymns of Prayer
Time and Eternity

Among the twenty members of the hymnal committee,
which did its work with considerable dispatch, was Jonas
Stadling (1846-1935), secretary of the group. He furnished
most of the new materials consisting of both originals and
translations. After becoming a Baptist in 1874, he studied
at the Baptist Seminary in Stockholm and Uppsala University.
His activities included travel, lectures, and the writing of
both books and numerous songs of "abiding quality and appeal."

The intent and aspirations of the committee for Psalmisten are expressed by Wiberg:

As for the real value of this hymn collection we can
readily expect that there will be difference of opinion. Preference, taste and conviction, especially in
spiritual matters, are admittedly so diverse, that even
the actually beautiful, true and good are often rejected as something shallow, false, and harmful. We
are, however, calm and glad in the awareness that
we have meant to do our best. That our ability has
in many ways been wanting, of this we are deeply
cognizant; and we could therefore have wished, that
the task entrusted to us as a hymnbook committee had

been put into more competent hands. With all the
shortcomings that may pertain to this achievement
we still dare to hope that the collection may appeal
especially to the Baptist churches in our land, on
the one hand because here are found a larger number
of hymns geared to Baptist faith and church order
than can be found in other collections; on the other
hand because the sale of the book will result in an
income designed to help indigent, aged and ailing
preachers and their families.[5]

The reception of Psalmisten by the Baptist conference
was hardly more significant than that of the Församling-
Sångbok. Though it was received with general enthusiasm,
its popularity dwindled and the Baptists grew tired of it rather
quickly. The earlier hymnal Pilgrims-Sånger continued to be
popular, after which the Palmquist Publication Company decided to publish Nya Pilgrimsånger. This new edition of the
old favorite, re-edited and enlarged, came from the press in
1892. Many new hymns which had never been in print before appeared in this new collection, which was to enjoy widespread popularity in free-church circles. A condensed translation of the foreword to Nya Pilgrims-sånger sheds further
light on its purpose, use, and place in public and private
worship:

"Pilgrim Songs on way to the heavenly Zion" was published the first time in 1859 and has since then been
issued in not less than forty-three editions. As these
comprised the first song collection of this kind in our
land, they have likewise been much loved and used.

Many genuinely basic songs which never can become
too old and which subsequently have been included
in other song books, first became known through this
one. There were, however, in Pilgrimsånger several
songs which now are seldom used, while on the other
hand new and valuable songs appeared from other sources and became generally known and liked. In response
to the promptings of many we have therefore undertaken a re-editing of the Pilgrim Songs, whereby these
could become more acceptable for both public and
private use. Of the old songs have been eliminated
only those that seldom have been sung; of the new
has been included a rich selecting from the many good
sources at our disposal.

That "the praise-worthy name of Jesus may be held in honor and many pilgrims on their journey homeward may be re-invigorated" was the final wish stated in the forward to the first edition of Pilgrimsånger-- a wish that verily has been fulfilled. May now the new Pilgrim Songs be fraught with blessing, and the good seed sown by it, bring harvests for eternity.[6]

After a few years some of the Baptist Church leaders again felt the need for yet another songbook. At the Baptist conference in Eskilstuna in 1897, a publishing committee, which was responsible for the initial publication of Psalmisten, was appointed to undertake another revision. Psalmisten, in its seventh edition in 1903, is the result. It contains about twenty songs from earlier editions, and includes selections from the Swedish Covenant Church hymnal and the National Evangelical Foundation's, Sions Toner. Additional songs were gleaned from song compilations from England, America, Denmark, Norway, Germany, and Finland.

The name of Teodor Truve (1838-1910) has already been mentioned in connection with the appearance of some of his songs in Psalmisten. Truve was born in Skåne where his father was a lumberman. Because of the relative poverty in his home, he had little chance for a substantial education. After a crisis in his spiritual life in 1857, he enrolled in the Bible course conducted by Gustaf Palmquist in Stockholm in 1860. Following this part of his education, he became an itinerant preacher throughout his home country. In 1862 he settled in Göteborg where he became assistant to the well-known F.O. Nilsson. His ministry in Göteborg extended for three years, after which he traveled to America where he studied at Madison (Colgate) University until 1868. Following his sojourn and study in America, Truve returned to Sweden where he served as pastor of the Baptist Tabernacle in Göteborg until his death in 1910.

In his lifetime, Truve became well known through his sermons and lectures on the Sunday school and temperance questions. In the literary field, he translated many articles concerning spiritual edification and edited a children's paper, "Bikupan," (The Beehive). But Truve is best known today because of the contribution he made to the cause of music for the Sunday schools of Sweden. His best-known work in this area is Sånger för Söndagsskolan och Hemmet (Songs for Sunday School and Home), which was published in thirty-two

editions of 360,000 copies. Truve's idea was to adapt the
songs to the level of the Sunday school pupil, and as a result this collection made a strong impact and lasting contribution to religious education in Scandinavia.[7] The preface to
the second edition indicates the popularity with which the collection was received:

> When the first edition of this book was put forth the
> publisher had a feeling similar to that of the sower
> when he sows a new kind of seed in his field: it
> was a trial venture. It succeeded above expectation,
> for the first edition, even large as it was, has in less
> than a year been sold out, and this in spite of the
> fact that the book was not on sale in the general book
> stores. In the Sunday Schools where the children
> have once heard some of these songs and have learned
> to sing these light melodies, there they wish to con-
> tinue singing them. Hence the publisher can only
> add: "Forbid them not."
>
> A new edition is now placed in the hands of the chil-
> dren with the wish that many children may be attracted
> to the Sunday school from the streets and alleys,
> highways and byways and then continue to sing until
> teachers and pupils in time will gather around the
> throne of God and there together with all saints and
> angels sing the "new song."[8]

In this particular volume it is difficult to ascertain which
songs were originals of Truve and which had been borrowed
from other authors and sources. A number of them had cer-
tainly been translated from the English by the author himself.
In the collection entitled Sankey-Sänger, which was published
in three parts in 1875-1877, it is generally agreed that the
greater part of them were translated by Truve. Besides this
endeavor with the Sankey collection, he also wrote many songs
for the 1880 edition of Psalmisten as has been indicated earlier
in this chapter. In one copy of this hymnal, he indicated
which hymns he wrote.

Although the Baptists of Sweden were not as prolific
in producing hymns as those of other countries, each attempt
at composing gave some impetus and encouragement to aspir-
ing hymnists. Although the number of hymn writers is modest,
those who expressed their faith in sacred verse and melody

made a significant contribution to the Baptist cause in Sweden
during the last century.

One of the early contributors to Swedish Baptist hymnody
was Karl Alinder (1859-1929). His formal theological training
was received at Betelseminariet in Stockholm and his service
among the Baptists included a number of churches in Sweden,
as well as special Sunday school missionary service in Oster-
gotland. His interest in the publication phase of the Baptist
outreach led him to work with the "Baptist missions bokförlag."
In conjunction with this position, he edited the "Barnens egen
tidning." Alinder's connection with the publishing house and
his enthusiasm for spiritual singing in the Sunday school
and church led him to publish several song collections for the
use of the Baptists of Sweden. His contributions in this area
included: Pilgrims Lof (1889), Sjung (1892), and Nya Pilgrims Lof (1901).

Josef Grytzel (1862-1908) is considered to have been
one of the foremost of the Baptist song writers of Sweden.
He was born in Dalarna and while a comparatively young man
was affiliated with the Baptist Church in Gävle, in which city
he also engaged in the bookbinding trade. Before any formal
theological training, he began to preach and soon became associated with the District Society of Skåne. Following a period
of study at Betelseminariet, he engaged in successive pastorates in Malmö and Stockholm. Ill health forced him to leave
the active ministry, but he carried on an extensive ministry
of writing, particularly hymn composition. Lövgren evaluates
his efforts by referring to him as an "assiduous writer, noted
especially within the Baptist denomination, whose songs are
of more abiding value than his other literary efforts."[9]

In addition to his own song contributions, Gryztell engaged actively in the compilation of the 1903 edition of Psalmisten. The following titles and first lines in English translation selected from among those of Grytzell in this book reveal
somewhat the thrust of Baptist hymnody of that day:

> Glorious salvation now sounded forth
> God's Love is Sure the Greatest.
> The Shining Sun of Righteousness
> God is Faithful, O My Soul
> "Suffer the Children," Yet is heard.
> Lord Jesus is the Vine of Truth

Flee from Sodom and its peril.
Atonement, Atonement, O Comforting Word
Spirit from Heaven, Comforting Spirit
Troubled heart, just look to Jesus.
Bubbling Springs of Elim.[10]

Sharing honors with Gryztell for his contribution to
Swedish Baptist hymnody is Jacob Bystrom (1854-1947). Although he was not as gifted a poet as Grytzell, Bystrom is
considered to have contributed more to the overall success
of the Baptist denomination than the former. Dr. Westin
places him next in importance to Anders Wiberg. Bystrom,
like so many others, attended popular courses for preachers
prior to any formal seminary training and engaged in a ministry
of itinerant evangelism throughout Sweden. Following his
graduation from Betelseminariet, he spent two years in America
studying at Colgate Seminary, which institution honored him
with a Doctor of Theology degree in 1914.

After a short pastorate in New York, Bystrom returned
to Sweden in 1884 and became pastor of several Baptist churches in succession. In 1889 his literary interests led him to
accept a position on the editorial staff of Wecko-Posten, the
official organ of the Baptists in Sweden. In 1919 he became
editor-in-chief and remained in this position until 1932. Besides this employment, he functioned as journalist, lecturer,
temperance promoter, and member of the Swedish Riksdag.

Bystrom also maintained a great interest in hymnody,
particularly as it pertained to the ongoing work of the Baptists. With Grytzell, he assisted with the compilation of the
1903 edition of Psalmisten and contributed some of his own
songs, although not in as great a number as the former. One
of his songs, "Go Preach," was inspired by his hearing a
rather mediocre sermon and remarking to himself that at least
the Gospel was preached! Other titles include:

O Glorious Day in Breaking
O Lord, Just Let Thy Glory be Present
Jesus Loves the Little Child
In Our Native Land

More than for his songs, Bystrom is remembered for his monumental work on hymnology Sånger och Sångare, which was
published in three volumes in 1936, 1940, and 1943, respectively.

Two graduates from Betelseminariet who made modest contributions to Baptist hymnody are Harold Waxberg (1864-1900) and John Peter Johansson (1863-1920). The former possessed a degree of poetical ability which never realized its fulfillment because his life was cut short by tuberculosis. In addition to two songs which appeared in Psalmisten, he published a collection of songs in 1899 under the title, "Trembling Leaves." Johansson, a Swedish Baptist pastor, was also highly gifted as a poet, although like Waxberg, very few of his songs have survived in later Scandinavian hymnals. Both of these men are represented by just one composition each in the latest Swedish Baptist hymnal, Psalm och Sång.

Karl August Moden (1868-1950) was originally associated with the Salvation Army of Sweden, but after training with this denomination and serving for a time as an officer he became a Baptist. After theological study he served many pastorates throughout Sweden. His last pastorate in Stockholm extended from 1898 to 1919 after which he assumed the position of mission secretary for the Swedish Baptists. His original song publications are few, but he is remembered best for his lasting contribution to the revision of the 1903 edition of Psalmisten.

Carl Gustaf Lundin (1869-1965) joined the Baptist ranks in 1882 and ten years later enrolled as a student in Betelseminariet. Upon graduation from the seminary, he became a pastor and served in subsequent years in this capacity in his native country in many important Baptist churches. In 1919 he entered a different type of ministry among the Baptists, first as Home Mission secretary and then in a similar office with the Foreign Mission society. Like others who have been mentioned previously, he took an active interest in matters pertaining to hymnody and hymnals and assisted significantly in the publication of the 1928 edition of Psalmisten. A number of his songs appear in this hymnal. Lundin was also a member of the committee which produced the inter-denominational hymnal Svensk Söngdaggsskolsångbok in 1929 in which several of his songs appear. He is also represented in the Psalm och Sång of 1966 by several original hymns and translations.

Another denominational leader and hymnist of distinction among Swedish Baptists is Nils Johan Nordstrom (1880-1943). His schooling included study at John Ongman's Bible School

in Örebro; Betelseminariet in Stockholm; Uppsala School of
Theology; and Northern Baptist Seminary in Chicago, from
which he received the Doctor of Theology degree in 1932.
Nordstrom's ministry was broadened and enriched by extensive travel and studies in England, Canada, Greece, and
Italy. He distinguished himself as a professor in the seminary in Stockholm for ten years, following which he became
rector in 1927. On the local level, Nordstrom rendered significant service in denominational affairs among the Baptists
in Sweden as well as among other free-church groups. He
was prominent as the author of a number of books, pamphlets,
and articles, his chief interest being Baptist history and biographies. His wider interest in the worldwide Baptist cause
brought him into responsible positions on the international
level among the Baptists, particularly in the Baptist World
Alliance. As a member of the songbook committee from 1923-
1928, he played an active part in the final revision and edition of Psalmisten to which he contributed a modest number
of songs. Some originals and translations appear in Psalm
och Sång.

Trygve Hoglund (b. 1902) has been a well-known figure
among the Baptists of Sweden for many years. Like so many
of the earlier religious leaders he left the life of a fisherman
and sailor, later to enter the Baptist ministry. After his
training at Betelseminariet, he became a missionary for the
organization known as the Skärgård Mission, and subsequent
positions included several pastorates in Sweden. His literary
productions included writings in newspapers and periodicals
in which hymns and spiritual songs have appeared occasionally.
Evidently the Christmas season has had great appeal to Hoglund since several of his hymns deal with this theme. Following are translated excerpts from three such hymns:

MY ADVENT

In me buildest Thou Thy Kingdom
My heart is Thine own throne.
Thou dost make the sinner equal.
He inherits with God's Son.

ADVENT

Night-enfolded time is with us

And waiting light is lit.
Worldwide mind of childhood
Born anew in Advent.
Human longs find their meaning
In flick'ring candle lights.
Churches filled with people
At muted organ sound.

CHRISTMAS NIGHT

Not heard
Where flock is resting
A sound in watch of night.
Just stirred
By lightest movement
From waft of gentle breeze
Is the light fold of shepherd's wide attire
As leaning pensively upon his staff he stands.

Simon Oberg (b. 1897) made a significant contribution
to the Baptists of Sweden through his pastoral ministry and
his musical endeavors. Oberg composed many of the songs
for the Swedish Youth Hymnal published in 1930 as well as
four texts for Strangbandet (Stringband) which was also
issued during the same period.

Oberg has shared the experience and background to
the writing of one of his hymns which appears as number
four in Psalm och Sång entitled "The Triune God." For twenty
years he served as pastor of the "Tabernaklet" in Stockholm
during which time he ministered to a very large group of
Estonian refugees. The robust faith of these Estonians was
a source of encouragement to their "adopted" pastor; and
from the inspiration he received by this association, he wrote
this hymn for their Easter Conference in 1946.

Gunnar Holm who was organist at the "Tabernaklet"
made a choral arrangement of the hymn for mixed voices.
It was subsequently sung by many choirs in Sweden in the
early years after its publication. When Psalm och Sång was
published, Oberg's song was selected for this hymnal; P.E.
Styf supplied the musical setting. A free translation of the
first stanza indicates the general message of this hymn:

The people, O Lord, rejoice
That the powers of evil are frightened
And retreat at thy word;
Thou dost keep thine own,
Thy love explains everything,
Thou dost make known thy Holy Spirit.

Foremost among present day hymnists and song writers
in Sweden is Rev. Erland Wendel-Hansen (b. 1916). He was
born in Denmark where he received his early education and
began his early literary career. In later years he moved to
his mother's home country, Sweden. After training for the
ministry at Betelseminariet, he pursued further study at the
University of Stockholm in the history of religions and philosophy. Although he taught at a gymnasiet and Betelseminariet, his main ambition has been the pastoral ministry. He has
been pastor of several prominent churches in Sweden and is
now retired from the pastorate of the Baptist church in Bromma,
a suburb of Stockholm.

Wendel-Hansen developed an interest in hymnody at a
very early age, and by the time he was eighteen years old,
he had written more than 100 hymns or poems in Danish.
After moving to Sweden, he continued his interest in writing
and translating hymns; however, with the exception of some
short collections of spiritual poems in one or two anthologies
and some numbers in the new Psalm och Sång he has published very few of his original works except as some have
appeared occasionally in newspapers and periodicals. His
other writings and publications include such topics as Christian baptism, biographies of religious leaders, the Bible, and
Bible history.

According to his personal testimony in correspondence,
he had ambitions to contribute to the new hymnal translations
of hymns by foreign authors such as Bunyan, Spurgeon,
Adoniram Judson, and Köbner, but organization and editing
of the book prohibited anything extensive in this category.
His special interest has been in the production of baptismal
hymns. In a letter to the writer, he has expressed it thus:

As a Baptist pastor and author, of course, I have a
great interest in the special baptismal hymns. And
in most of our Baptist hymnals, Scandinavian and
others, except for Germany, I have felt the loss of

a real gospel of baptism. It seems as if we Baptists
have been afraid of emphasizing any deeper meaning
of baptism than an act of confessing and imitating
Christ. Look now at nr. 276: "I know a way to
salvation." The Word has described it, and every
soul wandering that way shall never go astray. It
opens to every one, who believes in Jesus Christ,
and surely it leads through the river of baptism to
Heaven. And now as before, the Spirit urges everybody, who is seeking peace, to receive baptism in
Jesus' name repenting. How blessed it is to descend
with faith into the grave of baptism, throwing off
the burden of sin, never to see it again. And then
appear before God not in garmets of our own but
raised in the array of Christ, revived and risen.[11]

A free translation of the hymn gives insight to his particular
view of baptism:

I know a way to blessedness,
It's written in the Word,
And ev'ry soul who treads that way
Will never go astray.

It open lies to each and all
Who trust in Jesus Christ,
And leads through baptism withal
Through heaven's gate at last.

The Spirit urgeth as of old
Each one who seeketh peace
To be baptized in Jesus' name
Repenting self therewith.

How blessed in baptismal grave
In faith be lowered down
And cast away sin's heavy load
Ne'er to be seen again.

And then appear before one's God,
Not in one's own attire,
But dressed in Jesus' righteousness
Arisen, waked from sleep.

My thanks to Thee, O Jesus Christ

> For blest baptismal bath,
> For that good way which leads at last
> To Heaven's golden gate.

The author readily admits that this is a rather new and startling view of baptism for a traditional Baptist. A representative of Svenska Missionsförbundet, in reviewing the new Baptist hymnbook, was somewhat perplexed at this interpretation of baptism by a Baptist pastor. As a result, Wendel-Hansen was invited to defend his views as expressed in this hymn in the Svensk Veckotidning (The Covenant Post). His defense of this and other baptismal hymns in Psalm och Sång follows in part:

> In his perusal of the new all Baptist church songbook "Psalm och Sång" Oscal Lövgren has in "Svensk Veckotidning" particularly paid attention to baptismal songs and dwells especially on no. 276 "Jag vet an väg till salighet" (I know a way to blessedness), which he considers hazy, and sees in it an indication that the Baptists must have arrived at a considerably sacramental baptismal position.

> Now perhaps it could be said that Baptists in general should not be held responsible for one singular song; and after all it is not anonymous. With the Baptists as well as within "Missionsförbundet" no Baptists readily can accept pedobaptism as a correct Christian baptism, which admittedly does not prevent them from receiving infant-baptized Christians.

> But the view of baptism among the Baptists varies from an exclusively symbolic interpretation of baptism by which faith, so to speak, becomes alone sufficient unto salvation, to a more sacramental (hardly sacrementarian) view, where one would rather regard faith and baptism as two complementing sides in-- let us say-- regeneration, without permitting their temporal place to be regarded as unimportant on this account.... With the editor's permission I will here quite briefly attempt to give the background for this psalm's birth and an analysis of its theology. Incidentally this will reveal, on the whole, my own position on the problem: Faith-- baptism-- salvation.

The beginning may be sought in my earliest youth,
when I began to wrestle with the spiritual questions.
Even as a child--and I was not born in a Baptist
home--I took strong exception to the message in a
psalm by Grundtvig which often reappeared in the
school's morning worship, the last line of which runs:
"Our faith is our strong fortress; Its center is our
hope; In it we receive the Father's Spirit by means
of Jesus' child-baptism."

I simply could not take it. To be sure, faith is introduced at the beginning. But how could it logically
lead to pedo-baptism as a conclusion? This was to
remain for me a conundrum. My spiritual development
soon brought me to a Baptistic conviction, where baptism only received another place, but absolutely no
loss of importance. As I even at that time, and perhaps oftener than I do now, jotted down my experiences and musings in verse, I then made my first
outline for (based on) the psalm in question. The
melody I set to the text was the same we had sung
in the school with Grundtvig's words. Unfortunately
it did not become possible for the song book committee
to use it instead of the version published in "Psalm
och Sång".... The attentive listener can hardly mis-
take the intent of the message in the psalm.

In reality there is no way which leads to blessedness,
and that way is clearly depicted in God's Word. It
begins with faith in Jesus Christ, and it leads through
water baptism--and reaches its conclusion in heaven!

From a purely logical viewpoint I can state it this way:
The way of salvation is neither identical with the faith
nor with the baptism. But I can neither discover it
and begin to walk in it, and all the less continue to
walk in it apart from faith. Moreover the way of salvation is not the baptism. But that way even from the
start leads through baptism.

If the psalm seems hazy to some I hope it is not so
to all. It is a poor consolation that not even the
Gospels are fully clear to all in this respect, in spite
of efforts to clarify.[12]

In addition to the need for stronger interpretive hymns
on baptism, Wendel-Hansen has expressed his hope that in
the future new hymns might appear in other neglected subjects.

> Last but not least, in our Swedish hymnbooks I have
> always felt the lack of hymns about the life of Jesus
> as a human being, as well as popular morning and
> evening songs as we have them in Denmark from the
> hands and hearts of Grundtvig and Ingemann and
> others. I have written one or two hymns in their
> way and have also translated hymns of theirs. The
> morning hymn no. 605 "The dark night is over," may
> be an example. But it seems to me as if it were here
> a big field, and I wonder, if it could be a call and
> a challenge to some Christian poet to seek God in the
> earthly life of Jesus and not only in his divine birth,
> his mystical death and supernatural appearance, and
> to seek Christ not only in the frame of the Holy Land
> but also in the lands and lives of ours.[13]

Even though some of the hymns suggested by Wendel-
Hansen were not included in the Psalm och Sång, his ability
as a hymn writer and translator is duly recognized because
of an appreciable number of his originals and translations in
this volume.

The official songbook for the Baptist denomination in
Sweden and the Örebro Mission is Psalm och Sång, published
in 1966 and already referred to in this account. The former
songbook of the Baptists, Psalmisten, went through several
revisions and editions from 1880 until 1928, when the last
edition was published. Even though, as has been mentioned,
Psalmisten was received with a spirit of relative indifference
in 1880, it did continue to be the official praise book of the
Baptists until the recently published hymnal came off the
press.

The Örebro Mission's Andliga Sånger was first published
in 1931, and in an enlarged edition in 1935. It was intended
for use in revival meetings in a broad sense, but was accepted
as the official hymnal within the Örebro church. The 1931
collection contains 253 numbers while the later edition numbers 525 hymns and gospel songs. The foreword to Andliga
Sånger declares its aim and purpose:

The song collection here under consideration has as
its chief objective that of serving the evangelistic
work. We hope, namely, that yet many thousands
of dearly redeemed souls will be won for God's kingdom, and that the mighty wave of spiritual renewal,
which more than a couple of decades has swept forth
among God's people shall find its way to yet greater
hosts of people during the brief period of time that
yet may remain before Jesus comes. To the further-
ance of this glorious work of grace this songbook
would be of service.

... Some of the songs are weak from the theoretical
viewpoint, but since they have for a long time been
well known and preferably sung by both the older
and the younger among God's people, they were included in the selection of melodies, known and easily
sung melodies have been preferred to the more difficult ones, even if the latter from a purely musical
viewpoint could have been of greater worth. Our
effort has been to include the most practical and usable and exclude what infallibly would have become
"dead material."[14]

The scope of the contents is indicated by the table of contents:

Assembly and prayer
Revival and invitation
Golgotha songs
Sanctification
Assurance and jubilation
Labor and missions
God's people's future prospects
Solos
For special occasions

From the close of the 1950's, there had been agitation
and discussion concerning the possibility of a revision of the
Örebro hymnal and the combining with Psalmisten for a common Baptist hymnal. In the ensuing years, groundwork and
exploration were carried on in the interest of a new book.
The forword to Psalm och Sång explains the proceedings:

The renewal of the Christian treasure in song which

takes place continually and which was especially marked
in our land during the 1930's and the 1940's made
actual again the need of new song books. From the
Örebro Mission was brought forward the thought of
a common song book for immersionist people, a proposal which, however, could not be actualized. The
general conference of the Baptist denomination at its
meeting in 1953 took action to solve the question regarding a revision of Psalmisten. At the same time
inquiry was to be made as to the possibility of coöperation in the matter with the Örebro Mission, which
had a song book committee already at work. The committee with representatives from both sides, eventually
was appointed, began to function in the autumn of
1956.

The starting point for the work of the song book committee has been Psalmisten and Andliga Sånger, which
have been scrutinized most carefully in order to keep
the best. From other song books, Swedish and also
foreign, some rich material has been selected. Some
texts and melodies are new, or have not heretofore
been used as church song. To be rendered more
satisfactory formally certain songs have been revised.
In regard to the chorales, regard has been paid to
the latest research, and a number of melodies have
been brought back to their original form.

... The new hymnal, between the covers of which
are also found a selection of Bible texts for respon-
sive reading, has been given the name Psalm Och
Sång. This says something about the breadth and
varied character of its contents and the possibilities
for the song book for service in different situations.
It is our hope as well as that of churches and individuals, that in it they will find expression for praise
and aspiration, for testimony and eagerness to serve.[15]

The new hymnal Psalm och Sång is the latest expression
of the hopes and aspirations of the Baptists of Sweden represented in the conferences of the two groups involved in its
publication. This writer was present at the conference sessions in Stockholm, in June 1966, when the new hymnal was
presented and dedicated. It was received with great enthusiasm and a spirit of anticipation. The contents of this
volume are analyzed in some detail in the next chapter.

Besides the official denominational hymnbooks of Swedish Baptists, there appeared two auxiliary hymnals for special use in which the Baptists had a direct and a corporate interest, respectively. In 1919 they published a hymnal for revival and youth meetings entitled Samlingstoner. The need for such a hymnal had been felt for a long time, and its publication grew out of a number of smaller and inadequate hymn booklets which were published over a period of time. A committee was appointed in 1918, and a year later the hymnal was released for its intended use. Its contents for the most part are similar to the American gospel songs.

In summer 1925, a committee was appointed by the Baptists, Missionförbundet, and the Methodists for the publishing of a joint hymnal for use in the Sunday schools of Sweden. A year later the National Evangelical Foundation and the Swedish Alliance each added two representatives to the committee. The result of this committee's work was the Svensk Söngdaggsskolsangbok of 1929, so named because of its intended use as a song book for the children of Swedish Sunday schools. Compiled primarily for the younger set, it has been used to good advantage for children and young people in both home and church.

Hymnody of the Free-Baptists of Sweden

The Free-Baptist denomination in Sweden was founded and organized by Helge Åkeson. He studied for the Lutheran ministry, but through his own understanding of the Bible, he came to the Baptist position on the concept of the church and baptism. He joined the Baptists in 1857 and soon became a preacher among them. Because some within the Baptist tradition considered his doctrine of the atonement of Christ to be heretical according to Baptist theology, he was excluded from the fellowship and thus the denomination of Free-Baptists was formed in 1872.

One doctrine propounded by Åkeson and his followers was that of an ultimate restoration of everyone after God's judgment has been meted out. This borders on Universalism and was unacceptable to the "hard core" Baptists. The Free-Baptists met with strong opposition due to their stand against the bearing of arms and active participation in war. Many were subjected to prison terms, but because of their persistent

stand, laws were subsequently enacted which allowed for the
fulfillment of military obligations without actual combat service.

Although there are several hymnals by the same name
in Sweden, the official organ of praise of the Free-Baptists
is Pilgrimstoner. The first song book was published in 1886
under the title Pilgrims Cittran. It contained 380 songs and
was issued in six editions. The book was revised in 1913,
and at this time the name was changed to Pilgrimstoner. It
contained a total of 560 selections. About one half of the
songs were written by Free-Baptist authors. Like so many
other Swedish hymnbooks, a considerable number of the songs
contained in it are based on Swedish songs previously published in Sweden or from American sources. The music edition of Pilgrimstoner was published in 1915; a revised edition
of both text and music was issued in 1957, containing 560
selections.

From among the many authors whose hymns appear in
Pilgrimstoner, several are worth noting for their contribution
to this hymnal. Foremost among them is Anders Hansson
(1863-1925). As a youth he joined the Free-Baptist Church
and for a number of years served as an itinerant preacher.
He edited the official publication of his denomination, "Upplysningens Vän" (The Friend of Enlightment), from 1894
to 1916. He began to write hymns and sacred songs early
in life; in Pilgrims Cittran about seventy of his original poems
were used in musical settings. In Pilgrimstoner of 1913 his
poems number approximately 150, eighty-two of which were
included in the 1957 edition. Lövgren in his biographical
sketch of Hansson has observed that his songs bear the mark
of the influence from English and American song writers, whose
songs began to infiltrate into Scandinavia during the 1880's.[16]
Even though Hansson severed his connections with the Free-
Baptists in 1925, his songs have made a lasting contribution
to the worship of that group.

Another hymn writer of prominence among the Free-
Baptists is Erik Eriksson (1879-1918). Even though he did
not identify himself as a preacher in a formal way, Eriksson
did serve frequently in that capacity among the Free-Baptist
churches in Sweden. When Pilgrimstoner was published in
1913 he took an active part in this work, which was actually
a revision of the old Pilgrims Cittran. The contents included
thirty original texts and revisions by Eriksson. Some of his

originals had formerly appeared in "Upplysningens Vän."
Nine original songs by him were selected for use in the 1957
revision and edition of Pilgrimstoner.

Joel S. Friden (b. 1890) joined the Free-Baptist denomination in 1906. In 1944 he became editor for the denominational paper "Upplysingen Vän." As a song writer
and composer, he had a large share in the compilation of
Evangeliska Toner in 1937 and the 1957 edition of Pilgrimstoner. Thirteen of his hymns appear in the latter book:

1. Kom, o Gud, med kraft fran höj den
    Come, O God with pow'r from h-vn

2. Det finns en lycka some ej försvinner
    There is a joy which never ceases

3. Fatta beslutet, du t ekande hjärta
    Hesitant heart, do make your decision

4. Dig vi nu lova, o Fader i höjden
    Father in heaven, now we are praising Thee

5. Framåt, frälsta skara, fram i Jesus spår.
    Forward, O saved people, Forward in His steps

6. Hör nu, min vän, jag till dig har en hälsning
    Listen, my friend, I for you have a greeting

7. Fraft from höjden, så han sade
    From on high comes pow'r, said Jesus

8. Med Jesus farm på livets stig
    With Jesus forward on life's path

9. O hyr ljuvt ljöd ej sånger i Sion en gang
    How blest the singing sounded in Zion one time

10. Ur djupet jag ropar, O herre, till dig
    From the deep do I cry, O Lord unto Thee

11. Dyre Jesus, du som känner
    O dear Jesus, Thou who knewest

12. Jesus, du är livets bröd
    Jesus, Thou art bread of Life

13. Nu idag en årgräns du paserar
    Now today a milestone you are passing[17]

The Free-Baptists seemed to have engendered real

inspiration for poetry among their members since a sizable
number have contributed to they hymnody of this particular
denomination. Detailed biographical material is unavailable;
however, Lövgren has supplied enough information in his
"Lexikon" for thumbnail sketches of many Free-Baptist hymnists, most of whom contributed two or more hymns during the
past several years. As these sketches reveal, these hymnists
came from many walks of life.

Anders Anderson (1867-1921) served as a missionary
in South Africa for the Free-Baptist denomination.

N. Olof Anderson (1866-1937) was a tailor by trade
but also a respected song writer in the Free-Baptist
Church.

Hilda Cedarholm (1866-1928), a member of the Free-
Baptist Church in Furaboda, contributed four hymns
to the 1913 Pilgrimstoner.

Daniel Johan Danielson (1851-1910), a farmer from
Lau in Gotland, contributed four hymns to Pilgrims
Cittran of 1886.

Fredrika Jonsson (1956-1905) was a school teacher
and a member of the Free-Baptist Church in Hova.
A wedding hymn and one on the Bible appeared in
Pilgrimstoner of 1913.

Lisa Jonsson (1856-1905), a school teacher by pro-
fession and missionary in South Africa, is best known
for her hymn on practical holiness.

Mats Karlsson (1855-1916) was a Free-Baptist pastor
and hymn writer from Leksand. His hymns have
been used in both Pilgrims Cittran and Pilgrimston-
der.

Doris Lundgren (b. 1903) has been both an evangelist and children's missionary. Both hymnals, Evangeliska Toner (1937) and Pilgrimstoner (1957) contain
several of her hymns.

Axel Teodor Nordstrom (1863-1944) served as pastor
in several churches of his denomination and was
active in its work in America as well. Pilgrimstoner
contains two of his hymns.

Mattias Strömberg (d. 1900) is well represented in

both the early and later hymnals by several of his
hymns. He was both a popular preacher and song
writer among the Free-Baptists.

Johan Teodor Vesterberg (1859-1926) was active in
the Free-Baptist Church in Stockholm from 1887.
Four of his hymns were selected for inclusion in
Pilgrimstoner.

Gustav Östman (1867-1953) was a leading personality
among the Free-Baptists of Sweden. Until 1892
he served as a hired man and tiller of the soil,
then became a miner until 1899. At the turn of
the century he became a traveling preacher within
the Free-Baptist group and in 1916 assumed the
editorship of "Lilla Missionaren." He was one of
the most prolific writers and song composers in his
denomination. Eight of his hymns are to be found
in Pilgrimstoner.

Two observations are in order concerning the hymnody
of the Free-Baptists of Sweden. From the translations of
titles and first lines of many of their hymns, it appears that
their stand against conscription for military service, as well
as their doctrine of the possibility of a universal reconciliation, has not been overly enunciated in their hymnody. Also
noticeable is the exclusion of their hymns from the latest Baptist hymnal of Sweden, Psalm och Sång. One could come to
the conclusion that they are not in good standing with the
regular Baptists, although hymns of several of the latter group
are to be found in Pilgrimstoner.

Hymnody of the Swedish Missionsförbund

Svenska Missionförbundet was formed in 1878. As has
been previously pointed out, the break came when certain
students in the mission school of Evangeliska Fosterlanstiftel-
sen began to propagate Waldenström's theory of the atonement
which was Arminian in theology. These students were refused appointments as missionaries under the society. A number of small groups adhered quite strongly to Waldenström's
theories and celebrated communion among themselves apart
from the State Church in spite of repeated warnings of the
consequences. Waldenström and his followers were expelled
from the society, and thus the new Missionsförbundet was or-

ganized and it experienced rapid growth and expansion. Within the ranks of this new denomination were many gifted song writers who contributed greatly to the hymnody of the free-church movement in Scandinavia.

One of the most richly endowed of this group of hymnists was Joel Blomqvist (1840-1930). He was born into the home of a tailor in Stockholm who frequented the small free "spiritual circles" of that city. At the age of nineteen, Blomqvist moved to Uppsala, where he received employment in the shop of a gold painter, Carl Widman. This man was connected with the so-called Widmanian Hall, where a small group of believers met for spiritual worship, edification, and sharing. In a short time, Blomqvist joined their ranks and served as organist and song leader for their meetings. He traveled on preaching missions with the group from Uppsala, playing and singing his own songs as well as those of others in the group.

He became recognized early as an outstanding musician, author, and composer. In 1967 he published a small collection of his own compositions entitled Kanaan. In 1874 Blomqvist accepted a position with the Uppsala City Mission. During the early years in this association, he wrote a number of new hymns, both texts and melodies, which he compiled into a collection called Sabbatsklockan, published in 1877. The music edition was issued in 1878, containing fifty of his originals. Many of these, which are still in use in present-day Swedish hymnals, deal with such subjects as the Sabbath day, the life of spiritual devotion, advent, revival, and youth. His songs were extremely popular in the pietistic revivals in Sweden. The year 1877 was a time of great productivity in writing for Blomqvist. He testifies to unusual inspiration during this time and the urge to write as many as five or six songs in one day. It is estimated that he wrote 400 hymns and as many musical settings during his lifetime. One of Blomqvist's hymns, "Sabbath Day of Rest and Cheer," for which he wrote both words and music is presented here in a translation by A.L. Skoog:

> Sabbath day of rest and cheer!
> Day divine, to us so dear!
> Come, O come to old and young,
> Gath'ring all for prayer and song.
>
> Now the week to toil is o'er,

And in peace we sit once more
In thy presence, gracious Lord,
List'ning to thy holy word.

Lord, our God, we seek thy face,
Bless us with thy saving grace;
May thy heralds ev'rywhere
Fervently thy truth declare.

Let thy mighty word hold sway
Over men on earth today;
Our poor souls, good Shepherd, feed,
Into pastures green us lead.

May, O Lord, the day be near,
When we pass from trials here
Into thine eternal rest,
In mansions of the blest.

His song collection of 1877 was followed by another, Fridstoner, containing only twenty-five numbers. In 1883 he published a small edition of Nya Sånger and in 1889 his hymnal for youth, Ungdomstoner.

Lövgren describes the style and content of his hymns:

Blomqvist in his song writing never makes lyrical excursions beyond the bounds of reality. Neither is for him dogmatic orthodoxy of greatest importance. At the time of doctrinal controversy he had his own dogmatic views; but these he kept in the background. For him there are more important things to be put first. His songs bespeak a struggling and praying soul. He feels how the will and the mind are weighted down with the many things of the world. He longs and prays and agonizes and strives to overcome that which weighs down the wings of his soul and sullies the spiritual garment. Many of his songs can be characterized as prayer and sanctification songs. He preaches in the first instance to his own soul, "Separate thyself more completely unto God; leave all in His hands and for His service." He also has a message for those who have not yet begun to walk in God's pathway. From the beginning of the 1880's he devoted himself entirely to song and preaching.

His singing was noted for liveliness, captivating power
and heartiness--so goes the testimony of his son.[18]

When Missionsförbundet was organized, E.J. Ekman
(1842-1915) served as its chairman. During his ministry in
Ockelbo, he had been greatly exercised in his own conscience
concerning serving communion to those without spiritual dis-
cernment, even though they had been confirmed. This situation precipitated his break with the State Church. In 1879
he withdrew from the ministry and became the principal of
a mission school in Kristineham. This position was followed
by his assuming the post as Mission Superintendent and editor
for Missionsförbundet. When in later years he deviated from
the doctrine of eternal punishment and leaned toward Universalism, he was compelled to withdraw from his position with
Missionsförbundet. Although he was not a song writer of
great distinction, he did publish a collection called Fridsbasunen
in 1884, which contained some of the few numbers which he
wrote. Among these are two hymns on heaven and eternal
rest. Lövgren remarks that "it seems remarkable that this
strong-willed and powerful man could write songs of such
mild-minded resignation."[19]

Another minister of Missionsförbundet who was noted
as a compiler of hymns, as well as a poet, is Anders G.
Floden. Born in 1883 in Västergötland, he came to America
in 1914, where he pursued theological studies and became a
Missionsförbund pastor in Duluth and Winnepeg. During an
interim period in Sweden, 1919-1921, he served as an evangelist with both the Pentecostals and his own denomination.
While in America, Floden published a songbook, Klocktoner.
The second and third editions of this collection were published
in Sweden in 1930. The book comprises forty selections, most
of which are by Floden. One of his songs has a particularly
captivating title, "Varförbygger du Noa en båt?" (Why Are
You Building, O Noah, a Boat?).

Johan A. Gustafson (b. 1889) has distinguished himself
in Missionsförbundet as a pastor, editor, denominational secretary, and hymn writer. Foremost among his contribution to
the hymnody of the free churches of Scandinavia has been
his significant work as chairman of the committee for Sånger
och Psalmer, his denomination's latest hymnal. Gustafson has
been a diligent writer of meditations, novels, poems, and
hymns. He describes this method of writing as similar to his

inspiration for the preparation of a sermon: first a theme,
perhaps the line of a verse relative to a spiritual experience,
sometimes after meditation, but usually in connection with
some appealing melody. [20] The following English translations
of some of his titles and first lines give an idea of the scope
of his hymn texts:

> Bore you my burden, suffered for me.
>
> God is my refuge, fortress and strength.
>
> Hear me when my heart is crying.
>
> Abide the glow of morning.
>
> Speak to me, dear Savior.
>
> Just as of old He travels.
>
> Thrust thy own truth into my inmost self.

In addition to his work as a hymnologist, Oscar Lövgren
(b. 1899) has made a lasting contribution to the free-church
hymnody by his several hymns, among which is the one on
baptism, "För dopets helga gåva" (For the baptismal gift).
It had long been Lövgren's desire for a hymn about baptism
that could be sung at baptismal services regardless of the age
of the candidates. (His interest in baptismal hymns has already been pointed out in connection with the work of Rev.
Wendel-Hansen.) This hymn was revised by the author for
the hymnal Sånger och Psalmer in 1950. His interest in hymnody is shown by his distinguished work as secretary of the
committee for the above-named hymnal. Free-church hymnody
is deeply indebted to him for his three-volume work and the
Lexikon used in this study, as well as other works in hymnology.

Foremost among the hymn writers of Missionsförbundet
was Nils Frykman (1842-1911). As a public school teacher
in Norrköping, he was caught up in the revival spirit of the
1860's and, in time, became active in the affairs of the church
and revival meetings. Until the age of thirty-three, Frykman
had never penned a song, but the revival activities in Sweden
stimulated his capabilities along this line, and, in a short
time, his unusual poetic gifts were recognized by those with
whom he was associated. His career as a hymnist began with
his revisions of some of the older songs, which then led him
to produce some of his own. One of his first originals appeared
in the paper "Wermlands Allehanda" in 1876.

This was a time of religious upheaval in Sweden. Crowds of believers and seekers gathered in farmhouses where they preached, prayed, and sang of their faith and the desire for a fuller spiritual experience. In such an atmosphere, Frykman drew his inspiration for his countless songs which he was to write. The mood of the revival may be sensed in the following lines from some of his well-known hymns, which are still included in Swedish and American hymnals:

> Everyone can be saved, if to God he turneth.
>
> This command, straight from God, holds for every nation.
>
> Our mighty God works mighty wonders.
>
> Jesus' precious bride, wouldst thou reach the haven?
>
> I an content and happy,
>
> I now can freely breathe.

Most of these songs were written around 1881, at the time Frykman had been warned of his possible excommunication as a public school-teacher for his Waldenströmian views on the atonement and the Lord's Supper. His "Luther-like" determination is seen in a stanza of one of his hymns in a free-English translation:

> Let Satan roar on freely, and let the world assist,
> I'll not before them tremble; God's purpose will prevail,
> God's Word will be victorious, and so will everyone
> Who's under the Savior's command.

In time Frykman resigned his teaching position under pressure because of his obvious deviation from the teachings of the State Church. Now and again he brushed with the law over his lack of loyalty to the Church, but in process of time, like many reformers, he won his case and was exonerated of the charges. Songs vital to his faith continued to flow from his pen and find their place in the hearts of many in the free church.

Near the close of 1887, Frykman received a call to become pastor of the Swedish Mission Tabernacle in Chicago, which he accepted. In 1897 he published a small collection of

some thirty-five numbers called <u>Harpoklangen</u> (Harp Chimes).
In <u>Sions Basun</u>, an early hymnal of the Mission Covenant
Church in America, over 100 of Frykman's hymns are to be
found. These testify to his popularity as a hymn writer in
America.

Frykman moved to Minnesota in 1889, where he served
five small churches in the Covenant denomination. In 1907
he retired to Minneapolis, where he remained until his death
in 1911.

Andreas Fernholm (1840-1892) was to experience a check-
ered career as far as his church affiliation was concerned.
After graduation from the theological department of Uppsala
University, he was ordained to the Lutheran ministry in 1866.
Before his ordination, he became assistant to H.J. Lundborg
in Grythyttan from whom he received deep religious impressions. Fernholm also became acquainted with free-church
ideas through his mentor, who had visited in England for a
time. After serving two short pastorates, he returned to
Grythyttan following the death of Lundborg. At this time he
prepared the way for the breakthrough of the free church
by encouraging the formation of communion societies. In 1871
he left his pastorate to establish a school for lay preachers
in Kristinehamn. The following year he retired from the ministry of the State Church.

Fernholm's views on church polity led him to the Baptist denomination. After an active ministry of several years
among Swedish Baptists, he joined Missionsförbundet in 1880
because of his view of atonement which was similar to that
held by Waldenström. His previous journalistic activity aided
him greatly in the publishing of <u>Forbündet</u>, which he jointly
edited with E.J. Ekman. There followed for him several op-
portunities for the editing and publishing of other journals
and periodicals.

Fernholm's efforts in the field of hymnody earned for
him a place of distinction among free-church hymnists. In
1873 he published a collection of songs on baptism which reveal that he was well-versed in the Baptist view on this ordinance. While serving as co-editor with Ekman, he wrote
a baptismal hymn for Ekman's songbook, <u>Fridsbasunen</u>. This
hymn was so written that it could serve for either adult or
child baptism. His best-known hymn is the one based on
the parable of the sower:

Låt våra ögon upp, o Gud,
Att vi dit ord må fatta
(Open our eyes, O gracious God,
That we the word may fathom.)

Although Johan Erik Nystrom (1842-1907) never actually
held membership in Missionsförbundet, he did play an important part in its hymnody, particularly in the compilation of
its songbook. He maintained a close working relationship with
this denomination even in the capacity of an official missionary.

Nystrom was born to pietistic parents who identified
themselves with the Scott-Rosenius group in Stockholm. After
considerable struggle for an education, he did attain to the
Doctor of Philosophy degree in 1866, with a major in Greek.
During one of the enforced interruptions in his schooling,
he came into contact with the Baptists in Stockholm and, in
time, identified himself with them. He became an instructor
at the Baptist seminary in 1867, and in the meantime, he edited
a Bible concordance which gained wide acceptance and passed
through many editions.

Like Fernholm, he eventually severed connections with
the Baptists because of his views on open communion. After
missionary work in Beirut, Lebanon, he returned to Sweden
in 1881 to serve subsequently with Missionsförbundet, after
another short term of service with the Baptists. This new
affiliation led him into missionary service in North Africa,
where he died in July of 1907.

Although Nystrom became a hymnist in his own right,
his main interest and talent lay in translation and publication.
The songs of the American Ira Sankey captivated the free-
church groups in Scandinavia and many translations were
made of these songs. Nystrom had unusual success in these
translations. His collection of the Sankey songs, known as
Sånger till Lammets Lof, went through ten successive editions
with the addition of many new songs, principally by Sankey.
Its popularity was attested by the publication of three editions in 1875; the last edition of 1881 contained 292 selections.
This was without question Nystrom's first work of importance
in Swedish hymnody. His second work of significance was
the Svenska Missionsförbundet Sångbok of 1894, which occupied most of his time on furlough in 1892-93. More will be
said concerning this volume and Nystrom's relationship to its
publication later in this chapter.

Selma Sundelius Lagerstrom (1869-1927) was one of the
most prolific of women hymn writers in Missionsförbundet.
Her early home life was anything but pleasant as she was subjected at times to her father's violent and cruel treatment.
For some time she visited in the nearby manse at Torsby to
escape from him. In this situation she came in touch with
the evangelical revival and in time became stabilized in her
Christian faith. Early in the 1880's, she came to live with
the Hultkranz family in the Gillberga parish and while there
met Johannes Lagerstrom, whom she subsequently married.
After their marriage the Lagerstoms settled in Kristinehamn
and later in Stockholm.

Mrs. Lagerstom's literary talents were put to use early
in the service of Christian hymnody. Some of her first songs
appeared in the collection Fridsbasunen of 1882, published by
E.J. Ekman. Her well-known Easter hymn "Christ Is Living"
was contained in the 1884 edition of the same hymnal. Several
of her songs first appeared in the paper Sanningsvittnet in
successive issues. The following list of first lines in translation are a cross section of the subjects on which she wrote
her hymns:

Joyful news comes from Jesus to his precious bride.

Jesus, make me still contented.

"I'm coming soon," so Jesus said.

Yes, your names are written up in heaven.

Soon the great eternal portals open quietly for me.[21]

In 1896 she published her own collection of songs,
Blommar i törnbräcken (Flowers in the Thorn Hedge), a title
which was appropriate for her own life and experience. The
gloom and sadness of her early life returned in later years
to plague Mrs. Lagerstrom, and these experiences found expression in the sacred verse which came from her pen. Although troubled by a recurrence of childhood gloom and sadness, nevertheless through the medium of her poetry, she was
able to express her faith in divine Providence.

A hymn writer of great note in Missionsförbundet was
Carl Boberg (1859-1940). Like others he was caught up in
the evangelical awakening of his day and became one of its
outstanding teachers and preachers, with a special appeal to
Swedish youth. In addition to his unusual ability in this area,

his gift for writing manifested itself early. In 1889 when the
preacher and editor of Sanningsvittnet, P.A. Palmer, died,
Boberg was asked to assume the editorship of this popular
and influential publication. He had served on the staff since
1882. His influence in government was felt in the service
which he rendered as a member of the Riksdag's first chamber
from 1911 until 1924.

Boberg began to write religious verse while a student
at Kristinehamn. His first poem to be published was the well-
known song "Look up, O weary hard-pressed brother." Others
of his early songs found their way into the first collection of
Fridsbasunen, among them his communion hymn, "O Lamb of
God, for us so freely offered." One of the stanzas of the
hymn, now eliminated in later books, expressed the motiva-
tion for the private observance of the communion outside of
the State Church:

> O Savior, now because of Bible precept,
> We gather all around thy precious table,
> Remembering thy death for us.[22]

Another area of controversy which engaged his attention was
Waldenström's theory of the atonement of Christ. His align-
ment with Waldenström resulted in continual warning from some
of his friends. His youthful courage and assurance in the
rightness of his stand is expressed in his hymn which begins:

> David sang, "The Lord's my helper,"
> So I also now can sing.

Two seasons of the church year, Advent and Easter,
provided Boberg with the inspiration for expression in sacred
song. He also produced hymns on a variety of other subjects
and moods: evening hymns, sorrow and joy, funeral and baptismal hymns, devotional life, and heaven. The unusually
large number of songs in the current hymnal of Missionsförbundet testifies to his popularity as a hymnist. His style
of writing is summarized by Lövgren:

> Boberg's songs show clarity in thinking, simplicity
> in composition, romantic feeling and language rich
> in symbols. In easy rhyme he proclaims God's un-
> ending grace and goodness. His verse is very sing-
> able. Seldom does one find a word that disturbs the

ear. Very little does he say about God's holiness and
serious demands. He has a tendency to spread out
without going deeply. His fine lyrical precision and
poetic feeling rendered him most efficient as a member in song book committees.[23]

The events and work which led up to the publication of
Sånger och Psalmer, the official hymnal of Svenska Missionsförbundet, provide an appropriate close to our study of the
hymnody of this denomination. When the denomination was
formed in 1878, a number of small collections were in use by
the mission churches and societies which were to merge into
the one large group. Among these song books were some well-
known titles: Pilgrim Sånger (Palmquist's), Andeliga Sånger
(Ahnfelt), Sabbatsklockan (Blomqvist), Sånger till Lammets
lof (Nystrom), and Fridsbasunen (Ekman). All of these collections were published by private concerns, and there was
a strong desire that the new church should have a hymnal
distinctly its own. The matter was discussed in the conference in 1891, but it was not until 1892 that the project was
taken up in a serious and spirited manner under the direction of Erik Nystrom. Nystrom was entrusted with the main
responsibility of bringing a brand new book to publication.
Svenska Missionsförbundets Sångbok was in print in 1893 but
was not officially presented to the church until 1894.

The difficulties in compiling and publishing the new
hymnal were considerable since Nystrom was not able to use
translations of familiar hymns which had been used formerly
by other publishing houses. In many instances he had to
make entirely new translations. Cases in point were his own
translations of the Sankey songs and some of the well-known
songs of Lina Sandell. Consequently, he had to make new
translations of songs translated by him earlier. Many other
Swedish originals were revised by Nystrom with measurable
success. This procedure produced a splintering in the field
of sacred song but no alternative was opened to the committee
because high purchase rights prohibited any other course of
action.

In spite of these adverse circumstances, Nystrom and
the committee produced a book of considerable worth to Missionsförbundet. It was never his intention or desire to produce merely an anthology of sacred song but rather a book
of suitable texts and melodies for use in the various services

of the Church. This he succeeded in doing and the end
result, according to Lövgren, was comparable to the Wallin
Psalmbook. The book contained 703 selections and was printed
in a total of 693,500 copies. The music edition numbered
37,250 copies.

As early as 1901 the question was raised concerning a
revision of the new hymnal. Many felt that more of the läsare
songs should be included. The revision did not appear, however, until 1920. It contained a total of 782 selections with
the addition of 350 songs, many of which were not new. Most
of these added came from Sankey's Sånger and Hemlandstoner.
A total of 548,000 copies of the revision were printed and
25,000 of the music edition.

During the period 1939-1944, a number of discussions
were carried on regarding the production of a common hymnal
for use at least with the Swedish Baptists and the Methodist
denomination. Nothing materialized from these deliberations,
and the 1920 song book came up for revision instead. A
process of elimination and addition resulted in the use of new
hymns, many of which came from Psalmboken. A free translation of the foreword of the new publication Sånger och Psalmer
describes its contents and design:

> Sånger och Psalmer now before us with text as well
> as music succeeds the music edition of Svenska Mis-
> sionsförbundet published in 1921. By and large it
> builds on the same material. But when 258 numbers
> in the old song book have been left out and 263 new
> songs have been added the deviation from the old one
> is considerable.

> The old songs have as a rule been allowed to retain
> their old melodies. In some instances, however, sub-
> stitution has seemed necessary, when the old melodies
> have proven too difficult and have rendered the use
> of otherwise good song texts impossible. In some
> instance melodies have been substituted when they
> have been entirely unsuitable. Thus as a rule the
> national song melodies have had to give place to more
> suitable ones. The effort to retain in the greatest
> possible degree the melodies which of old have belonged
> to the texts has resulted in the retention of some mel-
> odies that the committee for musical reasons wished to
> eliminate.

The melodies which S&nger och Psalmer have in common with Svenska Psalmboken have usually been kept
unchanged. But deviations have, however, been made
in regard to melodies which the Choral Book Committee took over from the Swedish revival circles and in
that process did some revisions in a choralizing direction. The melodies not taken from the Choral Book
have usually been re-harmonized by the Committee.
In certain instances the melodies have been re-rhyth-
metized to make them suitable as congregational songs.
In place of the chorus arrangement in the old book
they have here been transposed to a more suitable
key.

The committee has striven to make the songs as sing-
able and playable as possible. A dotted line in the
music indicates place for prelude.

A valuable consideration is that in this book the music
has all the way through been supplied for every song.
Reference to other numbers have thus not been needed.
In that all verses of the song text have the music
throughout the annoyance of having music and text
separated is eliminated.[24]

Hymnody of the Swedish Methodists

The contribution of Swedish Methodists to Scandinavian
hymnody has been modest in comparison with those of other
denominations but of no less significance. The development
of the Methodist Church in Sweden has already been presented
in chapter two in the work of the brothers Olaf and Jonas
Hedstrom, the latter of whom became the pioneer and founder
of Swedish Methodism in the United States. Victor Witting
(1825-1906) has also been indicated as having had great influence in the development of the Swedish Methodist church
in his homeland and also in America.

Witting's career as a leader in Methodism was carried
on intermittently in both Sweden and the United States. Among
his several duties in the United States, he served as editor
of the Swedish-American Methodist periodical, Sändebudet.
In 1869 he made what was to have been a brief visit to Sweden;
but after his arrival, he became intensely involved in the work
among Swedish Methodists as one of the early pioneers.

Witting was a diligent writer, particularly in the religious field, and was especially active in writing and translating hymns and gospel songs. He was not a poet of any great consequence even though he contributed many usable poems. Many of his songs have had to be revised through the years for their continued use. Three of his original songs, which appear in the Methodist "Psalmbok," have been popular with the people of his denomination; two of them deal with the joy of spiritual certainty. The opening lines of each are as follows:

"Hear, oppressed, cast your look upon God's Lamb, who bears your sin."

and

"Thanks and praise to Thee, O Jesus! Thou didst save my sinful soul."

In 1870 he published his missionary hymn, which begins:

"O say, can you see what His promises mean?"

Jacob Th. Jacobsson (1840-1912) was born in Gotland and as a young boy settled in Klintehamn where he conducted his own business enterprise. A later move took him to Kalmar, where he became an ironmonger and as serious a student as time would permit. In his early years, he joined the Methodist church in which he engaged in devoted and faithful service. He became a lay preacher while still carrying on business pursuits. His preaching included the area of temperance, and he was instrumental in the formation of temperance societies in Sweden. He was a frequent lecturer in America also.

Jacobsson was a sedulous and talented writer. His works include a large number of poems and songs with sacred text all in the interest of Christianity and temperance. Many of his works, including his songs, were translated into English and widely circulated among interested people. His burial song appeared in the periodical Lilla Sändebudet on May 11, 1882, and has been one of the best known and widely used of its kind, appearing at the present time in several Swedish hymnals. Its opening lines set the victorious note characteristic of the entire hymn:

"War is now ended,
You have won the battle."

According to Lövgren, Jacobsson's best known and most highly
prized hymns were those written to be sung just before the
sermon. One of these found its way into <u>Svenska Psalmboken</u>,
as well as several other hymnals. One stanza shows its practicality for such usage:

O Holy Father, come Thou and be near us
Cause us to feel the power of Thy teaching.
Thou, who canst give us more than we are asking,
Hear us, O Father!

Carl August Stenholm (1843-1884), although a bookbinder
by trade, engaged in an active ministry among the Methodists
of Sweden. Early, his talents for service in the church became manifest, foremost were his speaking ability and his capacity for writing. One of his early assignments was in the
city of Norrköping, where he engaged in pioneer work for
the cause of Methodism. His subsequent labors were carried
on in Göteborg and Jönköping. His writing ability led him to
become editor of <u>Lilla Sändebudet</u>. Stenholm visited in America, and for a short period of time was pastor in Illinois. He
never felt quite at home in a foreign land and upon his return
to Sweden assumed preaching in several cities.

The songs in the Methodist "Psalmbok" are originals
of Stenholm. Their respective opening lines are:

"Healthful fountain, flowing from the throne of grace,"

and

"Oh come to the fountain, whose waters rush forth."

It is assumed that he is the author of a rather serious song
which begins:

"Time speeds away like a fast flowing stream,
Years upon years flee away."

Gustaf A. Gustafson (1865-1922) in his early church experience affiliated with the Salvation Army and attended its
denominational training school. Later he transferred to the

Methodist church and became one of its preachers. After
study at the pastoral school conducted by the Methodists in
Sweden, he served as pastor in several parishes in Sweden
and one in Finland. In 1916 he became editor of the Methodist paper and directed the publishing house.

Gustafson distinguished himself in many ways in his
activities with the Methodists but especially through his writings. Lovgren calls him one of the foremost hymn writers
within the Methodist church in Sweden. In the revision of
the Methodist hymnal of 1919, he is represented by many substantial contributions, foremost among which are his original
texts. The following opening lines and titles give some indication as to the scope of his hymn texts:

> Thy life Thou in death has given.
>
> Look, O Lord, upon Thy warriors.
>
> Look, O Lord, Thy church is meeting.
>
> In spring attire, as thine own bride.
>
> O God, when all goes haywire.
>
> O God, Who in the highest dwells.
>
> O what joy my heart is feeling.
>
> Down at the Cross, O Jesus Christ.
>
> I found at the cross full salvation.

Several other hymn writers among Swedish Methodists
have contributed to their hymnody in significant amounts but
about whom just scant biographical material is available. Their
names, dates, and the number of their hymns in the Methodist
hymnal are as follows:

> Mickael Peter Lindqvist (1832-1923)--2
> Karl E. Norstrom (1859-1918)--3
> Otto H. Strömberg (1867-1936)--6
> Mathilde Will-Ojerholm (1858-1903)--2

Methodism in Sweden actually received its start from
returning Swedes who had been influenced by American Methodism. One of the earliest hymn books to be used by Swedish
Methodists was one published in America by Victor Witting,
<u>Andliga Sånger for Bone, Klass och forlagnda Möten</u> (Spiritual

Songs for Prayers, Class and Protracted Meetings). In 1868 another collection was published in Göteborg called Sånger på vägen till Zion, and in 1870 Psalmer och Lofsånger, which contained texts from Psalmer och Sånger published in 1860 in Cincinnati.

The hymnal Methodist-episkopalkyrkans Svenska Psalmer made its appearance in 1892, the work of J.M. Erikson, K. Lundgren, and L.G. Berglund. The music edition edited by E. Lindgren was issued in 1893. The first revision appeared in 1919, the work of G.C. Gustafson and K.E. Norstrom. The music edition followed in 1921. The latest revisions in both text and music came in 1951 and 1958, respectively.

Hymnody of Helgelseförbundet

Helgelseförbundet (Holiness Covenant) denomination, as has been mentioned in Chapter II, was an outgrowth of the Methodist doctrine of holiness and complete sanctification. Although it has not had a phenomenal growth, it has had considerable influence on the free-church movement with its emphasis on a "full" spiritual experience. Its very few hymnists have contributed significantly to the hymnody of the free-church movement in Scandinavia and may rightfully be considered among those included in this study.

One of the early hymnists of Helgelseförbundet was Eric Berquist (1855-1906). Influenced by a lady relative who induced him to attend a Lutheran service, he became active in the evangelistic ministry of the Church, especially as it pertained to the outreach and education for children in the things of the faith. His poetic gifts were in evidence early in his life, and he was particularly interested in religious poetry. His interest in children led to his publishing the volume Barna-Sånger (Songs for Children) in 1887. The publication of the official hymnal of the denomination, Förbundstoner, was due in large measure to Berquist's efforts and influence. The first edition, issued in 1890, consisted of twenty selections over his pen-name "Eric," and sometimes "Onkel Erik." The hymnal went through fifteen editions until the time of Berquist's death, each edition being somewhat larger than the previous one. He has been well represented in the various editions of the Förbundstoner.

Emil Gustafson (1862–1900) was another hymnist of note in Helgelseförbundet. In early life he was a farmer, but while still a young man, he committed himself to evangelical work and particularly writing. Recurring trials of severe illness caused him to be rather introspective and quiet. This disposition is reflected in the many songs which came from his pen during his short lifetime. Several of his hymns are meditative, "reflecting the hidden life of the soul and the sanctification of the man's whole being." A few of the titles in English translation illustrate the truth of this statement:

A Childlike Heart in Stillness

Come, Rejoice, My Happy Heart

My Jesus, Take Charge of My Heart

I Am Mine Own No Longer

In 1886 he published his own collection, Betlehemsstjäran. His popularity as a hymn writer in his denomination is to be seen in the inclusion of forty-four of his songs in Förbund-stoner.

Jon Sonneson (1869–1950) was active as an evangelist with Helgelseförbundet, as well as a teacher and editor. He edited the music for Förbundstoner and published the music paper Harmoni. His many original hymns as well as his trans-lations became popular among the members of his own particu-lar church group. In addition to the texts, Sonneson composed many melodies of his own and revised many others used in the hymnal.

Carl A. Bjorkman (1873–1942) is another noteworthy author from this denomination. Bjorkman's decision to engage in religious work came at a very early age, and he never deviated from this chosen path. After a special evangelist's course in Göteborg completed in 1894, he engaged in an active ministry in Uppland, Marke, and Skåne for ten years. Dur-ing this time he wrote many of his songs which were published in 1896 in the hymnal Sånger till Lammets Lof (Songs of Praise to the Lamb). Another volume compiled especially for young people, Ungdomsstjärnan, became an unusual success within the denomination. It was issued in a total of 300,000 copies. Bjorkman's contribution to Förbundstoner amounted to twenty-four selections.

Concerning the contribution of these hymnists, it is
of significance that the emphasis of their hymnody on holy
living and Christian victory made their hymns popular with
the Pentecostals of Sweden. Many hymns of each found their
way into the hymnals of the Pentecostal group.

Hymnody of the Pentecostal
Church in Sweden

The Pentecostal revival in Sweden celebrated its fiftieth
anniversary in 1957, which was considered the "year of jubilee." At this time, the past fifty years were reviewed and
their accomplishments brought before its constituency. Levi
Pethrus (b. 1884) has already been cited as the greatest
leader and inspirational force in the organization and development of the Pentecostal church in Sweden, particularly as
pastor of "Filadelfiakyrkan" in Stockholm.

Pethrus was born in Turhem into the home of a paper
manufacturer, and at fifteen became a member of the local
Baptist congregation. He decided at an early age to enter
the ministry and from 1904 until 1906 studied at Betelseminariet in Stockholm. He served as pastor in Lidköping from 1906
until 1910, and in 1911 he assumed the pastorate of Filadelfiakyrkan. After an unusually long term of service, he resigned as regular pastor in 1958 but continued to be active
in the service of this outstanding free-church congregation
until his death in 1974.

Not only was Pethrus the denominational leader "taken
for granted" among the Swedish Pentecostals, but he also contributed notably to the hymnody of this group of people. Besides being a hymnist, and perhaps the only outstanding one
within this church, he, together with Paul Ongman, published
the first edition of Sergertoner (Victory Songs) in 1914. This
has continued to be the official hymnal of all the Pentecostal
congregations to the present day. Although he filled an important role as writer and publisher, relatively few of his
many hymns and melodies appear in Segertoner.

The first edition of this hymnal was of modest dimension,
including only sixty-nine selections. Part two, issued the
same year, contained 120 hymns. By the sixteenth edition

in 1922, Segertoner included 337 numbers, and the enlarge-
ment of 1930 numbered 452 hymns. The edition of 1960 was
enlarged to 604 numbers. At the beginning of its publication,
Segertoner borrowed many of its songs from Barratt's Maran
Ata, including a sizable number of translations of American
revival songs. Paul Ongman supplied many songs for the edition of 1930. It is of significance that in the edition of 1960
one can see the tendency to incorporate more hymns and melodies of Swedish origin, although by and large this book ex-
hibits the continued tendency toward eclecticism. From the
foreword to the 1960 edition, the following excerpts in translation indicate the scope and purpose of this hymnal:

> To a great extent these songs are an outgrowth of
> the revival; in the first place Segertoner has been
> compiled to serve the people of this revival. The col-
> lection has in the meantime been supplemented with
> songs belonging to the spiritual inheritance, which
> for the benefit to God's people has come down from
> revivals in past times. Initially Segertoner was
> meant to fill the need of songs likewise for solo, choir
> and string music; but in view of the fact that special
> song collections for such purposes now are available,
> the songs not specially suitable for unison singing
> have been screened out. Together with some songs
> of less practical worth 78 songs have thus been eli-
> minated and 230 new ones have been added. In this
> matter we have taken into account the replies to a
> questionnaire sent out to the Pentecostal churches in
> connection with the revision of the song book. Among
> the songs added there are some borrowed from the
> common Christian song treasures. At the same time
> we have seen to it, that the song writers and com-
> posers within the Pentecostal movement circles are
> represented. In the selecting of new songs regard
> has been shown for the need of songs for special oc-
> casions and festivities....
>
> During the past forty-six years Segertoner has been
> widely spread, and its songs have been sung in prac-
> tically all religious groups. This is presumably due
> to the fact that it contains many new songs, and also
> as a result of the spirit of revival and renewal which
> characterizes this song collection. Our prayer and
> anticipation is, that Segertoner in the same manner

and with the same outreach will continue to serve in
God's work with yet increased blessing.[25]

Free Church Hymnody of
Norway and Denmark

    The three main free-church groups of Norway cannot
boast of a great number of outstanding hymnists. In Norway
the State Church has carried on an evangelical ministry along
with the free groups, which in part may explain why the
smaller denominations have been willing to accept and use
much of the hymnody of the larger body, especially those
hymns which reflect their own particular theological slant and
practical emphasis.

    Mention has already been made of the ministry of T.B.
Barratt in connection with the establishment of the Pentecostal
church in Norway. Educated in England, he preached his
first sermon at the age of eighteen. For a time he studied
music with Edvard Grieg and art under a Norwegian artist.
Uncertain about his choice of vocation, he finally entered the
Methodist ministry. His break with the Methodist church and
his joining the Pentecostal movement have already been ela-
borated on in a previous chapter.

    Early in his ministry, Barratt used his artistic and li-
terary talent in the writing of hymns. In his collection of
songs of 1887, Evangeliske Sange, one of his own hymns was
included, "Come Here Each Thirsty Soul." Presumably at
the time of his early interest and experience with Pentecostalism (1906-1907), he wrote the hymn "Fire From Heaven, Come."
Not only in his own hymnal, but in several of those of the
free-church tradition, Barratt is well represented by a number
of songs and translations. The official hymnal of the Norwegian Pentecostal groups, Maran Ata, was compiled by Barratt and includes many of his original hymns; a sizable number are in the Swedish Pentecostal hymnal, Segertoner.

    Werner Skibstedt (b. 1894) is claimed by the Norwegian
Pentecostals as one of their outstanding hymnists, although
he came to them in a roundabout way. Born in Norway of
Swedish parents, he became a Baptist at an early age and
joined the Baptist Tabernacle in Fredrikshold, where the
family lived. A short time later, he became interested in the

Pentecostal movement and, subsequently, joined with it and
became one of its preachers, both as a pastor and an itinerant minister. Skibstedt has to his credit over two hundred
spiritual songs. For many of them he also composed the
music. He has related that for many of the songs he received
the inspiration to write the melodies before he wrote the text.
Several of his texts and musical settings appear in the Maran
Ata collection.

Because of his being well represented in many Norwegian
hymnals, Harry A. Tandberg (1871-1951) is worthy of mention
in this study. Tandberg was born in Chicago of Norwegian
parents who had settled in that city. Shortly after he was
born, his father lost his life in the great Chicago fire, and,
as a consequence, his mother returned with her son to Norway
to resume life again in her home country. At an early age,
Tandberg attached himself to the Salvation Army and became
an ardent supporter of its work. One of the key positions
which he filled was as children's and youth worker for the
Salvation Army. His interest and talent in writing led to his
appointment as editor in chief of his denominational publication in Norway. His ability as a writer was used well in the
many hymns and songs which he provided for his denomination and which have found their way in great numbers into
the various free-church hymnals of Scandinavia.

The Methodist Church of Norway lays claim to one of
the talented women hymnists of that country, Elevine Heede
(1820-1883). During a period of study in Paris, she made
her home with the family of a Methodist pastor who exerted
great influence on her and, subsequently, she joined the
Methodist church. From 1874 she engaged in work for the
Methodist publishing house in Oslo and taught in a school
for prospective preachers. For the Methodist hymnal of Norway, she wrote and translated approximately 200 songs, many
of which are to be found in other denominational hymnals of
Scandinavia.

Hymnists among the Baptists of Norway are very few
in number, which fact may be accounted for by the relatively
few members in this denomination. A careful perusal of Evangelisten, the hymnal of the Norweigan Baptists, shows the names
of only three of their number in the directory of hymnists
who contributed to this collection. P.Z. Helbostad (1852-
1939) minister, teacher, and editor at one time of the Baptist

Banneret is represented by just two hymns. He wrote many
hymns, translated a number of songs for use by his denomination, and supplied the Norwegian people with translations of
the works of Charles Haddon Spurgeon, the famous English
pulpiteer. His greatest contribution to Norwegian Baptist
hymnody was his editing of Evangelisten, which has had wide
use among the Baptists constituency of Norway. The Øhrn
brothers, Jacob Andersen (b. 1863) and Mons Andersen (b.
1856) exhibited outstanding leadership among Norwegian Baptists. They are still represented by several descendants in
the ongoing program of this denomination. Both were Baptist ministers, mission leaders, and pioneers in the Baptist
work in their native country. Like Helbostad, they wrote
many hymns and songs and translated several which appear
in Evangelisten. Each is represented in the hymnal by five
hymns on various topics. Missionary to the Congo, Frithjov
Iversen, (b. 1895) is represented in Evangelisten by just
one song, although he has been an author of some repute in
Norway, particularly among the Baptists.

Oscar Lövgren has observed that very few hymns have
come to Sweden from Denmark or Norway, although in more
recent years contributions from these two countries have been
more frequent. This is understandable since a cursory examination of even a Danish free-church hymnal reveals that
apart from the hymns of Grundtvig, Kingo, and Brorson,
and some of the other early hymnists, the Danes have contributed little to their hymnody, particularly of the free-church
vintage. Because of the evangelical spirit of the State Church,
as has been cited in the case of Norway, the Danish free
churches have availed themselves of the hymns from the larger
body. The Danish Baptist hymnal Salme-Og Sangbog testifies
to this fact.

Among the many free-church hymnists of Scandinavia
whose hymns appear in the Baptist hymnal of Denmark, the
Danish Baptists are in a small minority. Dr. Julius Köbner,
a pioneer minister in Baptist work in Denmark (see Chapter
II), has contributed enough hymns to the present collection
to more than compensate for the lack of other contributors
among Danish Baptists. Several of his hymns are included
in Salms-Og Sangbog, perhaps more than one would find of
any one author in most Scandinavian hymnals, with perhaps
two or three exceptions, and those among the State Church
hymnists.

In addition to his own hymns and translations, Köbner
gave the Danish Baptists a hymnal entitled Troens Stemme
(Tunes of Faith) in 1870. This was a step forward in providing the group with a song book of its own. This book
afforded instruction and inspiration for forty-six years, during which time it went through several editions with but
relatively few formal changes. In 1892 the hymnal Den nye
Hosanna was published, named after an earlier Sunday school
book Hosanna.

The earlier hymnals reflect the decisive German and
Anglo-American influence, but in course of time, the Danish
people became interested in their own national heritage and
peculiarity. The result was a growing appreciation for the
Danish psalms and a dissatisfaction among Danish Baptists with
Troens Stemme and Hosanna. They desired and requested
a hymnal of their very own. At the annual conference in
1912, it was recommended that a song book be compiled which
should retain a number of the Köbner psalms and include
translations of Anglo-American favorites and the best Danish
psalms. The first edition appeared in 1916 and the latest
in 1960. The final paragraph of the foreword states clearly
the intent and purpose of this hymnal:

> We thus send this "Salme-og Sangbog" forth to the
> Danish Baptists, confident that the Lord of the chur-
> ches, Who has intrusted his great work into the hands
> of His children, will also bless and use this Book for
> His glory and for the edification of His Church.[26]

One other name among Danish Baptists is worthy of
mention at this juncture, Søren Hansen (1819-1899). Although
Hansen contributed only one hymn to the hymnal, his position among Danish Baptists justifies the inclusion of his name
in this study. Arne Jensen in his history of the Danish Baptists quotes from the oration of Hansen's funeral:

> To write his history is to tell the history of the Dan-
> ish Baptists in the first fifty years. He is one of
> our pioneers, he has preached the gospel through
> many years in various places throughout our country,
> and he knew almost all the Baptists in Denmark in
> his time. With a rod in his hand and a basket with
> books on his back he has gone more miles than any-
> body else. He has a talent as a poet.[27]

His one hymn, Al Magt i Himmel, also appears in the hymnal
of the Norwegian Baptists, Evangelisten.

The official hymnal of the Danish Missionsförbund is
entitled Salmer og Sange. This collection is actually a revision of the old Evangeli Basun in a slightly abbreviated
form. Using the earlier hymnal as a "kernel," the editors
added many new psalms and songs, the texts of which were
made to conform to the official Danish Psalm Book. Evangeli
Basun was first issued in 1855, and two other editions followed in 1896 and 1935. Regarding the change of name after
the use of the first one for so many years, the committee
makes this defense:

> It is not the name but, rather, the content that
> should be decisive; and we have wished to follow the
> line staked out for us by our forebears. We began
> as a movement for awakening, and we wish to con-
> tinue as an awakening voice among our people. Hope-
> fully this new song book is a testimony thereof.[28]

Many hymnists from Scandinavia, the European main-
land, England, and America are represented in this hymnal,
both from the established church and the free-church denominations. The following are mentioned specifically as from
the Missionsförbund of Denmark:

Jorgen Peter Santon (1878-1944) was a preacher in
his denomination and author of eighteen hymns in
this hymnal.

Jens Jensen-Maar (1856-1932). Only one of his hymns
is included in this collection.

Emil Larsen (b. 1900). Eleven hymns and translations by this Förbund minister are used in the
hymnal.

Viggo Ramvold (B. 1914) a minister of his denomination has translated and written several hymns, eight
of which are included in this collection.

Jens Marinus Sørensen (B. 1880) is represented by
one hymn.

The first hymnal of the Danish Methodist Church was
issued in 1876. Before that there had been a few collections

in use in the churches of the denominations, but the official book, Salmebog till Brug i Kirken, Skolen og Hjemmet (Psalmbook for Use in Church, School and Home) was the answer to a long-felt need. Because of the shortcomings of this hymnal, a commission was appointed to make preparation for the issuing of a more satisfactory volume for use by the Danish Methodists. The result was the Salmebog for Metodistkirken I Denmark published in 1901.

This hymnal remained in use until 1952, when a new volume by the same name was published. This latest hymnal was the work of combined commissions, one of which had been appointed in 1945 to prepare a collection of "lighter" songs. For the sake of economy, it was decided to publish just one hymnal and the present one is the final result. The number of the more "churchly" psalms was greatly reduced over the 1901 hymnal, and many more of the gospel songs were added. The foreword to the 1952 hymnal expresses some concern over the quality of its contents:

> The commission has nevertheless done its best, within the limits of its present assignment, to bring forth the best of our rich Danish psalm treasure, and take in as much material--especially from Methodism's psalm compositions--as we found usable.
>
> We express our wish, that this psalm book may be used for the glory of Jesus Christ, and that it may serve God's kingdom work through our Church for many years, and that many will join us in prayer to the intent that this may come to pass.[29]

The following authors from the Danish Methodist Church have contributed to the 1952 hymnal:

Anton Bast (1867-1937)
Adolf Braestrup (B. 1880)
Alberta Eltholtz (1840-1929)
Carl Frederik Eltholtz (1840-1929)
Svend Kristian Johansen (1856-1943)
Johannes Kofod (b. 1900)
Niels Mann (b. 1889)
Benjamine Mohrbutter (b. 1840)
Niels Peter Nelsen (1861-1942)
Karl Jensen Schou (1841-1889)

Christian J.M. Thaarup (1851-1918)
Christian E. Willerup (1815-1866)

Most of the hymnists in the foregoing list were members
of the clergy of the Methodist Church; only one Alberta Eltholtz, has been accorded a biographical sketch in Lövgren's
Lexikon. She was a nurse and an active worker in Sunday
school and temperance societies. The Danish Methodist hymnal
is replete with hymns written by laymen and clergymen of
the Lutheran church, as well as those from the free-church
groups in Europe and America.

When the Danish Pentecostal Fraternal meeting was held
in Copenhagen in 1945, the wish was expressed for a revision
of their hymnal, Evangelitoner. The intention was that many
hymns be eliminated which were not in frequent and current
use, and more worthy hymns be substituted for those discarded. In the recent revision, attempts have been made
at linguistic improvement and stricter adherence to the original forms of many of the hymns. A perusal of this hymnal
reveals that it contains hymns by Pentecostal leaders in Scandinavia and many of the gospel-song type from America and
England. Kingo, Brorson, Grundtvig, and Ingemann are well
represented among its 441 hymns.

Summary

The development and expansion of the free-church
denominations in Scandinavia is the story of a simultaneous
growth of their hymnody. In many instances the hymnody of
these groups had small, modest beginnings, but with the help
of hymnists in the more evangelical wing of the State Church,
growth in the production of new hymns was assured.

Since a church's hymnody is a reflection of its doctrines
and teachings, it was only natural for the clergy to lead the
way in the production of such hymns. The roster of clergy-
hymnists is long. Their hymns reflect not only the doctrinal
leanings of their respective groups but also the emphasis on
standards of personal piety desired by them for each adher-
ent.

The production of hymnals in itself provides a fascinat-
ing study for layman and professional alike. From the incep-

tion of a particular religious group through its development
to the present time, the need for constant revision of its
hymnal is ever present. This is a mark of progress. All
of the major free-church denominations of the Scandinavian
countries have given much time and attention to the compilation and revision of their respective hymnals, and with few
exceptions the present editions in use date from no earlier
than 1950.

Nowhere is ecumenicity more clearly exemplified than
in the hymnals of the various Protestant (and even Catholic)
churches. Not only do denominations borrow freely from each
other's store of hymns but they freely import hymns from
other countries. Thus is enunciated the universal message
of the church in all ages.

NOTES

1. Selander, op. cit., p. 48 (translation).
2. Ibid., p. 247.
3. Oscar Lövgren, Psalm och Sånglexikon (Stockholm: Gum-
   messon's Bokforlag, 1964), p. 532.
4. Psalmisten (Stockholm: A.L. Normans Boktryckeri-
   Aktiebolag, 1880), foreword to the first edition.
5. Ibid.
6. Nya Pilgrimsånger (Stockholm: P. Palmquist's Aktiebolags
   Boktryckeri, 1894), from the foreword to the book.
7. Lövgren, Våra Psalm ... , II, p. 150.
8. Theodore Trued Truve, Sånger för Söndagaskolan och
   Hammet (Chicago: Nya Wecko-Postens Forlag, 1886),
   from the foreword to the book.
9. Lövgren, Våra Psalm ... , III, p. 165.
10. Lövgren, Lexikon, pp. 247-249.
11. Letter from Rev. Erland Wendel-Hasen, Swedish Baptist
    Pastor, August 9, 1967.
12. Free translation--Wendel-Hansen, Veckotidning.
13. Wendel-Hansen, Loc. cit.
14. Andliga Sånger (Örebro, Örebro Missions förenings För-
    lag, 1931), from the Foreword.
15. Psalm och Sång (Stockholm: Svenska Baptistsamfundet
    och Orebromissionen, 1966), foreword to the book.
16. Lövgren, Lexikon, p. 263.
17. Ibid., pp. 207, 208.
18. Lövgren, Våra Psalm ..., III, p. 239.

19. Lövgren, Lexikon, p. 171.
20. Ibid., p. 255.
21. Lövgren, Våra Psalm ... , III, pp. 292, 293.
22. Ibid., p. 319.
23. Ibid., p. 333.
24. Sånger och Psalmer (Stockholm: Missionsförbundets Forlag, 1951), foreword to the book.
25. Music till Segertoner (Stockholm: Förlaget Filadelfia, 1960), from the foreword.
26. Salme-og Sangbog (Holboek: Dansk Baptist-Forlag, 1916), foreword to the book.
27. Arne Jensen, Baptisternes Historie i Danmark (Kobenhaum: Baptisterne Forlag, 1961), pp. 163-165.
28. Salmer og Sange (København: Missionsförbundets Forlag, 1954), foreword to the book.
29. Salmebog For Metodistkirken I Danmark (København: Kurer-Forlaget, Metodiskirkens Forlag, 1953), p. 6.

CHAPTER V

THE RECIPROCAL INFLUENCE OF STATE- AND FREE-CHURCH HYMNODY IN SCANDINAVIA

Background of State-Church Hymnody

Sweden

The Koral-Bok companion to the 1849 edition of the Wallin hymnal contains a concise but comprehensive history of song in the Christian church, and more particularly the church in Sweden. The writer of this history cites what is supposed to have been "the first Christian song in the mother tongue of the Scandinavian people," namely "Solsången" (The Sun Song).[1] It was written "in the old heroic form and recorded in Iceland by 'Saemunder den vise' (d. 1133)."[2] Although Latin hymnody gained ground during the Catholic period, it never could blot out the "inherent love for song in the mother tongue."[3] The following translated quotation elaborates on the musical activities of the Swedes in the ensuing years.

> Fairy-like Mary-songs, legend-song, May-songs, Bible history-songs and little psalms were sounded forth for centuries from the lips of the people in the Scandinavian Northlands. When the people in Delarna in 1527 complained that spiritual songs were sung in Swedish at the worship services, Gustaf I could with reason reply "that it is the custom in the entire kingdom throughout all parishes, that one usually sings praises to God in the Swedish language." At the close of the Middle Ages a number of the Church foundation psalms were translated into Swedish and published in "Den Svenska Tideboken" (Vorfruwe, Helghe Andz och Helga Kors-Tydher 1525). The one by Erik

Olai (d. 1486): "Een rikir man ok welloger han" is
so far as known the first Swedish original psalm by
a known author.[4]

Latin songs in adulation of Swedish Saints continued to
be performed on Saints Days. The praise song to the Virgin
Mary "Ave Maria Stella" was held a favorite among the Swedish people and a trace of the melody is still to be seen in the
Lutheran mass of Sweden. Sequences by Notker Balbulus
are found in Swedish translations among which is the well-
known "Veni Sancte Spiritus" (O du Helge Ande). Bernard
of Clairvaux (1091-1153), Thomas of Aquine (1225-1274),
Thomas of Celano (d. 1255), and other prominent Latin writers
of the Middle Ages have enriched the hymnody of Sweden as
their songs have been accepted in the state-church hymnals.

Among the hymns of the pre-Reformation period, those
of John Huss have been reworked and placed in the Swedish
Psalmbok. A contemporary of Luther, and the most famous
of the "meistersingers," Hans Sachs, (1494-1576), wrote several hymns, two of which were included in the Swedberg
Psalmbok of 1695. Like the Reformation in Germany, the
same movement awakened considerable interest in vernacular
singing in Sweden. Quite naturally the chorales of Martin
Luther became popular in the north country and found their
way into the hymnals and then into public worship. Similar
practice obtained in Sweden as in Germany in the unison singing of the chorales which were often accompanied by the choir
and/or organ. The latter agents were never allowed to "over-
sound" the congregational singing. Several other authors who
followed Luther also contributed to the hymnody of Reformation
Sweden. The contributions of Swedish hymnists who were
leaders in the church at this time have already been discussed
in chapter one, including such writers as Olavus and Laurentius Petri, L. Petri Gothus, P. Johannes Gothus, et al. Many
of the sixteenth-century hymnals were the work of these men.

Hymn singing in the seventeenth century was borne
along with the continued publication of hymnals and service
books for the Swedish State Church. The Radical Handbook
of 1614 cut off the Gregorian elements and paved the way
for congregational singing.[5] The Enchiridion (Swedish Psalm
Book) of 1622 by Petrus J. Rudbeck was a significant volume
in that line of hymnals which led to the Swedberg book. Rudbeck, a pastor, professor at Uppsala University, and lecturer

in theology at Vasterås became well known by his "wedding
ode," which appeared in this collection. Rudbeck also included
suitable psalms with texts for each Sunday of the church year.
The Enchiridion contained, in addition to the congregational
psalms, a calendar, the catechism by Luther, home exhorta-
tions, a prayer book, church orders, the Gospels and Epistles,
the story of Christ's passion from the four Gospels, and the
story of the destruction of Jerusalem by Flavius Josephus.

Part-singing grew in popularity and practice during the
seventeenth century in Sweden. Much of the music was supplied by the "Havkape" of Stockholm where many of the country's musicians were trained. The German church of Sweden
was the home of great chorale composers including Gustaf
Düben Sr. and Joachim Düben. Gustaf came to be known as
the royal court master and organist in the German church in
Stockholm, and a leading personality in Swedish musical life
in the latter third of the century. Joachim, a military man
and leader in the Riksdag, came under the influence of Pietism while imprisoned in Russia. As a result, he published in
1727 his Uthwolde Andeliga SåNGER (Select Spiritual Songs).
German influence spread to the principal cities, where composers supplied organ music and musical sources for settings
by local masters. Praetorius and Schutz are well represented
by such settings.

The seventeenth century was thus a fruitful period for
the production of original chorales in Sweden. Particularly
toward the end of the century, native composers appeared in
significant numbers.

Johann Crüger (1598-1662) was a most important German
composer who contributed to the Swedish chorale tradition.
Lundholm has mentioned that his "musical meditations" on all
of the church "tones," which make use of the solo organ and
double choir were used in the school in Vasterås in 1626.[6]
The well-known Praxis pietatis melica must have exerted great
influence in Sweden since so many of Crüger's chorales were
used widely in Swedish churches. Lundholm has further observed that thirty-one parts and variations in the chorale book
of 1819 were taken from this collection.

Swedish church music generally followed the pattern as
developed in Germany, with the more sinple settings for use
by the congregation, and more ornate music arranged for the

choir with organ and orchestral accompaniments.[7] The organ
was rarely used, but when it was used it was nearly always
in alternation with the congregational singing of the chorale.

It is worth noting that French influence on Swedish
church melody is to be seen in the use of music by Crequillon,
Clemenson Papa, and Jannequin, and Italian influence is exhibited in the use of music by Giovanni Gabrielli. During the
later seventeenth and early eighteenth century, antiphonal
singing was practiced in the Swedish church, no doubt because of the influence of the Venetian composer and his school
of composition and performance.

According to Lundholm, the eighteenth century in
Sweden was a period of secularization, and the building of
the chorale melodies was not imposing. Church leaders became interested mainly in the texts. The Celiska Psalmbok
of 1765 and 1767 (See Appendix D.) represents not only a
reaction against the texts of previous books, but also a desire for more simple musical arrangements for the chorale
texts. These melodies in the "gallant" style did not come
into general church use because of the strong conservative
element among those who still exerted real influence on the
church life of the day. The Swedish people quite generally
set themselves against the profane settings with their overly-
ornamented melodies. Even though some of the less worthy
texts were used, the older melodies were retained as musical
settings.[8]

The use of the organ with congregational singing reached
its height during the early part of the eighteenth century
because of the influence of the German masters. Not only
were organists in places of prestige in the church, but they
also were recognized as teachers of music and music theory.
They developed the ability to play the chorales from the
figured bass and became proficient as singers of chorales
and "lesser songs." It was necessary for them to be able
to play the violin for folk dances, and they needed a working knowledge of the other stringed instruments and wood-
winds for teaching purposes. Many excelled in the writing of
chorale settings and familiarized themselves with the many
facets and methods of performance.

Lundholm points out that the eighteenth century closed
with a real renaissance of the a cappella style of chorale

singing. Royalty became interested in the musical development of the Swedish people. The Royal Academy was established and daily concerts were held at the Royal Court. The
opera house was opened and the production of the first Swedish opera took place in 1773. Swedish composers looked to
other countries, particularly France, for their inspiration,
and French melodies were collected for use in both sacred
and secular compositions.[9]

The question of an official chorale book was still un-
settled at the beginning of the nineteenth century. Several
musicians produced a number of chorale collections and ultimately established the four-voiced style. Johann Christian
Haeffner (1759-1833), court composer, conductor of the Stockholm opera, music director at Uppsala University, and organist of the German church in Stockholm was one of the first
to produce a collection of chorales. His 1808 collection contained twenty-five old and nineteen new settings. A second
book by Haeffner in 1820-21 containing nearly 300 chorales,
among which were only ninety-six new melodies, was to influence significantly the development of the hymnody of
Sweden. Lundholm's analysis reveals the use of a number
of the Greek modes treated in typical nineteenth-century
romantic style, with a simple unadorned melodic line.

Haeffner's collections came under severe scrutiny, and
opinions varied regarding their worth and practicality. Criticism arose concerning the slow tempos, monotonous style,
and poor harmonizations which included parallel fifths and
hidden octaves. However, Haeffner's work inspired other
composers to write chorale settings in spite of the severe
criticism leveled against him. One of the first to follow in
the footsteps of Haeffner was Johan Dillner (1785-1862), a
highly gifted pastor of the military. He composed and collected a number of songs for four voices which he published
in 1858 under the title Occasional Pieces from the Countryside.
Dillner also may be classified as a music educator because of
his interest and methods in the teaching of singing. He is
known as the inventor of the one-stringed instrument, the
psalmodikon, which, in its simple construction, consisted of
a plain wooden box on which was fastened a single string.
(See Appendix G.) Many of the churches at that time did
not have organs, and this instrument became a great help in
congregational singing, as well as a source of musical pleasure
in the homes. In the preface to the instruction book on play-

ing the psalmodikon, the author laments the poor singing in
the church at that time. He points out that music education
has been entrusted to the schools, and that the churches had
not accepted responsibility for improving congregational singing.[10] Dillner saw the psalmodikon as particularly designed
for church use, easy to construct and its numerical notation
easy to read for the average church members.[11]

Dillner's method of part singing was successful and became popular in schools like the Uppland Seminary in Uppsala.
His chorale book of 1830, which used cipher symbols instead
of regular notation, was widely used as well as his settings
to the Syreen hymnal, which appeared in 1846. The latter
book contained four-voiced harmony based on the major scale.
This was according to the Royal Edict of 1845, which stated
that four-voiced music was to be practiced in the seminaries
throughout Sweden with such books to be furnished for this
purpose.

The Royal Edict of 1845, with its emphasis on four-
voiced harmony, led to the rise of many editions of chorales
settings for male voices. These were important in that they
took care of situations created by the changing boy's voice.
One of the first editions for male voices was published in 1848
by J.P. Bronham. In this book the melody was placed in the
tenor voice. This edition was followed by several others such
as the one by August Lundh in 1866 for three voices, and
Alard's chorale arrangements of 1864 which placed the melody
in the top voice.

In the meantime, Haeffner's book continued to be criticized and new collections were published to counteract its influence. Abraham Mankell (1802-1868), professor of church
music at the Stockholm Conservatory, issued his Koralbok
för folkskolan eller det förenklade Psalmodikon, written for
four voices in a more simple style than Dillner. Franz Ber-
wald revised the Haeffner chorales as did J.A. Josephson.
Ministers were very active in their protest to Haeffner's work
while the organists continued to be very passive about it.[12]

Many of the newer collections were subjected to severe
criticism as the more "lively" chorale settings were in demand,
probably because of the strong sectarian influences which
prevailed. The influence of the free-church movement was
strong with its emphasis on the sentimental, lively type of

spiritual song. Chorale singing was truly at a low ebb. The
general situation is typified by the collection by Per Ulrik
Stenhammer (1829-1875), a rather self-taught musician, who
composed a number of choruses and solo songs. His Congregational Songs were received with wide acclaim. More will
be said concerning this hymnal later in the chapter; suffice
it to point out that its contents were of inferior quality.

While the chorale went through a period of struggle
during the nineteenth century in Sweden, the end of the century witnessed its renaissance. In 1889 the "Friends of Church
Song" was organized to restore the Protestant chorales to their
original settings as the early Swedish church leaders had sung
them. New interest was generated in the chorale collection
of 1697, and new and more traditional styles of chorale settings were published.[13]

In the early part of the twentieth century, further steps
were taken to restore the chorale to its rightful place. A
committee was appointed in 1916 for the express purpose of
formulating and presenting new chorales. The work was completed in 1921 with the Korolbok till Nya Psalmer, a trial collection to be used with the Wallin book of 1819. It contained
many new melodies but it also borrowed extensively from
German, English, Danish, and American sources.

An analysis of the chorale of Swedish vintage reveals
the extensive use of the folk song in its development. The
chorales for the Wallin Psalmbook of 1819 show a decided use
of folk melodies with their small intervals and close adherence
to the scale line. It is not uncommon to find a mixture of
modes in a chorale arrangement; a melody may begin in the
minor mode and end in the parallel major. Music that was
used for festive celebrations tended toward the major tonality.
Lundholm points out that Swedish music tends to show more
Danish than Norwegian influence in the plaintive, sorrowful,
and tranquil melodies which are used.[14] German influence
is seen in the use of the music of Bach, Crüger, Scheidt,
and others whose melodies served as guidelines in the development of the Swedish chorale. In some instances, the Latin
and German influences combined in the chorales of the Swedish
people. While no really outstanding chorale composers wrote
in Sweden, the music of this north country did draw on the
rich legacy from foreign countries for its enrichment and development. When, in some instances, native Swedish melodies

were used, they showed the influence of neighboring countries
which experienced the Protestant Reformation. C.R. Osbeck
has enunciated in a straightforward manner how dependent
Sweden has been on foreign influence and contributions for
its hymnody. Writing in the post-war era of 1924, he had
this to say concerning a wrong ascription of a German hymn
to Swedish original:

> That the immortal stanza by the German author, Niko-
> laus Decius, "Guds rena Lamm, skyldig pa korset,
> for oss slaktad," has been listed as of Swedish origin
> is perhaps of no particular importance ... but in
> these days of hate for Germans we could do well in
> giving the land of Luther and Oncken due credit.
> Moreover, if we Swedes were to give full acknowledge-
> ment for what we have received by way of religious
> thought from Germany and England, there would not
> be much left for us to boast of as our very own.[15]

Denmark

According to Julian, the first hymnal of Denmark and
Norway, in fact of the whole North, was the one published
in 1528 by Claus Martenson Töndebinder (1500-1576), considered by Julian to be the Father of Danish hymnody. It
contained translations from Latin, German, and Swedish sources, as well as originals. It was recast in 1529 by the author
and two others, Arvid Petersen and Hans Spendemager; its
final form contained prayers, psalms, hymns and canticles,
in keeping with the principles of the Danish Reformation.
The title in English translation presents its contents and
purpose:

> A new handbook with psalms and spiritual songs of
> praise, derived from Holy Writ which now are sung
> in the Christian assembly to God's praise and men's
> salvation.[16]

Bishop Hans Hensen of Ribe published a reproduction of the
book in 1544, and Hans Thomisson edited a similar edition in
1569 (see page 136). These books were used for more than
a century in both Denmark and Norway until the attempted
revision by Kingo.

In 1573 appeared the Jesperson Graduale which was used

mainly by the cities of Denmark for "high mass and holy days."
Twenty-one of the twenty-six parts were from the Roman Mass,
and this book represented a compromise between Gregorian
music and popular congregational song. The Jesperson Graduale marked the transition into vernacular singing and became influential until 1650. The last edition was brought out
in 1637. This was a new day for the Church when the "Psal-
masse" was established throughout Denmark and Norway.

Several significant publications followed that were to
enrich the worship of the Lutheran church in Denmark. In
addition to Kingo's Graduale and the Salmebog of 1699 the
following were published by and used for the Danish people:

> Den Ny Salmebog of 1740, projected by Adolf Bror-
> son and completed by Erik Pontopiddan. (See page
> 144.) Hjortsvang has remarked that this hymnal
> completed the decadence of the chorale begun by
> Kingo's Graduale.

> Salmebog eller en Samling af gamle or ny Salmer, till
> Guds Aire og hans Menigheds ophyggelse was pub-
> lished in 1778 and became known as the Guldberg
> Salmebog.

> In 1797 the Evangelisk-kristalig Salmebog till Brugved
> Kirke Kirke og Hus Andagt was released for the
> Danish Church, but was never widely accepted and
> merely served as a transitional book for later pub-
> lications.

> Sangvark till den Danske Kirke (Grundtvig) was pub-
> lished in 1839 (see page 150).

> Inspired by the Grundtvig hymnal, a new official
> hymnal was produced in 1855 entitled, Salmebog
> till Kirke og Hasandagt. This was in reality a re-
> vision by Ingemann of an old Kingo Hymnal and
> became known as the Roskilde Konvents Salmebog.[17]
> (See page 130.) The desire grew year by year
> for a richer supply of psalms for the Danish chur-
> ches until supplements were supplied to the Roskilde
> collection in 1873 and 1890, the former remaining
> very popular throughout Denmark.

> The Samebog for Kirke og Hjem of 1897 in the final
> publication growing out of "proposals" of 1885, 1888,
> and 1892.[18]

In the 1897 book, many of the Roskild "Konvent"
psalms were omitted and a few from the "proposals" were inserted in the compilation of this book. The hymnal has gone
through several editions. The Danish Lutheran hymnal in
America has retained the title of the mother-church hymnal
in English translation, The Hymnal for Church and Home
and includes in its contents many hymns and melodies from
the old Danish hymnal.

In addition to the hymnals, several melody books were
forthcoming for use with the various collections of hymn texts.
For the Guldberg hymnal of 1778, a book of musical settings
was published in 1781; in 1801 H.O.C. Zinck published his
Koralbog for use with the same. In 1853 and 1878, collections
of chorale settings were issued for use with the "Konvent"
hymnal and its supplements, respectively. The hymnal of
1897 was supplied with proper settings by V. Bielefeldt in
his collection of melodies of 1901. Besides these books, several chorale books for use with the Danish hymnals followed
in close succession from 1888 until 1920. Attempts were made
in some of the melody books to restore the chorales to the
rhythm of the sixteenth century; others favored the blending
of the free melodies with the traditional chorale tunes. The
most comprehensive collection of musical settings was the one
entitled Meinhedens Melodier till i Kirklag Hjem, published
in two editions in 1914 and 1920, containing over 1,278 melodies and a supplement of forty tunes.[19]

Norway

The Norwegian Lutheran Church generally followed
Denmark in the compilation of its hymnbooks and the organization of its hymnody. The hymnals of Thomisson, Pontoppidan,
and Guldberg were used freely by the Church in Norway as
a basis for its hymnals. Mention has already been made of
the Lanstad hymnal, Kirke Salme Bogen, first published in
1865 (see page 160). Its popularity is attested by the fact
that six hundred of Norway's one thousand congregations used
it. The Salmebogen till Kirke og hus Andagt, which appeared
in 1911, was merely a revision of the Danish hymnal just previously mentioned. Another collection which received considerable use in Norway was John Nicolae Frantzen's Christe-
ligie Psalmer till Husandagt of Skole brug, published in 1851.

Cartford has observed the "undertones" of Gregorian

chant in Norwegian music, particularly in the modal cadences
which are frequently used. He also points out the influence
which church music had on the folk music of Norway, citing
that missionary work gave a particular flavor to folk music.
It would seem that this process is the reverse of what is nor-
mal in that folk music usually influences the music of the
church. He suggests that the open fifth in much of the music
in Norway illustrates this point.[20]

The Reformation in Norway resulted in a new emphasis
on congregational singing as obtained in the other Scandinavian countries and Germany. The layman was provided with
a wide field in which to express his newly found faith. The
old chants were harmonized, in some instances resulting in a
mixture of Latin and Nordic flavor, and the entire realm of
hymnody was a broad field for composition. New tunes were
created, and old settings from Germany, Sweden, and Denmark
were arranged "to suit Norwegian tastes." Many tunes were
written to texts by Kingo and Brorson. Den Store hvide
Flok (The Great White Host) of Brorson became popular among
the Norwegian people. Lindeman discovered the tune, and
Grieg made it famous by his arrangement for male voices.
Cartford cites this as a "exhibit A" of a folk tune "lifted bodily
from folk music into the hymnbook."[21]

Perhaps the most influential composer in Norway was
Ludwig M. Lindeman, although, as Cartford discovered in
his study, little is known of his life apart from Norwegian
accounts. He was born into a family which contributed to
the musical life of Norway as did the Bach family in Germany
and the Couperins in France.[22] Ole Andreas Lindeman, the
father, was a traveling virtuoso pianist and one-time organist
in the Domkirke in Trondheim. Ludwig was the most gifted
of the sons, who were all musicians. An admirer of Johann
Sebastian Bach, he studied theory, piano, and organ and
wrote preludes and fugues on Bach. Ludwig was a respected musician and teacher in his native country and held
honored posts in both areas. In time he was recognized as
Norway's leading organist and was signally honored by being
asked to give a recital on the organ in Royal Albert Hall in
London in 1871.[23]

Ludwig Lindeman began to work on his folk song collection in 1840. This activity was to occupy his time in the
next twenty-five years. He collected in excess of 2,000 folk

tunes from various sources and published over 600 in carefully harmonized musical settings. His three-volume set Aeldre
og nyere Norske Fjeld melodier (Old and New Norwegian Moun-
tain Melodies) won for him acclaim from a noted contemporary,
Franz Liszt.[24]

Lindeman's best known and most significant contribution
to the musical culture of Norway has been in his composing
and arranging of hymn tunes. His originals and arrangements
total approximately 200. Cartford asserts that these were
really his only popular works even though he was recognized
for his other contributions to the musical life of Norway. In
1859 he edited Luther's Geistliche Lieder for the Norwegian
people and in 1871 edited the new church Koralbog, which was
used with the Lanstad hymnal. The latter was received with
great favor and enthusiasm. Cartford asserts that Lindeman
felt at home with the light, picturesque texts of Grundtvig
and Brorson and that his "fantasy-like quality of Norwegian
folk music is infused into his hymn tunes." He "bridged the
gap between the staunch old chorales and the new pietistic
hymns of the revivalistic period in which he lived."[25]

Although Lindeman's chorale settings were generally
popular, he did enter into controversy with his more conservative critics because of his tempo indications, dotted rhythms,
and the liberty he allowed for free improvisatory organ accompaniments. One of his critics, Erik Hoff, produced a
hymnal in 1878 in an effort to thwart the influence of Lindeman, but the latter remained popular while he lived. He
could write music of the revivalistic type for Hauge's songbook and in the conservative tradition for Lanstad's hymnal.
After his death, the traditional chorales were quite generally
restored to their original forms.[26]

Lindeman presents his intentions concerning his harmonizations, style, and performance of his chorale settings in the
foreword to the 1877 edition of his Koralbog and, in a sense,
defends himself against his critics:

> In regard to the harmonizing I have tried to preserve
> the required ease and poise as well as clarity and
> variety, in order that the melodies, lighted up and
> enlivened, may stand forth as a connected whole.
> Since the harmonizing of the melodies can be accom-
> plished in many ways, it follows of itself, that the

organist, when he possesses the required musical and
harmonistic insight and skill, as well as for the sake
of greater variety, at least for every verse--make
use of altered harmony. Where on the other hand,
such cannot be posited, it is important that the prescribed harmony should carefully be observed.

As for the congregational responses indicated in the
Choral Book it could be wished that the more capable
in the congregation would learn these to the point
where they could be heard independently apart from
the congregation itself.[27]

The Koralbog was published in an American edition in
1899 and accomodated itself to the need for a book containing
"all melodies needed in a Psalm Book for Lutheran Christians
in America," as well as for use with the Lanstad hymnal and
other Psalm books of the various Synods in America. It was
designed for use both by the choir and the organist.[28]

As has been mentioned in chapter four, the list of
hymnists from Norway in the late nineteenth and early twentieth centuries is not imposing. Their contributions, however,
are of significance to the study of the relationship between
state and free-church hymnody. To the list should be added
the following hymnists: Carl G. Aagard (1852-1927), chaplain, pastor and writer, and author of the famous "Sailor's
Hymn"; Ole Teador Moe (1863-1922), pastor and author of the
well-known hymn "Jesus, the Only One, Holiest, Costliest";
Alette Hayerdahl (b. 1862), pastor's wife; Johan Halmrast
(1866-1912), journalist and author of the popular hymn "O
Blessed Morn, Nothing Like it."[29]

The Influence of State-Church Hymnody on the
Hymnody of the Scandinavian Free Church

Sweden

Early Baptist hymnody began in 1859 with the publication of Pilgrims Sånger by Gustaf Palmquist. An analysis of
its contents has already been given in Chapter IV. Since
this collection was intended for use in the more informal evangelistic services, it is not surprising that hymns from the State
Church are scarce among its contents. Laurentius Petri, Jakob

Arrhenius, Brorson, and Malmstedt are represented by a very
few hymns in this hymnal even though the greatest percentage
of the hymns are from the pietist and free-church authors.
Nya Pilgrims Sånger contains some chorales such as "Vom Him-
mel hoch," "Ein feste Burg," and the Philipp Nicolai chorale
"Wie schon leuchtet der Morgenstern." Nicolai's setting has
been adopted by the Swedish people as their very own because of its close association with the Christmas text "All Hail
to Thee O Blessed Morn."

    The first official Swedish Baptist hymnal, Psalmisten,
in its early editions, contained a sampling of hymns from the
Swedish Psalmbook, as well as some from the official hymnal
of the Finnish State Church. Subsequent editions indicate
more of a return to the chorales of Lutheranism. The edition
of 1904 contains an appreciable number of chorales by Nicolai,
Nicolaus Decius, Martin Luther, and Johann Herman Schein.
The latest revision of Psalmisten of 1928 includes the chorales
of the following composers in addition to those appearing in
the 1904 edition: Melchior Teschner, Gustav Düben, Johan
Schop, Johann Crüger, and Jacques Regnart. Although
Psalmisten is strongly Swedish in its selection of hymns, a
number of Danish and Norwegian hymns have been given a
place within its pages.

    The latest publication of the Swedish Baptists, Psalm
och Sång (1966) is quite revolutionary. Although the percentage of state-church hymns in this hymnal is not phenomenal, it does indicate a rather strong affinity with the old
hymns and chorales on the part of a separatist church. From
German Lutheranism alone, there are approximately fifty chorales in this new hymnal; of this number fifteen are by Johann
Crüger, who, as previously stated seems to have been the
favorite composer of the Scandinavian people through the years.
Teschner, Luther, Nicolai, and Heinrich Albert are next in
order of popularity. Others include Franz Gruber, Adam
Krieger, Hans Leo Hassler, Melchoir Vulpios, Michael Praetorius, and Georg Neumark. German poets and authors are included in Psalm och Sång in a sizeable number; specifically
there are twenty-three by them, with Martin Luther represented by five hymns. The hymns of such well-known writers
as Benjamin Schmolck, Count Zinzendorf, Paul Gerhardt, Christian Gregor, Johann Franck, Joachim Neander, and Elizabeth
Cruciger are also found in this latest Baptist hymnal.

Scandinavian composers and authors are well-represented in Psalm och Sång. It is appropriate to include at this juncture short biographical material on a few whose contributions to Swedish hymnody have been of some significance and whose hymns are contained in this hymnal.

Carl Axel Toren (1813-1904) was confirmed by F.M. Franzen, the poet and hymn writer. Toren was greatly influenced by Franzen to enter the Lutheran ministry. After theological studies he was ordained as a clergyman by J.O. Wallin in 1839. He contributed to the hymnody of the Church by his own compositions and as a member of the Psalmbook committee of 1883. Two of his translations appear in Psalm och Sång.

Severin Cavallin (1820-1886) entered the Lutheran ministry as a result of his strong religious home background. A prolific writer, he published his own sermons and religious poetry. He was instrumental in the compilations and publication of several Psalmbook proposals, having served with distinction on the committee of 1883. Several of his translations of well-known psalms have appeared in free-church hymnals.

Robert T. Kiblberg (1848-1908), a Lutheran minister, served in various capacities in the wider ministry of the Church. In addition to pastoral duties, he served as a catechist in the Katrina congregation in Stockholm and assistant teacher and preacher at the Deaconess Institute. He arranged music for the choir and was the translator and arranger of hymns and chorales.

Johan Alfred Eklund (1863-1945) was ordained a priest in the Lutheran Church following his theological studies at Uppsala University. He served with distinction as Cathedral Dean in Kalmar and as Bishop of Karlstad. In church hymnody he was noted not only as a writer of hymns but as a member of the psalmbook committees in the early years of the twentieth century. He translated Danish, English, and German psalms representing the period from the seventeenth and eighteenth centuries. Sixteen of his originals and translations are contained in Psalm och Sång.

Much space has already been given to Johan Olof Wallin, the greatest figure in the hymnody of the State Church, as well as the free-church bodies of Sweden. A study of Scandi-

navian hymnody leaves one with the impression that he is
claimed equally by both groups. Naturally his strong pietistic
leanings and sympathy reflected in his hymns have endeared
him to the separatist groups. In Psalm och Sång alone over
fifty of his hymns are included. No other hymn writer is
as well represented. This is the strongest link between the
hymnody of the Lutheran tradition and that of any free-church
denomination. Running a close second to Wallin is the poetess
Lina Sandell-Berg, whose total contribution to Psalm och Sång
numbers forty-six hymns. The grand total of nearly 100 hymns
of these two authors testifies to their continuing popularity
with Scandinavian people, both of the state-church and free-
church traditions.

The hymnal of the Free Baptist denomination in Sweden,
Pilgrimstoner, also reflects the influence of the hymnody of
the State Church but to a lesser degree than Psalm och Sång,
perhaps only because it contains fewer hymns. Among the
composers, one will find the names of Nicolai, Regnart, Luther,
Desius, Schein, C.H. Rinck, and Vulpius. Authors in this
hymnal from the Lutheran communion include Arrhenius, Cruciger, Franck, Gerhardt, Laurentius, Luther, Olavus Petri,
Swedberg, and Decius, Similar situations obtain in the Helgelseförbundet hymnal, Förbundstoner, and the official hymnal
of the Swedish Methodists, Metodist krkans Psalmbok. With
only slight variations, the same list of authors and composers
may be gleaned as from the hymnals discussed previously.
Both also include hymnists and composers from the State
Churches of Denmark and Norway.

The hymnal of Svenska Missionsförbundet, Sånger och
Psalmer, compares in size and in scope of its contents with
the recent Baptist hymnal of Sweden. Similar relationship
to the Lutheran hymnody is readily discernible in these two
free-church hymnals, both monuments to the work of capable
committees. In addition to Danish, Norwegian, and Finnish
authors and hymnists of the State Church, those already mentioned from the German and Swedish Lutheran tradition are
also contained in this hymnal.

Among the composers of hymn and chorale settings,
several appear in great numbers. Johann Crüger leads the
list with nineteen chorale settings, followed by Martin Luther
with fifteen, Gustaf Düben and Heinrich Albert, each with
ten, Teschner with seven, and Nicolai with five. Approximately

twelve more composers from the State Church are included in
the hymnal; many melodies are used as settings for Wallin
psalms. In addition to arrangements and settings by the composers just mentioned, there are over sixty German melodies;
many of these are used as settings for Wallin texts. Approximately eight of Jesper Swedberg's hymns and translations
are found in Sånger och Psalmer, a similar number to those
found in the Baptist hymnal. Both J.O. Wallin and Lina
Sandell-Berg are represented by scores of texts as is the
case with the Baptist Psalm och Sång. Wallin's originals and
translations are in excess of fifty while Mrs. Berg's original
poems and a few translations number more than sixty.

      The hymnody of the Lutheran church, while not omitted
entirely from Segertoner, the Swedish Pentecostal hymnal,
does not appear in as great abundance as in the foregoing collections. In spite of the predilection of the Pentecostal denomination for a lighter type of hymnody, the Fildelphia hymnal
does contain an appreciable and worthy selection of hymn texts
and chorale melodies of the State Church. Most of the authors
and composers mentioned in connection with the hymnals already discussed have been accorded a place among the 600
hymns in Segertoner. Twenty-seven hymns from the state-
church hymnists are included, which indicates that this branch
of hymnody has not been neglected entirely by a less formal
denomination, although the percentage is relatively small compared to other hymnals of free-church affiliation.

Denmark

      The hymnists of the Danish Lutheran Church are well
represented in the hymnals of the free churches in Denmark.
Reference has already been made to the many hymns written
by state-church hymnists, both in Norway and Denmark, which
met the demands of several free-church groups. From among
the scores of hymnists, the following appear frequently in
the hymnals of the denominations included in this study. The
biographical material is taken from Lövgren's Lexikon:

      Scholler Birkedal (1809-1892) entered the ministry under
the influence of Grundtvig after having trained as an apothe-
cary and having taught in public school. After dismissal
from the church because of his severe denunciation of its
politics, he continued unabated in preaching to promote home
gatherings. His songs were popular in his native Denmark
and were translated into Swedish.

Casper Johannes Boye (1791-1853) was born in Norway but spent most of his life in Denmark after his seminary training in that country. He served as pastor in several parishes including the Garnison Church in Copenhagen. His songs were popular in Denmark and were translated into Swedish and Norwegian; they have been equally popular in these countries.

Andreas P.V. Gregersen (1723-1801) received his early inspiration in music from his visit to Herrnhut in 1742. He was ordained into the ministry in 1757 and served both as deacon and bishop in his church. In addition to his work as an author of many hymns, he became a publisher of church hymnals and songbooks.

Niels Johannes Holm (1778-1845) was a private teacher and priest in Fyen, but because of earlier contact with the Brethren Church in Germany he became vitally interested in the work of this group. He labored intermittently with the Brethren Church and became popular among the free churches. His song "Hvar saliger den lille flokk" (Now blessed is the little flock) has been popular in Scandinavia.

Peder Jacobsen Hygom (1692-1764) was an ordained priest of the Danish Lutheran Church. Because of his strong leaning toward Pietism, he influenced the several congregations he served. His service to the Danish people was mainly the translation of hymns.

Jacob Peter M. Paulli (1844-1915) was at one time the pastor and dean of the influential Church of Our Lady in Copenhagen. He was a popular preacher who attracted large crowds to this church in the capital city. His conservative stand was evident not only in his preaching but also in his interest in the Inner Mission of Denmark. His hymns are found in nearly all of the free-church hymnals.

Ernst Christian Richardt (1831-1892) engaged in work in theology, journalism, and teaching before finally settling in the work of the ministry. He was popular as a song writer, particularly for his song "Tornerose," a symbolical poem which became the campaign song for the resistance group in Denmark-Norway in 1940-1945.

From among the 533 selections in the Danish Baptist

hymnal Salmer og Sangbog, nearly half are from state-church
hymnists. Included in this number are the hymns of Grundtvig, Kingo, and Ingemann. Pietistic writers of other countries also are represented by a considerable number of hymns.
The Danish Baptists have leaned heavily on the hymnists of
their native State Church, as well as on those of Germany,
Sweden, and Norway. Hymns of Luther, Gerhardt, Schmolck,
Decius, Tersteegen, Freylinghausen, Neander, von Lowen-
stern, Melancthon, Wilhelm of Weimer, and Nicolai are among
the contents of this hymnal. Luther and Gerhardt have the
greatest representation of hymns among this group. While
Lina Sandell-Berg and J.O. Wallin have been popular among
Sweden's free-church people, the Danish Baptists have not
taken to their hymns up to this point in their history.

The Danish Missionforbund's hymnal Salmer og Sange
shows considerably less influence from the State Church in
Scandinavia or Germany as compared with the Baptist hymnal.
The hymns and translations of Brorson, Grundtvig, and Ingemann are included in the amount of twenty-six, forty-eight
and nineteen respectively, but beyond the hymns of these
authors, this hymnal contains only forty-one selections by
state-church hymnists.

The Danish Methodist hymnal presents an interesting
study in comparison with those already considered. Nearly
all of the hymns from the Lutheran Church contained in this
hymnal are from Danish hymnists, with only a few from Norwegian and Swedish poets. Outside of Scandinavia only the
names of Luther, Neander, Nicolai, Zinzendorf, Schmolck,
and Philip Spitta are to be found in the directory of contributors. The list of state-church poets, mostly from Denmark,
contains the names of sixty hymn writers. The Methodists
of Denmark have drawn heavily on the Danish Lutheran Church
for their hymnody.

The Danish Pentecostal Church has used very few hymns
by state-church hymnists in its hymnal Evangelietoner. Grundtvig, Brorson, Ingemann, Luther, and Gerhardt are represented by a few hymns; Paulli, Richardt, and Boye have contributed a small number, but the percentage by even nominal
members of the State Church is very low compared to the
hymnals of the other bodies.

Norway

Previous reference has been made to the more popular
state-church hymnists whose names appear in the free-church
hymnals of Norway. In addition to Johannes Johnson, Moe,
Lanstad, Wexels, and Kirsten Hansen, there are approximately
fifty other hymnists from the Norwegian, Swedish, and Danish
Lutheran Churches whose hymns have been selected for the
Baptist hymnal Evangelisten. There are forty-four texts by
German hymnists in this collection. Hassler, Weissel, Zinck,
Schop, Nicolai, Teschner, Vulpius, Luther, Neander, Crüger,
and Rinkart are a few of the prominent German authors whose
hymns are being used by Norwegian Baptists.

Ludwig Lindeman leads the way as the prominent composer among the Norwegian people, particularly in the free-
churches. In Evangelisten there are fifteen entries of his
chorale settings, more than from any other single composer.
In addition to Lindeman, several other composers from Scandinavia are represented.

Sions Harpe, the official praise-book of the Methodist
Church in Norway, presents the same picture as Evangelisten.
Lindeman's settings are the best represented and the most
popular. Chorales of prominent German and Scandinavian composers are just nominally used. The popularity of Scandinavian authors is noticeable in the Methodist hymnal. Lina
Sandell's hymns number fifteen while the composite figure of
other Scandinavian hymnists is approximately twenty-one.

The Misjonsforbund hymnal of Norway, Salmer og Sanger,
compares favorably to the hymnals of the Swedish Baptists
and Missionsförbundet in its drawing upon state-church hymnists and composers. Ludwig Lindeman alone has forty-one
entries in this hymnal. Among the well-known composers,
H.O.C. Zinck contributed twelve hymns in this collection;
Nicolai and Schop follow in close succession with nine and
eight chorales, respectively; Hessler and Crüger are both
represented by three setting; Luther, Teschner, and Vulpuis
each are represented by two chorale melodies. Many Scandinavian composers and collections have been the source of
supply for Salmer og Sanger.

Among the hymnists of the State Church in Scandinavia,

those from Sweden are in the most prominent place with forty-
one texts used in Salmer og Sanger. Lina Sandell-Berg's
poems number twenty-six in this hymnal. Danish and Norwegian hymn writers have supplied a total of twenty-nine
selections while fourteen hymns of Martin Luther are included
in this hymnal.

An analysis of the hymnal of the Norwegian Pentecostal
Church reveals that this denomination has had the least to do
with the hymnody of the State Church. The only author worth
noting at all is Lina Sandell-Berg whose hymns number approximately fourteen. Quite naturally the warmth of her expression and simplicity of style have had an appeal to this
group. The number of other authors and composers from
the State Church at large is of little or no consequence in
Norwegian Pentecostal hymnody.

Summary

Although the break with the State Church in all of the
Scandinavian countries was decisive and complete, the various
free-church denominations have never completely overthrown
the traditional Lutheran hymns and chorale melodies. Hymn
texts and tunes are still found to a greater or lesser extent
in all hymnals of the major free-church tradition. As the
analysis of hymnals has shown, the Baptists of Sweden and
Denmark and the Mission Covenant Church of all three countries under study have made considerable use of hymns and
musical settings from the State Church. The Scandinavian
Methodists have also included an appreciable number of hymns
from state-church hymnody in their collections. It is quite
natural to expect that the Pentecostal churches would find
the least use for hymns of the state church tradition, although
even among this group there is not a total absence of such
hymns.

Background of Free-Church Hymnody
in Scandinavia

One of the first references to the influence of Pietism
on Scandinavian hymnody was in connection with the Swedberg
Psalmbook of 1695 (see Chapter I). Although the accusations
against Swedberg were prejudiced and unfounded, Arrhenius
and Ollon, who also contributed to this hymnal, leaned toward

pietistic expressions in their hymns (page 92). The foreword to the Thomander-Wieselgren Koral-Bok gives a rather
clear and concise evaluation of the hymns in this volume and
their relationship to Pietism.

> Among the Swedish and Danish psalm composers of
> this period are found "great ones of first caliber."
> The Scandinavian psalm writing is now having its
> glorious summer. Bible-true, powerful, deep and
> lofty, while at the same time plain and hearty, the
> psalm in Swedish, Danish and Icelandish, peals forth
> among all ages and ranks. It is not pietistic; but
> its spiritual appeal and worth really harks back to
> the psalm singing of the previous period. Pietism did
> not immediately gain progress in Sweden. First in
> 1706 did it seem necessary through the royal proclama-
> tion to warn against this movement and stipulate
> punishment for its adherants, a measure which sub-
> sequently was sharpened by the sadly notorious "con-
> venticle promulgation" of 1726. That certain psalms
> from that time have a pietistic flavor cannot be denied,
> and few, if any of that kind can be found in the
> Swedish Psalm Book of 1695, the Psalm Book full of
> living faith so important to the church.[30]

With this bit of controversial information as background,
one of Swedberg's hymns is submitted for comparison with one
by Arrhenius. The latter's hymn definitely shows a bent
toward the more intimate relationship between a man and his
God as expressed in Pietism.

> O Lord, give heed unto our plea,
> O Spirit, grant Thy graces,
> That we who put our trust in Thee
> May rightly sing Thy praises.
> Thy Word, O Christ, unto us give,
> That grace and pow'r we may receive
> To follow Thee, Our Master.

> Touch Thou the shepherd's lips, O Lord,
> That in this blessed hour
> He may proclaim Thy sacred Word
> With unction and with power.
> That Thou wouldst have Thy servant say,
> Put Thou into his heart, we pray.
> With grace and strength to say it.

Let heart and ear be opened wide
Unto Thy Word and pleading;
Our minds, O Holy Spirit, guide
By Thine own light and leading.
The law of Christ we would fulfill,
And walk according to His will,
His Word our rule of living.[31]
                              --Jesper Swedberg

Jesus is my Friend most precious,
Never friend did love as He
Can I leave this Friend so gracious,
Spurn His wondrous love for me?
No! nor friend nor foe shall sever
Me from Him who loves me so;
His shall be my will forever,
There above, and here below.

Bitter death for me He suffered;
From all guilt He set me free;
To His Father He hath offered
Everlasting prayers for me.
Who is he that would condemn me?
Christ hath saved me by His grace;
Who can from my Savious draw me?
I am safe in His embrace.

Now I am convinced that never
Life or death can sever me
From my blessed Lord and Saviour;
Present things, nor things to be,
Height nor depth, nor fear nor favor,
Naught that heaven or earth affords
Makes the sacred promise waver:
"Ye are Christ's, and He's the Lord's."[32]
                              --Jacob Arrhenius

     Besides the hymns of Pietism native to Scandinavia,
many were imported from Germany to enhance the treasury
of pietistic song. Among the many German poets and translators who were influenced by Pietism, the following from the
seventeenth and eighteenth centuries have been included in
Swedish hymnals to the present day:

     Carl H. von Bogatzky (1690-1744)
     Christian F. Gellert (1715-1769)

Johann F. Herzog (1647-1699)
Philip F. Hiller (1699-1769)
Johann J. Rambach (1693-1735)
Christian F. Richter (1676-1711)
Johann A. Rothe (1688-1758)
Benjamin Schmolck (1672-1737)
Gerhard Tersteegen (1697-1769)

The pietistic emphasis in the hymns of these authors is typified in a stanza of one of Gellert's hymns:

When I approach Thine altar, Lord,
May I this comfort cherish,
That on the cross Thy blood was poured
For me, lest I should perish.
Thou didst for me God's law fulfill,
That holy joy my heart might thrill,
When on Thy love I'm feasting.[33]

During the nineteenth century, a sizable number of
"popular" hymnals were released for use by the various church
groups in Scandinavia. For the most part the "free-churchly"
influence is seen in the rather sentimental, lightly sung, and
lively spiritual songs which marked a low ebb in the chorale
tradition.[34] The following books listed by Olson are but a
few of the many which were made available during the Romantic period. In one or two instances there are repetitions from
Chapter IV.

Andeliga Sånger från America
Församlings Sångboken (78 songs arranged for mixed
    voices by Haeffner)
Ahnfeltsångerna
Canaan
Sions Nya Sånger
Nöd och Nåd
Fridsånger Album
Sabbatsklockon
Davidsharpan
Fridstoner
Andeliga Quartter
Sionstoner
Stridssånger[35]

Much of the music in these collections was of folk song

character. Swedish music is a combination of the gay and
serious; Danish songs tended toward the major key, and the
Norwegian melodies are predominantly in the minor key. Some
songs reflect the influence of dancing tunes and some border
on the love-ditty. While there is a preponderance of national
folk idioms, some song books such as Missionsånger (Uppsala
1887) makes use of both German and English folk melodies.
The parody technic was adopted by some composers, especially
for the Salvation Army song books. The publication by C.J.
Stockenberg, Kyrkosong i Skolan uses 100 chorale melodies
which are parodies of folk tunes.[36]

   The collection by Stenhammer, Congregational Songs,
referred to earlier in this chapter, contains seventy-eight
chorales by Haeffner and ninety-two from English and American song collections. Much of the music is in lively 6/8
time. The Swedish texts have been altered to fit the melodies from collections such as Jubilee Singers and Redeeming
Love. American composers such as Ira Sankey and Philip
Bliss are well represented in this collection, as well as native
composers of Scandinavia with their original melodies and harmonizations.

   Hymnals and collections from the various free-church
denominations made their appearance at the close of the nineteenth and early in the twentieth century. Many of these
have been referred to earlier in this study.

   In Norway the influence of Hauge in the early nineteenth
century resulted in a decline in the music of the church. In
addition to those of Lindeman, the free-church movement
brought into use many other hymn settings which did much
harm to the singing of the traditional chorales.

Influence of Free-Church Hymnody on the
Hymnody of the State Church

   This study has revealed that the free church exerted
a reciprocal relationship on the hymnody of the State Church
in Scandinavia. The life and hymns of J.O. Wallin and Lina
Sandell-Berg and their relationship to the hymnody of both
branches of the Church have already been dealt with in some
detail. Little has been said concerning the influence of Pietism and the free-church movement on them personally, which

caused them to express in warm, personal terms the reality
of their faith. Many others like them who did not separate
from the state-church body felt the influence of the new denominations and expressed warm sympathy with their cause.
Two hymnists who are representative of this group are Anna
Ölander (1861-1932) and Carl Wilhelm Skarstedt (1815-1908).

Anna Ölander was born into a pastor's family. In her
early years she began to write poetry and stories; and between 1890 and 1920, she published several collections of her
own works under many different titles. She had a special
interest in writing for children and young people. One of
her hymns expresses an exhortation to youth: "Youth in
the spring of life; time is short." At the request of Karl
Fries, she wrote a large number of original texts and also
translated many songs for the K. M. F. U. (Y.M.C.A.) song
book which was published in 1900. Among her originals are
the following titles:

Thy Word, O Jesus, Let Us Be Still

Do All You Can for the Great Countless Masses

God, Above All Lands and People

Earth Can Give No Satisfaction

One of her foremost hymns which has found its way into many
song books to the present day is "If I Gained the World But
Lost the Savior." Lövgren analyzes Anna Ölander's religious
faith and outlook as follows:

Anna Ölander's holiness message savors of the Angli-
can type. It is easy to find resemblances between
hers and, for example, Frances Havergal and Mary
James, of the Methodist persuasion. Sanctification is
not a goal she considers herself to have reached, but
something to strive for. Seriously she tries to lift
her wings over worldly things, but she does not attain to the heights she would like to. [37]

She may be considered to have been a member of the low-
church branch of Lutheranism which was very sympathetic
to the pietistic cause.

Carl Skarstedt studied at Uppsala University and was

ordained to the Lutheran ministry in 1841. He attained to
the Doctor of Philosophy degree in 1842. His varied ministry
included that of pastor, teacher, dean at the Halmstad's Educational Institute, and docent at the University of Lund.
From 1865 he was professor in practical theology and biblical
exegesis at the latter institution. In his youth he became
interested in the doctrines and preaching of Schartau which
accounted for his own personal piety and pietistic outlook.
At the turn of the century, he allied himself more with the
low-church emphasis exemplified in Thomander and Wieselgren.
His strong interest and attachment to foreign missions caused
him to publish anonymously in 1861 the collection Christliga
Missionsånger (Christian Mission Songs).[38]

     In seeking to determine how extensively free-church
hymnody has been used by the state-church bodies, representative hymnals from the State Church in Scandinavia and
related groups in America have been analyzed by this writer
through an examination of these individual books. In addition
to the composers and poets who definitely identified themselves
with the free-church groups, several from pietistic circles in
Germany and Scandinavia, such as Lina Sandell-Berg and
J.A. Freylinghausen, have been included. For all practical
purposes they belong to this category, since their contributions to both the state and free-church hymnody are of equal
importance. In addition, English and American songs have
also been considered.

Sweden

     Den Svenska Koralboken of 1939 contains the texts of
the Psalmbok of 1937, as well as the musical settings for use
with the latter volume. Over 600 selections are included, representing texts and melodies from the early years of the Christian Church through the twentieth century. Since information
on authors was unavailable, the task involved comparing the
contents of both the Lutheran book and the latest Swedish
Baptist hymnal to determine the authorship of at least the
hymns used in both books.

     The hymns of writers with pietistic leanings and sym-
pathies in Scandinavia include such names as Lina Sandell-
Berg, S.J. Hedborn, Jeanne Oterdahl, Olof Kolmodin, Carl
O. Rosenius, Lars Linderot, Hans A. Brorson, and Anders
Frostenson. The 1939 hymnal also contains the hymns of

other hymnists from the State Church who expressed themselves in the warm pietistic style and who had an appeal to
the pietist and free-church groups. These include Sigrid
Dahlquist, Paul Nilsson, Natanael Beskow, Emil Liedgren,
Erik G. Geijer, Wilhelm A. Wexels, and Johan L. Runeberg.
Pietistic writers from outside Scandinavia are represented by
a relatively few hymns in the latest Swedish Lutheran hymnal.
Johann A. Rothe and J.A. Freylinghausen have one hymn
each in this collection; two Huguenot melodies were also used.

   Hymns by authors directly connected with the free-
church groups of Scandinavia have not been selected in great
numbers. The one hymnist whose name appears more than
any other is Betty Ehrenborg-Posse with four hymns and
translations. Oscar Ahnfelt stands next to Mrs. Posse with
a representation of three hymns and tunes. The Methodist
hymnist Jacob T. Jacobsoon can lay claim to one hymn in this
hymnal.

   English and American poets and composers have a fair
representation in the Lutheran hymnal of Sweden. The hymns
and tunes of such well-known persons as Charles Wesley,
Isaac Watts, Thomas Toplady, William Cowper, Reginald Heber,
and Sarah Adams from England, and Philip Bliss, Lowell Mason,
and Lydia Baxter from America, have been accorded a small
place among the several hundred in this volume.

   Among the well-known hymns from all sources connected
with Pietism and the free-church movement, the following are
contained in this monumental work:

   Rock of Ages--Toplady, Hastings

   Blott en dag (Day by Day)--Lina Sandell-Berg,
      Oscar Ahnfelt

   Nearer My God to Thee--Sarah Adams, Lowell Mason

   Abide with Me--Francis Lyte, William Monk

   Trygare kan ingen vara (Children of the Heavenly
      Father)--Lina Sandell-Berg

   Home Sweet Home (an adaptation by Lina Sandell-
      Berg with the familiar melody)

Denmark

Salme Bog for Kirke og Hjem is the official hymnal of
the Lutheran Church in Denmark. The edition made available for this study is that of 1927. The hymns of Brorson,
Grundtvig, Kingo, and Ingemann dominate the contents of
this hymnal as they do in the hymnals of the Danish free
churches. As has already been noted, Brorson had the
strongest pietistic leanings of these national poets. The
strong national spirit is exemplified by the use of so many
hymns of Danish authorship in both the free-church and
Lutheran hymnals. A cursory examination of the contents
reveals that although Brorson has a considerable number of
hymns in this hymnal, those of the other national poets, particularly Kingo and Grundtvig, exceed his in number.

Other Scandinavian poets of pietistic tendencies whose
hymns are included in this hymnal include Peder J. Hygom,
bishop of Aarhus, Israel Kolmodin, Christian F. Wadskiaer
who worked on the Pontopiddan psalm book, Jacob P.M. Paulli,
a participant in the work of the Inner Mission, and Hans
Agerbek whose poems and preaching exerted considerable influence on those seeking a more "complete" religious experience.

Several pietists from the Halle school are represented
among the hymnists in the Danish Lutheran hymnal. The
most noted is J.A. Freylinghausen who contributed both texts
and melodies. Others from Halle include J.J. Breithaupt, a
theological professor, J.D. Herrnschmidt who succeeded August
Francke as professor at the University of Halle, and C.F.
Richter, one of the noted song writers of the Halle pietists.
Musical settings from the Dormstadter Songbook of 1699 are
also included in this hymnal. This was a pioneer work in
the hymnody of Pietism and a forerunner of the Freylinghausen
collection. Hymns by Johan A. Rothe of the Herrnhut group
and Laurentius Laurenti of Bremen are included in this selection. Laurenti is reputed to have been the greatest of the
pietistic hymn writers.

Among the many chorales from pietistic sources in the
Menighedens Melodier collection are several from the Pontoppidan book, including some by C.F. Breitendich who made
many two-voiced settings for the Pontoppidan book. Christian
Gregor, the noted Moravian composer and Herrnhut organist

and publisher also is represented. Several songs by Christian Richter, the talented preacher and song writer in the
song circles of Halle, are found in this collection.

America is represented by just a few hymn melodies,
so the influence from this source has not been extensive or
significant. "Stand Up, Stand Up for Jesus" by Duffield and
Webb and "Ring the Bells of Heaven" are borrowed from San-
keys Sånger. W.H. Doane, the popular American song writer
has contributed the well-known tune "Ring the Bells of Heaven."

The latest chorale book from Denmark examined in this
study is Den Danske Koralbog edited by Jens Peter Larsen
and Magens Woldike, published in 1954. Two pietistic sources
have furnished melodies for this collection. Ten tunes of
Freylinghausen and just one from the Pontoppidan book are
included. From America come six melodies composed by Lowell
Mason, Joseph Barnby, J.B. Dykes, and W.H. Monk.

Norway

The Norwegian State Church continues to make use of
M.B. Lanstad's Kirkesalmebok and the Koralbog for Den Norske
Kirke. From among the many hymns of the pietistic and free-
church writers, a comparable number to those chosen for the
other two Lutheran hymnals are included in these books. Johann Rothe, J.A. Freylinghausen, and Carl H. Bogatzky represent the contributions of German Pietism. Foremost among
the Norwegian hymnists in the number of entries in their hymnal
is William A. Wexels, whose contribution to Scandinavian hymnody
has already been discussed in detail. Ten of his hymns appear
in Lanstad's hymnal. Others of the free-church, conservative
hymnists of Norway whose "spiritual songs" have .been included
are Johannes Johnson, Elevine Heede, and Ole T. Moe. Hans
Brorson and J.P. Paulli represent the Danish contribution
found among the selections in this hymnal. Pietistic, Swedish
influence on Norwegian Lutheran hymnody is seen in the inclusion of several hymns by Lina Sandell-Berg and J.O. Wallin and, in addition, hymns by Olof Kolmodin, Betty Ehrenborg-
Posse and Lars Linderot.

Pertinent to this aspect of this study is an analysis of
each of three Lutheran hymnals of America with Scandinavian
background and the Concordia Hymnal of the Lutheran Free
Church. These were examined relative to the content of free-

church and pietistic hymns of Scandinavian origin found in
them. The hymnal <u>Hemlandssånger</u> first published in 1892
is really in a class by itself because of its close association
with Swedish hymnody in the early days of Swedish settlements in this country. The four hymnals are listed with representative free-church and pietistic authors:

> <u>The Hymnal</u> (Augustana Synod)
>   O. Ahnfelt
>   Lina Sandell-Berg
>   Hans Brorson
>   Agatha Rosenius
>   Carl O. Rosenius
>   Andreas C. Rutstrom
>
> <u>Hymnal for Church and Home</u> (Danish Lutheran)
>   Hans Brorson: 20 originals and 17 translations
>   Peder Hygom
>   Magnus Lanstad
>   J.P. Paulli
>   O. Ahnfelt
>
> <u>Hemlandssånger</u> (Augustana Synod-Swedish)
>   Joel Blomqvist
>   Olof Kolmodin
>   Lars Linderot
>   Magnus Malmstedt
>   Gustav Palmquist
>   Betty Ehrenborg-Posse
>   Carol O. Rosenius
>   Agatha Rosenius
>   A.C. Rutström
>   Peder Syreen
>   Teodor Truve
>   Peter Waldenstrom
>
> The following sources of musical settings are rep-
>   resented in this hymnal:
>   <u>Mose och Lamsens Wisor</u>
>   <u>Syreens Sånger</u>
>   <u>Fridsbasunen</u>
>   <u>Sionstoner</u>
>   <u>Pilgrimssånger</u>
>   <u>Pilgrimsharpen</u>

The Concordia Hymnal (Lutheran Free Church)
  Lina Sandell-Berg
  Hans Brorson
  Hans Nelson Hauge
  Magnus Lanstad
  Betty Ehrenborg-Posse
  Carol O. Rosenius

Summary

While both the State Church and the free-church denominations have borrowed from the hymnody of each other,
the balance has not been of equal proportions. This particular study has revealed a much heavier borrowing of state-
church hymns and musical settings by the free churches than
was true of the compilers and editors of the state-church
hymnals. This seems to point up the fact that the tradition
of state-church hymnody continues to exert considerable influence on the pietistic and free-church groups in the compilation of their hymnals. As has been asserted in a previous
chapter, the conservative leanings of the State Church in the
Scandinavian countries has provided more "spiritual" songs
from within its ranks. This is true particularly in Norway
and Denmark, and seems to be a logical outcome of such a
situation. While the number of borrowings from the hymns of
the free churches has not been as great, it is of real significance that the older established church should have seen
fit to recognize and utilize the hymns of a sizable number of
free-church authors and composers.

NOTES

1. J.H. Thomander and P. Wieselgren, Svenska Psalm-Boken
    Förenad Med Koral-Bok (Rock Island: The Lutheran
    Augustana Book Concern, 1892), p. ix.
2. Ibid.
3. Ibid.
4. Ibid.
5. Lundholm, op. cit., p. 15.
6. Ibid., p. 19.
7. Ibid., p. 20.
8. Ibid., p. 26.
9. Ibid., pp. 29, 30.

10. Johannes Dillner, Psalmodikon (Cedarholm, 1830), p. x.
11. Ibid., p. xiv.
12. Lundholm, op. cit., p. 32.
13. Ibid., pp. 78-80.
14. Ibid., p. 68.
15. C.R. Osbeck, Old Acquaintances in New Garb (translated from "Svenska Standaret," February 12, 1924).
16. Julian, op. cit., p. 1000.
17. Hjortsvang, op. cit., pp. 60-61.
18. Ibid.
19. Ibid., pp. 67, 68.
20. Cartford, op. cit., p. 6.
21. Ibid., pp. 8, 9.
22. Ibid., p. 15.
23. Ibid., pp. 15-17.
24. Ibid., p. 17.
25. Ibid., pp. 19, 20.
26. Ibid., p. 26.
27. Koralbog indeholdende Melodier til Salmebog for lutherske Kristne i Amerika (Minneapolis: Augsburg Publishing House, 1916), pp. 3, 4.
28. Ibid., p. 4.
29. Lövgren, Våra Psalm ... , III, pp. 391-398.
30. Thomander and Wieselgren, op. cit., p. xiii.
31. The Hymnal and Order of Service (Rock Island: Augustana Book Concern, 1925), Hymn No. 348.
32. Ibid., Hymn No. 470.
33. Ibid., Hymn No. 237.
34. Lundholm, op. cit., p. 33.
35. Olson, op. cit., p. 116.
36. Olson, op. cit., p. 117.
37. Lövgren, Våra Psalm ... , III, p. 142.
38. Lövgren, Lexikon, p. 640.

• CHAPTER VI

THE PRESENT STATUS OF SCANDINAVIAN
FREE-CHURCH HYMNODY

The hymnody of the Scandinavian Free Churches of the present time is in a state of progress, particularly among the major denominations. The constant revising and re-editing of the older editions of free-church hymnals and the publication of entirely new ones substantiates this conclusion.

Preceding chapters have dealt with the relationship of these hymnals to state-church hymnody. A final analysis of each hymnal is given at this point to determine the present hymnological interests of the various denominations represented and more recent developments within each group.

Sweden

Psalm och Sang

This hymnal represents one of the latest publications by a free-church denomination in Scandinavia. Although significant contributions by foreign authors and composers have been included in sizable numbers, the Scandinavian element has not been entirely neglected. In addition to approximately 180 entries of German chorale melodies, there are forty-five musical settings derived from Swedish sources. From the other Scandinavian countries, only six melodies have been used in this hymnal.

In contrast to the small percentage of Swedish melodies used in Psalm och Sång, Swedish and other Scandinavian poems have a significant representation. While only nineteen German authors are represented, sixty-six Scandinavian hymnists

have provided hymns for this Swedish Baptist hymnal. The
following listing according to countries shows the distribution
among Scandinavian hymnists:

Sweden		
Baptist Union		22
Örebro Mission		4
Missionsförbundet		18
	Total	44
Norway		9
Denmark		13
Finland		13
	Total	35

The most popular hymnists according to the number of
entries are Lina Sandell-Berg with forty-five originals and
translations, and J.O. Wallin who contributed fifty-one hymns.
While the German melodies are preponderant in Psalm och
Sång, several hundred texts from Scandinavia still give this
book a decided Scandinavian flavor.

Hymns from England and America, particularly those
of the revival period of the nineteenth century, have had an
appeal to the free-church people of Scandinavia. The hymns
of the many popular song writers are included in Psalm och
Sång, representing a total of approximately 120 selections.
Fanny Crosby, Horatius Bonar, Baring-Gould, William Booth,
Isaac Watts, Charles Wesley, Philip Bliss and many others
are well represented in this most recently published volume
of the Baptists of Sweden. Psalm och Sång continues to be
popular among the churches of the Baptist Union in Sweden
and the Örebro Mission. (See Appendix H.)

Pilgrimstoner

The Free Baptists of Sweden have been quite provincial
in their selection of authors and hymns for their official hymnal.
Approximately 136 Scandinavian authors have contributed 450
of the 560 hymns contained in this hymnal. Of the remaining
hymns, fifty-nine are of American or English origin. Sharing
honors with Lina Sandell-Berg and J.O. Wallin is Anders Hanson with eighty-two of his songs included in this publication,
the largest number by a single author. Besides Hanson, twenty

other hymnists of the Free Baptist denomination have hymns
in this collection. Their contribution numbers seventy-four
hymn texts collectively, with Joel Friden the next highest
contender to Hanson. Fifteen of his hymns are in Pilgrimstoner. Among the non-Baptists whose texts are in this
hymnal, Nils Frykman is represented by fifteen hymns.

Even though there is a sizable number of hymns by
foreign authors in Pilgrimstoner, the preponderance of those
of Scandinavian origin makes this hymnal decidedly Scandinavian in character.

Sånger och Psalmer

The official hymnal of Missionsförbundet in Sweden is
an example of one of the more progressive hymnals of the
Scandinavian free-church groups. Both the scope of its contents and the international representation of its authors and
composers indicate a broad outlook on the part of the compilers of this monumental work. Great hymns of the past and
present have been given a place within its covers.

Most of the authors of Scandinavian background are
Swedish, and total in excess of 125; these are represented
by nearly 350 hymns in addition to scores of translations by
some of the more prominent authors. Including translations
and original poems in the Scandinavian language, the total
number of works by Swedish, Danish, Norwegian, and Finnish poets amounts to more than half of the contents of this
hymnal. Among the hymnists of all the countries represented,
J.O. Wallin's hymns and translations total fifty-four, while
fifty-one of Lina Sandell-Berg's hymns are included in Sånger
och Psalmer.

Several hymn writers of Missionsförbundet have been
mentioned in chapter four. Although their contributions to
their denominational hymnal cannot compare numerically with
Wallin's or Mrs. Berg's, it is worth noting that the total number of hymns by these authors is approximately 100; this
figure includes some translation by Johan Erik Nystrom. Other
prominent hymnists in this group include Carl Boberg, Joel
Blomquist, Nils Frykman, and Selma Sundelius Lagerstrom.
Boberg is represented by thirty-two hymns; Frykman follows
close with twenty-six and Blomquist with thirteen. Mrs. Lagerstrom and Nystrom each have contributed eight hymns.

In addition to the entries from state-church hymnody, the Missionsförbund has included hymns from well-known British, and American sources. Watts, Wesley, Cowper, and Fawcett from England, and nineteenth century American gospel song writers have been given prominent place among the hymnists chosen for this volume. Hymn texts from the early centuries of the Christian Church, as well as old texts from Europe, have been translated; their place in this hymnal, as well as the inclusion of eight-three texts from the twentieth century, make this hymnal of inestimable value in providing this particular denomination with the great hymns of the past and present. Although there is a natural inclination toward Swedish hymns in this particular hymnal, it is worth noting that nearly half of its contents comes from sources outside of the Scandinavian countries.

The selection of melodies and musical settings from the early years of the church to the present time parallels the choice of hymn texts. Representation by countries shows the international flavor of Sånger och Psalmer. The sources for the musical settings and melodies used in this hymnal are presented in the following tabulation. Significant numbers from any one source are included in parentheses.

1. Early melodies: fourth and fifth centuries and Middle Ages
2. French (11)
3. Danish (5)
4. Swedish (39)
5. American
6. Huguenot Psalm Melodies (12)
7. Freylinghausen Sangbok
8. Herrnhut
9. Norwegian
10. Well-known English and American Melodies
11. Melodies from the following collections:
    Sånger till Lammets lof
    Brödraförsamling
    Hemlandstoner
    Sionstoner
    Pilgrimstoner
    Pilgrims Sånger
    Finska koralboken
    Ahnfelts Sånger
    Jubelklangen, 1896

Sions nya sånger, 1857
Fridsbasunen
Sanningsvittnet
Segertoner
12. Composers of the twentieth century (45)

Sånger och Psalmer remains ever popular among the churches
in the Missionsförbundet in Sweden.

Metodistkyrkans Psalmbok

The hymnal for Swedish Methodists presents an interesting contrast to the Baptist and Missionsförbundet hymnals.
It should be noticed that J.O. Wallin and Lina Sandell-Berg
share the honors once again, each having more hymns in this
hymnal than any other poet. Thirty-three of Wallin's are
used compared with forty-four of Mrs. Berg's. For a denominational hymnal, this of the Methodists does not draw heavily
on its own resources. Naturally one would expect to find
several of Charles Wesley's hymns among the nearly 700 which
make up this hymnal. Charles Wesley's hymns number twenty-
eight while four of his brother John's have been chosen.

The percentage of hymns of Swedish Methodist poets
is relatively small, which is somewhat the case of the contribution of Swedish Baptists to Psalm och Sång. Jacob Jacobsson has the largest number of hymns in the Methodist hymnal.
Thirteen of his hymns have been used while Victor Witting's
hymns number only four. While the Missionsförbund has drawn
heavily on the poems of its own members, the Baptists and
Methodists seemingly have not so availed themselves. While
there is a definite preponderance of Scandinavian hymns in
the Methodist collection, the choice of hymns has been spread
among many poets as is the case with the Baptist hymnal.
Practically all of the well-known hymnists previously mentioned
in this study are represented by one or two hymns.

American and British hymns have a peculiar attraction
to the Swedish Methodists, particularly the American. A
cursory examination of their hymnal turns up several hymns
by leading song writers, particularly of the American "revival
period" of the nineteenth century. Tunes and texts are in
significant amounts in this volume. Since Swedish Methodism
was greatly influenced by American Methodists, it follows naturally that American hymnody would have an appeal. Fanny

Crosby seems to be a favorite among Swedish Methodists as
is evidenced by the choice of thirteen of her hymns.   Isaac
Watts, John Newton, and Francis Havergal are representative
of the many British hymnists whose hymns have been selected
for this hymnal.

The music of the Methodist hymnal presents a wide
variety of types.   In addition to the musical settings from
collections, melodies and harmonizations of Scandinavian composers have been utilized for this hymnal.   The materials
are from sixty-five composers representing a total of 184 hymn
tunes.   Among those whose hymn tunes have been selected
in sizable number are Oscar Ahnfelt with fourteen; Erik Lindgren and Johan Lindberg have ten and nine, respectively.
The Methodists have used the music of several organists
throughout the hymnal.   In addition to the tunes of Erik
Lindgren who was at one time organist at Saint Peter's Methodist Church in Stockholm, music for the Methodist hymnal
has been supplied by the following organists:

> Johan Alfred Ahlström (1883-1910)
> Andreas Peter Berggren (1801-1880)
> Julius Alfred Dahlöf (1871-1913)
> Algot Eklof (1875-1938)
> Fredrik August Ekström (1819-1901)
> August Elfåker (1851-1914)
> Oscar Fredrik Lindberg (1870-1931)
> Ludwig Matthias Lindeman (1812-1887)
> Albert Esaias Lindstrom (1853-1935)
> Johan Erik Nordblom (1788-1848)
> Otto Olsson (b. 1879)
> Wilhelm Theodor Soderberg (1845-1922)
> Viktor Patrik Vretblod (1876-1953)
> G. Torsten G. Wall (b. 1902)
> Fredrik Wallentin (b. 1885)
> N. Henry P. Weman (b. 1897)
> Christoph E.F. Weyse (1774-1842)
> Ivar Wideen (1871-1951)

Besides the many organists whose hymn settings appear in
the hymnal, the roster of composers also contains the names
of musical directors, teachers, and pastors, many of whom
have been connected with the ministry of the State Church.
Also a significant number of American composers of the Gospel
Song era are represented among the musical settings of this

hymnal, i.e. Charlotte Barnard, Philip Bliss, Charles Con-
verse, William H. Doane, Charles Gabriel, Robert Lowry,
James McGranahan, George Root, Ira Sankey, George Stebbins,
and Issac Woodbury. The inclusion of musical arrangements
from these sources plus adaptations of melodies by Haydn,
Mozart, Beethoven, and Bortniansky makes the Methodist
hymnal an example of a well-rounded, well-balanced hymnal,
worthy of emulation by other denominations. No new hymnal
is planned at this time to replace the present hymnal of the
Swedish Methodists.

Segertoner

The Swedish Pentecostals have produced, through several editions, a substantial collection of hymns and gospel
songs which has been adapted to serve the needs and emphasis of their denomination. As has been indicated in Chapter
V, the number of state-church hymns is quite substantial
for this particular free-church group but is only a small percentage of the entire collection of over 600 hymns. Running
"true to form," Lina Sandell's hymns number twenty-eight,
more than can be claimed by any other single poet. Only
twelve hymns by J.O. Wallin have been used; as has been
previously indicated, Levi Pethrus, the Pentecostals' strong
leader, is represented by just sixteen hymns. Paul Ongman
runs a close second to Pethrus with sixteen entries, some of
which are arrangements and adaptations of borrowed melodies.

The hymns of Scandinavian pietistic and free-church
hymnists make up a considerable portion of the contents of
Segertoner. A variety of poets from various denominational
groups about which this study has been concerned is represented, although not in great numbers. The list of poets and
composers whose works appear in this hymnal in great abundance could well have been lifted bodily from an American
hymnal. The Pentecostals have been more inclined toward
American hymnody, particularly that of the nineteenth century,
than any of the groups under study. Fanny Crosby, Philip
Bliss, James McGranahan, William Kirkpatrick, William Bradbury, and Charles Gabriel are among the many from America
whose hymns and tunes have been adopted by the Swedish
Pentecostal Church.

Another significant feature of Segertoner is the presence
of over two dozen songs from the Swedish Psalmbook. While

it is true that the majority of these songs were written by
J.O. Wallin and others whose sympathy and emphasis were
with the free-church movement, nevertheless, it is worth noting that this extremely conservative group within this movement has seen fit to include these songs in its hymnal. This
is indicative of their universal and ecumenical appeal.

Denmark

The hymnody of the Danish Baptists has been dealt
with rather completely in chapters four and five, and little
remains to be said concerning its present status. The 1928
revision of Salme-og-Sangbog differs very little from that of
1916. The latest revision is from 1960. All editions contain
over 500 hymns, and as has been previously mentioned, approximately half are from state-church hymnists and the writers of the Danish pietistic groups. Because of the strong
nationalistic feelings among the Danes, only thirty-two poets
from England and America are included among the selections
in the hymnal, with usually just one hymn from each poet.
Borrowing has not been abundant. A study of their hymnal
reveals an apparently less progressive spirit among the Danish Baptists, perhaps, in reality, only a desire to remain nationalistic in their choice of hymns. The Danish Baptists an-
ticipate the publication of a new hymnal in the near future.

Salmebog

The Danish Methodists, likewise, exhibit a strong nationalistic feeling regarding their hymnody. Like the Baptists, the Methodists have drawn heavily on state-church hymnody as well as from other Danish sources. The Danish Methodists are well represented by twelve poets and approximately sixty hymns besides numerous translations. Alberta
Eltholtz shares honors with Lina Sandell-Berg as a prominent
hymn writer and translator among the Danes. While Mrs.
Berg has comparatively few of her hymns in this hymnal,
Alberta Eltholtz's hymns are twenty-eight in number. Anton
East and Nels Mann, who were Danish Methodist clergymen,
wrote several hymns of which nine by East and twelve by
Mann were selected for the official hymnal. All three of the
above-mentioned poets made substantial contributions to this
book by their several translations from various sources. Even
though the Methodist hymnal has drawn heavily on Danish

sources, a more progressive spirit than the Baptists is evident in the inclusion of many more hymns from English and
American sources. As has been indicated before, the borrowing from England and America has been mainly of nineteenth
century hymnody. Eighty-two hymns from sixty-nine English
and American authors are found among the contents of this
hymnal. These figures indicate that no one author has been
a favorite, except that nine of Fanny Crosby's hymns were
selected. The Danish Methodists have exhibited a desire for
"sampling" among the many English and American hymns.

Evangelie-toner

This hymnal of the Danish Pentecostals is in a class by
itself. Little favoritism is shown for any one poet with the
exception of T.B. Barratt, the Pentecostal leader in Scandinavia. Fifteen of his hymns are in Evangelie-toner. Fanny
Crosby is next in line as a favorite with twelve of her hymns
being selected for this hymnal. Two general observations
will suffice to evaluate the present choice of the Pentecostals
of Denmark: nearly all of the Danish hymns chosen are of
the free-church tradition with special emphasis on those of
J.P. Santon of the Danish Missionsförbund; there is a wide
variety of English and American songs, with the heavier emphasis on the American "gospel" song. This hymnal, because
of its contents having been chosen from among scores of
hymnists, is another good example of a "sampler" collection.

Salmer og Sange

The hymnists among the Danish Missionsförbund are few
in number. Merely a half dozen are mentioned in the directory of authors in Salmer og Sange. This denomination is
indebted to Jorgen Peter Santon (1878-1944) for eighteen
hymns in this collection, and Emil Larsen (b. 1900) and Viggo
Ramvold (b. 1914), both of whom contributed several translations from various sources.

As has been the case with the other denominational
hymnals, a large proportion of hymns are by authors from
other free-church groups in Scandinavia. Five hymns by
T.B. Barratt and six by Lina Sandell-Berg make these the
largest representations by single poets.

Anglo-American influence is seen in Salmer og Sange

in the seventy-seven hymns of American and English origin
chosen from the poems of an appreciable number of writers.
Fanny Crosby again has been revealed as a favorite poet in
the Scandinavian free-church people. Twelve of her hymns
are used in this collection. The names of well-known writers
previously mentioned are in evidence in this Missionsförbund's
book, presenting a cross section of evangelical hymns of England and the gospel songs of America, with perhaps greater
inclination toward the latter type.

     As far as can be determined, the Danish Missionsförbund
is the only free-church group in Denmark to have published
a new denominational hymnal recently. Published in 1976,
the first printing was sold out and a new edition is forthcoming.

Norway

Evangelisten

     The Norwegian Baptist hymnal Evangelisten shows an
almost equal balance between the hymnody of the Scandinavian
free church and American hymnody. American hymns total
approximately 115, with the hymns of Fanny Crosby and
Philip Bliss numbering nineteen and thirteen, respectively.
The total number of hymns by free-church authors is in
excess of 110. Six of T.B. Barratt's hymns are in this category. Lina Sandell-Berg is a favorite with Norwegian Baptists as is shown by the inclusion of twenty-one of her texts
in their hymnal. Hymns from Great Britain are in considerable number with the total of sixty-seven, including a half-
dozen hymns each from Havergal, Watts, and Wesley.

     Evangelisten exemplified further the influence from
America in the choice of many tunes from such composers as
William Bradbury, William H. Doane, Lowell Mason, George
Stebbins, and others from the church scene of nineteenth-
century America. In addition to American tunes, several
koralbog melodies are used, as well as folk melodies from the
European countries including Scandinavia.

Salmer og Sanger

     The Norwegian Misjonforbund hymnal represents a simi-

lar compilation, as does the Baptist Evangelisten, the only
difference being in the total contribution from the several
sources. Nearly 150 hymns of Scandinavian free-church
origin were chosen with the honors once again going to Mrs.
Berg whose hymns total twenty-six; the balance of these hymns
is quite well distributed among the hymn writers typified by
Joel Blomquist, Nils Frykman, T.B. Barratt, and Matias Or-
heim, the blind Norwegian hymnist, twelve of whose hymns
are included. Approximately seventy-five selections of American and British authors appear in this hymnal, and as has
been the case in the majority of hymnals examined in this
study, most of the texts are from the popular nineteenth-
century romantic era.

Over 100 musical settings from American gospel-song
composers have been used by the compilers of Salmer og
Sanger, one of the larger numbers in these hymnals used in
this study. This is another testimony to the popularity of
American tunes among the people of the Scandinavian free-
church groups.

Sions Harpe

The Methodist Church of Norway has produced a noteworthy volume in its official hymnal, Sions Harpe. The list
of authors contains the names of the popular ones who appear
in all of the free-church hymnals, and in addition to the names
of many lesser-known poets from Scandinavia. These poets,
numbering approximately twenty-five, set this hymnal apart
from those of the other denominations. Philip Bliss and Fanny
Crosby seem to be the popular American writers since more
of their hymns are included than of the other popular Ameri-
cans. Nearly equal honors are shared by Charles Wesley and
T.B. Barratt in the number of their hymns chosen for this
book. Nine of Wesley's are included compared to eight by
Barratt. Otherwise, the rest of the free-church hymns are
spread quite evenly among the several well-known writers.

Besides the abundance of hymn settings by well-known
American, British, and Scandinavian composers, several interesting and almost novel melodies are used in this particular
hymnal. The peak of American influence is seen in the use
of two popular tunes: "The Battle Hymn of the Republic,"
used with the text, and the melody to Stephen Foster's immortal song "Swanee River." The latter is a setting for one
of T.B. Barratt's texts.

The most striking inclusions from among the many American and British tunes and texts are the two national anthems
with their appropriate melodies: "Star Spangled Banner" and
"God Save the King!"   The texts are in English translations.
The choice of these songs brings the Norwegian people close
to American and British life and culture.   As with the rest
of the hymnals under analysis, there is a good selection of
folk tunes from Scandinavia, the continent, and even one
from Spain.

Maran Ata

The hymnal of the Pentecostals in Norway contains in
excess of 700 hymns.   In the back of the hymnal is a section
containing short selections which would compare to the American "Gospel Chorus" of a generation ago.   The complete hymnal, words and music, is so large that it has been published
in two volumes.   An examination of the contents reveals that
T.B. Barratt, the founder of Norwegian Pentecostalism, has
been the driving force and inspiration.   No previous author
exceeds Barratt in the number of hymns included in the volumes under study.   Allowing for errors, the number of Barratt's hymns in Maran Ata is in excess of 100.   Levi Pethrus,
who bears the same relationship to Swedish Pentecostals as
Barratt does to the Norwegian, has hardly a token number
of hymns in Segertoner compared with the number of Barratt's hymns in the Norwegian book.   Barratt's contact with
the "Four Square" group is reflected in the inclusion of one
of Aimee Semple McPherson's hymns.   The rest of the contents
consists of hymns by Scandinavian free-church poets and the
well-known English and American poets of the nineteenth century.

The melodies in Mara Ata are marked by the excessive
use of dotted rhythms and notes of short value, as is characteristic of many of the American "Gospel" songs.   Swedish
and Norwegian folk melodies provide a sizable number of musical settings as had been characteristic of the other free-church
hymnals.   Once again, the choice of distinctly American tunes
is noteworthy.   Not only is "Swanee River" used in this collection, but the southern American tradition is further seen
in the choice of "Old Black Joe" with an adaptation of the
text in Norwegian by T.B. Barratt!   (His contacts in America
must have made deep impressions on him.)   Tune and text
arrangements of such well-known American gospel songs as

"His Eye is on the Sparrow" point to the fascination this type
of song has had for the Norwegian Pentecostals.

Summary

The examination of these several hymnals has revealed
what has been taking place over the last several years among
the people of the Scandinavian free-church tradition. Almost without exception, they have been compiled with the view
to giving each particular denomination not only an anthology
of hymns in the Scandinavian, European, British, and American traditions, but a practical tool for public praise and
private devotion. It has been interesting to note the way
melodies and harmonies have been changed. A case in point
is the indication by perforated line of sections of the musical
settings to be used as introductions for congregational singing. The hymnals of the Swedish Baptists and Missionsförbundet are examples of this innovation. The hymnals of both
groups witness to the increased use of state-church chorales
and American hymns in interesting harmonic and rhythmic
arrangements.

Recent Developments in Scandinavian Hymnody

An interesting and timely article by Aron Hallenberg
appeared in (March 17, 1966), Vecko-Posten the official organ
of Swedish Baptists. What he has written about church music
and hymnody in Sweden was true to a greater or lesser degree in other Scandinavian countries at that time.

> Anyone who has dealt with church music during
> the last thirty years can testify to the fact that it
> has gone through a revolution during the last decade,
> or something similar. What during the thirties was
> unthinkable even as a subject for discussion in the
> realm of church music is now practiced without any
> wide protest: "Swinging" chorals, Gospel songs and
> Negro spirituals--and a liturgy entirely divorced from
> an accepted tradition.
> The interest in church music is keener than ever;
> and the subject is discussed and practiced more lively
> than for a long time. The young people are engaging
> themselves with the new style spiritedly. One can

without exageration state that it is the young people
who point the way to a new church musical style....

Churchgoers have all too long been lulled to sleep-
iness by the endless "row bands" of the Haeffnerian
chorales. Now there is a return to Luther's glad
chorales-which in the time of the great reformer were
looked upon as spiritual ditties quite in line with the
glad tidings they meant to set forth. These songs
had a refreshing tempo and a lively rhythm; but they
were forced into an intolerable strait jacket when the
Haeffnerian chorale book was issued 1821....

Then as a kind of reaction there came the happy
songs of mass revivals, often set to waltz time 6/8
beat....

The revival songs were rated as musically unworthy
at the time when the present chorale book was made
up. The lively melodies, often written in 3-beats,
were changed in rhythm, or exchanged with others,
often newer compositions. But innovations are never
accepted by churchgoers. Those who have grown up
with the "lasare" songs find it difficult to bear with
them in other versions....

Slowly but surely the demand for a more refreshing choral singing has won its way into the churches
--thanks, naturally, to purposeful endeavor on the
part of church musicians. The tempo of the chorales
has increased stage by stage, so that the psalms are
now often sung twice as fast as the case was thirty
years ago. In the new appendix to the chorale book
approved September 9, 1964, the rhythm to the chorales have been altered to the extent that they are near
to the ideals of Reformation times. The churches will
presumably encounter great difficulties before they
learn to sing rhythmically. As an example can be
mentioned the well-known "A Mighty Fortress is our
God," which in its old and now renewed form has become a declamatory "visa," quite different from the
straightened chorale, which generations of school
children have had to learn for future religious purpose....

It was noted above that youth relates itself to participation in church music entirely differently now than
in former times. Thereby some of the traditional
forms of expression take on a changed character.
Negro spirituals and alternate singing takes the place

of what formerly was called choir song and solo.
Bach is taken as a good example for "swing" also in
the church. The question is, moreover, if it isn't
Bach, who has attracted young people into the realm
of church music? The old Thomas chanter is even
today an unbelievably vital musician. His polyphonic
music is to young ears more attractive than the homo-
phonic pre- and postludiums of later epochs. The
linear music of Bach sharpens the mind and the rhythm is wholly in class with that which is put forth
by the masters of jazz music. Many "converted" jazz
musicians is a testimony to the fact that the path to
classical music proceeds from pop music via Johan
Sebastian Bach. This is a good recommendation for
the 18th century music composer who never neglected
to write "Solo Deo Gloria"--To God alone glory--on
all his manuscripts.[1]

What was taking place in 1966 reveals a trend that is
still being witnessed in both the State Church and the Free
Church denominations in Scandinavia. It is prophetic and
points to some very significant developments which have been
taking place right up to the present time. Some trace these
developments to the influence of American contemporary church
music.

State-Church Hymnody

In 1969 a Hymn Book Committee was established by the
State Church of Sweden to promote the writing and compilation of hymns "to meet the needs of the time." Specifically
there was a growing desire for a supplement to the official
hymnal of 1937 which would contain the more contemporary
texts and tunes. There had appeared in 1960 a collection
entitled Kyrkovisor For Barn (Church Songs for Children),
and in 1965, 17 Psalmer (17 Hymns). Several booklets of
hymns were published which were primarily directed to youth.
These were laying the groundwork for further developments
in the publications of state-church hymns. The activity of
the 1969 committee is presented in the preface to 71 Psalmer
och Visor, an experimental booklet of hymns for use in the
State Church of Sweden.

The hymn committee has during its activity on the
one hand compiled existing hymns, and on the other

stimulated writers and composers to new productions.
In the committee's treatment of received material the
texts and the melodies have been put before the members without mentioning the author or composer. The
anonymity has guaranteed a judgment as objective as
possible.

The committee has during its activity considered
as important to publish a small amount of its material
in order to get an idea of how different kinds of texts
and music are received in the churches, what responds
to the needs and what is possible to use. Thus the
experimental booklet came into being. It has no claims
on completion or definitiveness. The committee has in
its hands recommended texts which have not yet received melodies.

There is, in the experimental booklet, both older
and newer material. The committee has tried to give
the material a reasonable breadth, which is marked
in the title, 71 Psalmer och Visor (71 Hymns and
Songs). It is hard to draw a line between the one
and the other kind of spiritual song. This selection
does not cover the whole field where new hymns and
songs are needed according to the committee's view.
In proportion as the experimentary booklet is able to
inspire to new creation of such texts and music it
has filled an important mission.

The booklet is going to be tried within the framework for the liturgical experimental activity, which is
going on in certain churches. It is the hope of the
committee that also other churches will be using this
booklet.[2]

    The hymns are numbered in connection with the official
hymnal, beginning with number 613. Thus this trial booklet
could be used with the older hymnal, Den Svenska Psalmboken
(1937).

    The following free translations of two hymns in 71 Psal-
mer och Visor reveal an almost pietistic flavor in their simplicity and warmth of expression. One can also observe the
close scriptural basis for most of these hymns, which contain
one or two scripture references each.

MARIA SA JUDUS
("Mary", said Judas)
John 12:1-8

1. "Mary" Judas said, "What are you doing,
   when wasting the ointment? "
   "I'm pouring it over the foot of my Master,
   And I wipe it away with my hair," she said,
   "And I wipe it away with my hair."

2. "Mary, Mary you could have sold it
   And a lot of money you could have got.
   You could have bought clothes,
   You could have bought food
   To give to the poor," he said,
   "To give to the poor."

3. "Tomorrow, tomorrow I will think on them,
   Today my Saviour is here.
   I do not know when I will see him again.
   Now, my love I will give him," she said.
   "Now, my love I will give him."

4. "Mary," said Jesus, "The deed that you did
   Will be remembered--Its fragrance it will give.
   As far as the Gospel reaches on earth,
   And as long as I am with you," he said,
   "And as long as I am with you."

5. "You know where I am, there you shall seek me.
   With them that are frozen and ill,
   With starving, homeless, captives am I.
   You can see me and serve me there," he said,
   "You can see me and serve me there."[3]
   --Sydney Carter

ETT KRISTUSBREV TILL VÄRLDEN
(A Letter of Christ to the World)
II Corinthians 3:3-18

1. A letter of Christ to the world is everyone that re-
   ceives
   And in whose heart the Spirit of the Father and Son
   dwells:
   A Letter from eternity is sent out to those

Who have lost themselves and forgotten their Father's
home.

2. A letter sealed with blood about freedom and about
comfort,
Today to a worried and suffering human heart.
A letter that doesn't ask about doubt or faith,
But says: You are loved even if you live far away.

3. A letter that the Spirit writes on hearts, not on stone,
And not with ink but with splendour from God's hidden
glory.
And someone that we meet will have from you, O God,
Relief from his burden, a gleam of light from you.[4]
    --Anders Frostenson

The committee continued its work, which resulted in
the publication of a more "official" trial book entitled Psalmer
och Visor 76. The foreword to this collection describes the
work of the commission and the background and development
of the book.

Preface

Psalmer och Visor 76 is a supplement to our Swedish hymnbook, confirmed by the government July 1,
1976, after the church council of 1975 had been heard.
The supplement may be used together with the Hymnbook of 1937 and the metrical hymnbook of 1939 during the period from the first Sunday in Advent, 1976,
to the Sunday of Judgment, 1986.

Background

Kungliga Majestat (The Government) appointed a
committee in 1969, which assumed the name "1969 ars
psalmkommitte" (The hymnbooks-committee of 1969),
with the commission to work out a supplement to the
Swedish hymnbook to be used together with it until
a revision of the hymnbook has been done. The decision was induced by a petition from the council in
1968. The petition pointed, among other things, to
the strong changes that have happened in many areas,
after the present hymnbook was confirmed in 1937,
and to the need for hymns that in a better way re-
late to the situation in out time. It could also point

to the continued renewing of the hymn singing that
is happening among other countries.

In 1971 the committee published <u>71 Psalmer och
Visor</u> as an example of the goals and characteristics
of the continuing work. Through scientific research
the hymn committee sought to get a picture of how
this material answered the needs of individuals and
churches. The research showed that the material
had been received positively.

Motifs and Motif Areas

The texts carry a stamp of the idea of the pres-
sence of God. Man meets Him in the creation and is
there co-responsible. He meets him in Jesus Christ,
who is often portrayed in the texts as the One who
entered the most severe conditions of humankind and
who carries the suffering and need with us. He also
meets God in the presence of the wind of the Spirit
through the world, as something new and at the same
time, timeless, as something strange and yet well
known. God is present in the complicated and con-
fused patterns, that our life-conditions today offer,
and presents the possibility of hope.

Language and Music

The language in <u>Psalmer och Visor 76</u> is generally
more simple and more direct than in former hymn
poetry. The simplicity has nevertheless not been
pressed so far that important values and shades have
been lost.

In the same manner <u>Psalmer och Visor 76</u> displays
a large breadth in terms of the music. A guiding
principle has been that every text should have its
own melody, as the case usually is in other circumstances. In this way it has been possible to obtain
a greater amount of harmony between text and music,
and every hymn and song acquires its own individual
character. In the choice between simpler and more
complicated melodies the committee has as a rule preferred the former. Yet sometimes has a more complicated music been selected when the character of
the text made this suitable. In some cases alternative
music has been given. The intention has not been to
let the melodies compete, but to give a possibility to

vary the performance according to the situation where
the song is used, it is is sung by a choir or congregation, etc.

   As far as possible the harmony between text and
music has been taken into consideration in that a
translation of a Middle Age hymn has received a Gregorian melody, a free-church revival song has retained its original music, etc. Many of the songs
admit that the singing can be varied in that the choir
and the congregation alternate, refrains have been
added, etc.

The Use

   When Psalmer och Visor, as already the title suggests, clearly shows a breadth in terms of content
and style, so is this an expression of the conviction
that the song compilation ought to express the Christian message in a way that it engages both in breadth
and depth. Therefore, Psalmer och Visor contains
on the one hand text and music that is characterized
by great simplicity and accessibility, and on the other
hand material that is more demanding and satisfies
demands on higher quality.[5]

   Psalmer och Visor 76 was tested for a time in the churches and proved to be popular among the congregations of
the State Church of Sweden. It was the committee's purpose
that it be used in a variety of churches.

   The committee was directed to compile a second part
to Psalmer och Visor 76. The result of the work of this group
is the collection Psalmer och Visor 82, which is the second
part of the supplement to the 1937 hymnal. The Swedish
government has confirmed that the supplement of 1976 and
1982 may be used together with the official hymnal until the
"Sunday of Judgment, 1986." The 1982 supplement became
official for use on the first Sunday of Advent, 1982. The
foreword contains material on the background, contents, and
use of Psalmer och Visor 82. The following selected portions
of the foreword describe the features of the collection.

Background

   In the preface to Psalmer och Visor 76 the committee gives a short summary of the background to

the continuing hymnbook work until the proposition
of the first supplement to the hymnbook was completed.
There it also stated that the committee had as its
commission to work out a second part of such a supplement. In this would also be songs for the church
duties and a selection of Psalms from the book of
Psalm arranged for a presinger/a choir and the congregation....

Content

Psalmer och Visor 82 contains a number of newly
written and newly composed Psalms of the same kinds
as in Psalmer och Visor 76. The church council of
1975, which decided on the proposition of the committee to the first part of the hymnbook's supplement,
saw it important also in the second part of the supplement to give space for such material....

With the Hymns of the Book of Psalms in this
supplement we have made a connection to the striving
within many churches over the world to again use
the Book of Psalms as song texts for the congregations....

As an expression for the growing coöperation
between the churches within the Nordic countries
and with regard to the immigration mostly from Finland this supplement also contains some hymns with
texts in Danish, Norwegian, and Finnish, the latter
with parallel translation to Swedish. By inclusion
of a number of well-known Negro spirituals the affinity
with the world wide church has been underlined. This
is also shown by the many texts that have been inspired by songs from churches in other countries
and through the fact that many melodies have been
picked up from outside our country. In connection
with this we would like to point out that when stated
in the supplement "English text"--"Swedish text,"
this can mean that an English text has given suggestion to the Swedish text but it is not necessarily a
direct translation.

At a special heading the Church council of 1975
gave Läse-Psalmer; Psalmer och Visor 76 (Reading
hymns in Psalmer och Visor 76). The church council
of 1982 was of the opinion that every song and every
hymn ought to be possible to read for example at
personal devotional time and that it therefore would

be misleading to present only certain hymns as reading hymns. The hymnbooks committee shares this view but nevertheless we have in Psalmer och Visor 82 chosen to keep the heading "Läsepsalmer" because we want to follow the disposition in Psalmer och Visor 76.

The Use

The breadth of the material shows that one of the aims with this supplement is to offer songs that can be sung not only at the services but also at other occasions. This is up to the one who makes the choice of the songs to examine what is suitable to use. Because Psalmer och Visor 76 and 82 are to be tested in the congregations "until an extensive revision of the Hymnbook and Metrical Hymnbook is completed" it is urgent that the supplements be used as often as possible. It is only through frequent use of these songs that the presuppositions are created so that later on it can be decided what is wishful to contain in a forthcoming Hymnbook and what can be deleted....

With some songs, e.g. number 850, have alternative notation been made in order to make it possible to sing the song in a more easily played tone for the guitar.[6]

The following are free translations of two hymns contained in Psalmer och Visor 82.

HAN KOMMER, HAN AR NARA
(He Comes, He is at Hand)

1. He comes, He is at hand.
    Our waiting is over.
    Let all the torches be lightened,
    Meet the bridegroom with light.
    Break up, come with me on the journey
    To feast in heaven,
    Come with me, and fire-mark the way,
    Life up your heart, burn.

2. Now the flame of eagerness is blazing,
    Now there is no time for sleep,
    And nobody has time to borrow

What thoughtlessness has forgotten.
And all who are ready go away singing.
Soon only an echo is left
With those who are left.

3. A door that was open far away is shut.
   How deep is the darkness
   When heaven has passed by.
   It is important to grasp
   The time that no one knows.
   Therefore, pray and watch
   Everyday that the Lord gives.[7]
   --Olov Hartman

I ADAM ÄR VI ALLA ETT
(We Are All One in Adam)

1. We are all one in Adam
   And Adam's treachery was ours.
   We hid ourselves among the trees of Eden
   When the Lord looked for us.

2. We fled and then we were lost
   From God and from each other.
   We wanted to have our own way.
   Only solitude we found.

3. With your love you looked for us.
   You have given us your son.
   So help us listen to his voice
   And listening become one.

4. It is not that we have loved you
   But you have loved us.
   And Jesus, the light of the world, came hither
   For salvation, not for judgment.

5. O God, you created us for you,
   Forgive our guilt, our treachery.
   Let penance turn to praise, death to life.
   Let blind eyes see.[8]
   --Martin H. Franzmann

The State Church tradition of Psalmer och Visor 82 is
apparent in the index of hymns in the back of the book. This

index is arranged according to the church year beginning with
the first Sunday in Advent and concluding with Aftonbön
(evening prayers). There is also an index of hymns having
to do with the six-week Lenton season; each hymn is pre-
ceeded by one or two Scripture passages related to that particular hymn.

At this point, a word is in order concerning the contributors to Psalmer och Visor 82. Leading the list of poets
is Anders Frostenson (b. 1906). An ordained minister of
the State Church, he was at one time an associate pastor of
the Gustaf Vasa church in Stockholm. According to J. Irving
Erickson, Frostenson "has been a leading figure in the attempt
to revise the hymnody of the Swedish Church."[9] There are
thirty-three hymns of Frostenson in Psalmer och Visor 82.
No other contributors have as many titles to their credit.
Erickson points out that besides original texts, Frostenson
has revised many of the texts from other sources, and that
"his themes are many, and his lyrics have depth and power."[10]
It is of some significance that nearly all of the contributors
of texts are contemporary poets and authors.

Among the composers represented in this collection one
finds both early and contemporary names. The one with the
most musical settings is Roland Forsberg, one of the leading
musicians in Sweden today.

The first hymn in Psalmer och Visor 76 is No. 613 which
follows No. 612 in the 1937 hymnal of the State Church of
Sweden. As has been pointed out, this numbering is similar
to the 1971 supplement. The first hymn in the 1982 supplement is No. 751, which follows No. 750 in the 1976 volume.
Thus both hymnals may be considered as continuations of the
1937 hymnal. As the committee has indicated, these will be
used until 1986, when it is hoped that a new state-church
hymnal will be completed and will include the best and most
popular from the old hymnal and these very worthy supplements. In many of the church sanctuaries, the supplements
have an equal place of honor in the hymnal racks along with
the 1937 edition, and seem to be used just as frequently.

In Norway the State Church is in process of preparing
a new hymnal which should be completed before 1990. At
the present time, no new hymnal seems to be forthcoming for
the State Church of Denmark.

Free-Church Hymnody

The hymnody of the Free Churches of Sweden has witnessed a similar development to Psalm och Visor in the State Church with the publication of Herren Lever (The Lord Lives.) A committee from five free-church denominations worked on its compilation and publication. The five denominations represented include the Methodist, the Swedish Alliance Mission, the Swedish Baptist Conference, the Swedish Covenant Church and the Örebro Mission (Baptist.) Beside the official hymnbook committee, many others have shown interest in the project by assisting in the selection of hymns and the compilation of indexes. The preface to Herren Lever speaks to it as:

> ... An ecumenically interesting development, in regard to congregation singing within Swedish Christianity. From the 1950's a strong renewing has taken place through the growth of new songs and hymns in different denominations. The new spiritual song is ecumenical and border crossing in regard to its character.[11]

The editors of Herren Lever have expressed the wish that in the future some kind of a common hymn book might be forthcoming since "a great number of new songs in Herren Lever are also in Psalm och Visor 76.... The outline in Herren Lever does to a great extent follow the one in Psalm och Visor 76."[12]

The contents of Herren Lever include both older hymns which were missing for a time in the free-church hymnals, and have been reinstated with a "more lively rhythm" and the more contemporary hymns of both "Swedish and international origin."[13] The latter-type hymns are in the majority in this collection. It has been the intent of the committee that there be hymns that would appeal also to children and young people. The wishes of the committee are summed up in this way:

> It is the hope of the committee that this hymn and songbook will contribute to the renewal of the worship ... and so in that way make the people of God better equipped for service and witnessing among people. The Lord is alive![14]

The hymns in Herren Lever have been divided under these headings:

Praise Songs   The Times and Days of
                                    the Year
Father, Son, and   The Church Year
  Holy Spirit
The Word   The Church in the World
The Church   Future Hope

Well-known authors and poets from the Scandinavian countries are represented in Herren Lever, both from years past as well as those from the contemporary scene. Hymn writers from England and the continent have also contributed to this collection. The committee has deemed it appropriate to include some Negro spirituals and familiar Christmas carols. One is impressed by the great number of hymns which have direct Scripture reference as are also to be found in Psalmer och Visor 76 and 82. There are a sizable number of prayers and biblical texts to be read responsively. An index of poets is included, among whom Anders Frostenson has the most entries. There is also an index of composers and arrangers and a directory of the hymns alphabetically arranged.

Herren Lever is to be found in many free-church sanctuaries. Like Psalmer och Visor in the State Church, it has almost usurped the position of the regular denominational hymnals. The Missionsförbundet has seen fit to have it bound with the latest edition of its official hymnal.

The following free translations of hymns from Herren Lever are representative of its contents.

LOVA HERREN SOL OCH MÅNE
(Worship the Lord, Sun and Moon)

1. Worship the Lord, sun and moon
   All the stars that he has lightened!
   Worship the Lord heavens in high
   Which he has stretched over earth!

2. Worship the Lord, sea that roars
   Fog, rain and wind and snow!
   Worship the Lord, trees and stones
   Flower, leaf, petal and smallest seed!

3. Worship the Lord, mountains and heights,
    Book and spring, stream and river!
    Worship the Lord, bees and birds,
    All the animals on ground and in forest!

4. Worship the Lord in his church!
    He that lives swells among us,
    Everything he gives us. He shall create
    New heavens and a new earth.[15]
                                    --Anders Frostenson

                  DU SEGERN OSS FORKUNNAR
                  (You Proclaim the Victory to us)

1. You proclaim to us the victory
    You have redeemed us
    You our mouths praise
    O Jesus, our defense.
    You have broken the sting of death
    And loosened the bars of the grave
    And brought out the life.

2. You appear in honor
    And the world fills with light.
    Its beams bear relief
    Even in the hour of death.
    Joy is in the swelling of the angels
    On earth joy, reconciliation
    And an immortal hope.[16]
                                    --Erfurt, 1524

        In 1976 the Danish Baptists produced a supplement to
their regular 1960 hymnal entitled Ny Sang (New Song). The
purpose for the publication of Ny Sang is stated in the foreword:

        The addendum has as its main purpose to support
        the hymn singing in the services with some mostly
        newer hymns. Respect has therefore been paid to
        the poetical value and content as well as to their
        singability at the service. The thought is that the
        addendum is distributed together with the hymnbook
        at every service and the numbers in the booklet are
        used. Because the hymnbook has 700 numbers, we
        have found it practical to let the addendum begin
        with number 701.

Of course we hope that the booklet also will find its
way into other circumstances than the service. For
example, it can be used in the homes."[17]

The compilers of this supplement have indicated in the
foreword that certain hymns have been excluded because of
not having the possibility of surviving the test of time. A
certain confidence is expressed that the use of this collection
will be a rewarding and enriching experience for all within
the Baptist fellowship of Denmark.

Ny Sang contains 37 selections from a booklet entitled
Hymns and Songs for our Time published by the High School
of Loegumkloster. The committee for the latter volume acted
as consultants and advisers to the publication committee of
the Baptist book.

Two hymns are here quoted in translation.

NY SANG 711

1. One thing he knew about the way forward:
    That it ended in Jerusalem;
    And as the prophecy said,
    It ended there in cross and death.

2. This way he obediently chose to walk;
    He had a certain goal to reach.
    And no enemy's violence and guile

3. But the cry: "You son of David,
    Have mercy, hear a beggar's prayer,"
    It stopped Jesus on His way,
    He just couldn't say "no."

4. This is our comfort in life and death:
    He was moved by a beggar's poverty and need.
    And all our hope is concealed therein:
    He could not pass by.

5. This is the true love
    That wants the goal and knows the way
    But still stops when it sees
    His neighbor's need, his brother's woe.[18]
                                    --K.L. Aastrup

NY SANG 734

1. Every hour, every day
   Every second, every heart beat
   My life lies in the hands of Jesus.
   He is near, to the end of life.

   He is my life.
   He is the way.
   He is the door to golden heaven.
   He is my life.
   He is Christ light and glory.
   He is Savior mild and dear.
   He is eternity and now
   He is my life.

2. Joyous hours, dark days
   Luck, light--when sorrow comes:
   Whatever happens to me, he will give
   My life will be meaningful.

3. To my neighbor I am sent,
   I have to make Christ known.
   Wherever I go, I gladly confess:
   He turns my life to luck.[19]
                              --Berge Andersen

Sampsalm

        The topic of ecumenicity on several levels of the Church's
ministry has been very popular in recent and present days.
The so-called Ecumenical Movement has reached into many
countries among the various denominations. Ecumenical Praise
is a recent hymnal published in the United States, which has
sought to cross denominational lines. It is described as "fully
catholic in its spread of texts, tunes, poets, and composers...."[20]
The ecumenical spirit is also at work in Sweden among the
various State-Church and Free-Church denominations, and is
expressed in plans for an ecumenical hymnal with the suggested title Sampsalm. Two committees have been at work on
this project, namely, the 1969 committee, which has already
produced Psalmer och Visor 76 and 82, and the newer committee for this latest project. The initiative for Sampsalm was
taken by the Swedish State Church and the Swedish Mission

Covenant. The government of Sweden has authorized the
1969 committee, which is already working on a revision of the
state-church hymnal, to work within the frame of its commission and participate in the production of Sampsalm, an
ecumenical psalmbook. Fifteen denominations are cooperating
in this effort.

Representatives from these denominations will deal primarily with four aspects of the proposed project Sampsalm:
1) the motives or motivations for a common hymnbook; 2) the
possibilities for its publication; 3) what it will contain; and
4) how it will be shaped. Older songs will be reworked, and
new songs will be introduced.

When the work will be completed is uncertain. The
committee hopes that the basic part will be finished in 1985;
then each denomination will have to complete its own supplement. The hope is that each denomination will have its own
Sampsalm sometime before this decade is over. Note: This
information has been translated from correspondence from Mr.
David Rondin, a member of the Sampsalm committee.

An initial publication booklet concerning the proposed
selections for Sampsalm, also includes a commentary concerning the project and a list of participating denominations.
The following churches are involved:

> The Lutheran Free Church (Evangeliska Fosterlands
>   Stiftelsen)
> The Free Baptist Church (Fri Baptisterna)
> The Salvation Army (Fralsningsarmen)
> Similar to Evengelical Free-church (Helgelseförbundet)
> The Catholic Church (Katolska Kyrkan)
> The Liberal Catholic Church (Liberala Katolska Kyrkan)
> The Methodist Church (Metodist Kyrkan)
> The Pentecostal Movement (Pingstrorelsen)
> The Adventist Church (Adventistsamfundet)
> The Swedish Alliance Mission (Svenska Allians Mis-
>   sionen)
> The Swedish Baptist (General) Conference (Svenska
>   Baptist-samfundet)
> The Örebro Mission (Örebromissionen)
> The Swedish Salvation Army (Svenska Fralsningsarmen)
> The Swedish State Church (Svenska Kyrkan)
> The Swedish Covenant Church (Svenska Missionsför-
>   bundet)[21]

With the recent developments in hymnody within the
State-Church as well as the Free-Church denominations of
Scandinavia, a particularly in Sweden, some very interesting
advances have been made toward making people aware of
their heritage in church worship. Hymnody not only unites
individual congregations, but it crosses denominational lines
and makes Christians everywhere aware of their common heritage in Christian praise.

NOTES

1. Aron Hallenberg, "Church Music on the Swing," Vecko-
    Posten (March 17, 1966).
2. 71 Psalmer och Visor (Stockholm: A.B. Tryckmans,
    1971), from the foreword to the book.
3. Ibid., No. 620.
4. Ibid., No. 624.
5. Psalmer och Visor 76 (Lund: Berlings 1981), from the
    foreword.
6. Psalmer och Visor 82 (Arlov: Berlings, 1982), from
    the foreword.
7. Ibid., No. 795.
8. Ibid., No. 813.
9. J. Irving Erickson, Twice Born Hymns (Chicago: Coven-
    ant Press, 1976), p. 94.
10. Ibid., p. 94.
11. Herren Lever (Folköping: Gummessons Tryckeri, 1978),
    translated from the foreword.
12. Ibid.
13. Ibid.
14. Ibid.
15. Ibid., No. 800.
16. Ibid., No. 874.
17. Ny Sang (Baptisternes Forlag, 1976), translation from
    the foreword.
18. Ibid., No. 711.
19. Ibid., No. 734.
20. Ecumenical Praise (Carol Stream, Ill.: Agape, 1977),
    from the foreword.
21. Sampsalms förslag (Älvsjö: Sampsalms Expedition, 1982),
    p. 12.

CHAPTER VII

SCANDINAVIAN FREE-CHURCH HYMNODY
IN AMERICA

Background of the Scandinavian
Free Church in America

The founding and development of the Scandinavian free
churches in America paralleled the development in the countries in Scandinavia. The history of the Baptist and Methodist churches in particular indicates that the establishment
of these groups in Scandinavia was inspired and promoted
by native leaders who had been in America during the pioneer
days of the nineteenth century. Many of these leaders received their education in the United States and returned to
their own countries to aid in the establishment of the free
churches.

The Baptists

Before 1820 there had been little emigration from Sweden,
but between 1820 and 1850, about 11,000 Swedes came to
America. And in the decades following, considerable numbers
found their way to the new country. The first Swedish Baptist congregation in the Old Country was established in 1848,
and in 1852 the first Swedish Baptist Church in Rock Island,
Illinois, was founded under the leadership of Gustav Palmquist. The three Baptist leaders in America, Palmquist,
Anders Wiberg, and F.O. Nilsson, also became pioneers for
the new denomination in Sweden. The Swedish Baptist movement continued to spread westward with the heaviest concentration settling in the northern Mississippi Valley. By 1870
the Baptist numbered 1,500 members among thirty-four congregations, and by 1920 their were 320 congregations from
Maine to California with 22,000 members.

District and national organization was a natural result
of the spread of the Baptist movement among the Swedes.
The first conference of any magnitude was held in 1856 at
Rock Island, and in 1858 the four Swedish congregations in
Minnesota organized themselves into the first Minnesota Baptist Conference. The Swedish Baptist denomination continued
to grow and spread until, at the present time, the entire
constituency numbers in excess of 130,000 members scattered
among the approximately 800 congregations. It is known as
the Baptist General Conference.

The first Norwegian Baptist Church in America was
founded in Ottawa, Illinois, in 1842, at which time the pioneer
Baptist leader, Hans Valder, was baptized into that church.
In 1844 Valder was ordained as the first Norwegian Baptist
minister in America, and in 1853 he migrated to Minnesota
and founded the town of Newburg. The Norwegian Baptist
movement spread among the states of the Middle West.

By 1884 the number of Norwegian Baptists had grown
to approximately 500 members. The Norwegian Baptist Conference of America was organized in Fargo, North Dakota,
in 1910. Statistics show a rather continual growth to the year
1938, aided in great measure by financial help from the American Baptist Convention. The post-war period of the 1940's
witnessed the gradual decline of the Norwegian Baptists as a
group and their amalgamation into the American Baptist denomination.

It has been estimated that during the first thirty-five
years of work among the Baptists of Denmark, one out of
every six or seven of the Baptist converts migrated to America. The first Danish Baptist Church in America was organized in 1855 in Potter County, Pennsylvania, when nine
Baptists from the Vandlose Church in Zealand, Denmark,
banded themselves together for work and worship. They
were aided in this venture by an American Baptist colporter,
Rayer by name. This little church disbanded within three
years when the "call of the west" caused some of the members to move away to greener pastures.

The first permanent Danish Baptist Church in America
was founded in Racine County, Wisconsin, on November 10,
1856, when the small group of twelve charter members broke
away from the American church to form their own congregation.

The statistics of this once thriving group indicate a series
of mergers of the Danish churches with the American and
Swedish conferences, as well as the discontinuance of many
others. As in the Norwegian conference, this disintegration
took place during the postwar period and into the 1950's.

The Methodists

The Methodists developed their second-largest language
group among the Swedes. The beginning of Swedish Methodism stems from the work of Olaf Gustav Hedstrom and the
work on the Bethel Ship in New York Harbor. Hedstrom is
also credited with the establishing of the first Swedish Methodist Sunday school in America. In one decade the Methodist
mission to the Swedes developed from the single vessel and
one missionary to seven missions with seventeen missionaries.

Methodism spread among the Swedish immigrants under
the leadership of Olaf Hedstrom and his brother Jonas. In
1846 Jonas founded a Swedish Methodist society in Victoria,
Illinois, and from this early base, his missionary activites
spread through several Illinois cities and to New Sweden,
Iowa. In 1850 Olaf and Jonas combined their evangelistic
efforts in the Chicago area as a result of which a Chicago
mission was established. From 1870 and 1880 small groups of
Swedish Methodists were begun in Massachusetts, and in 1895
the New England Conference was organized.

Olaf Hedstrom realized the need for more permanent
work in the New York area and in 1972 "went ashore" with
his congregation. The edifice of Swedish Immanuel Church
was dedicated in May of that year.

By the time of World War I, the Swedish Methodist denomination had grown considerably until four annual confer-
erences were held, and the work was carried on by 167 ministers among 19,815 members, with 21,365 enrolled in its Sunday schools.

From this period the membership of the Swedish Methodist denomination dwindled until the post-World War II era
the group gradually dissolved. Most of the members joined
with the churches of American Methodism following the dissolution of the Eastern Swedish Conference in 1936.

Ole Peter Petersen, a young Norwegian sailor, became
associated with the Methodists in Boston in 1843. Greatly influenced by the preaching of Olaf Hedstrom, he returned to
his native Norway, where he did missionary work among his
people. Upon his return to the United States in 1850, he became a local preacher and missionary to the Norwegians in
upper Iowa. From this humble beginning, the work spread
into Wisconsin, Minnesota, and the Pacific Northwest. In 1884
the Norwegian-Danish Methodist Conference was organized,
and by 1932 extensive work was being carried on in thirteen
states besides work in Norway and Denmark. In 1943 this
conference was dissolved, and its members scattered among
the American Methodist Church.

The Evangelical Covenant Church

The Covenant denomination in America was the result
of a growing dissatisfaction among many Swedish immigrants
with the increased ritualism of the Lutheran Augustana Synod.
This situation developed because of the great number of immigrants who had been influenced by Rosenius and his brand
of Pietism which stressed revivalism rather than education
as a means of evangelism. This "Mission Friends," as they
became known because of their establishing of Mission Societies, gradually broke away from the Augustana group. One
of the earliest leaders in this separatist movement was Carl
A. Bjork, a cobbler and soldier, considered by many to be
the founder of the Evangelical Covenant Church in America.
Bjork carried on a ministry of home meetings; as a result, a
group broke away from the Lutheran communion and called
Bjork as their pastor in 1867. This new Mission Society was
the beginning of the Covenant movement. A similar group
was organized in Chicago in 1868. The Evangelical Lutheran
Mission Synod and the Evangelical Ansgar Synod were organized in 1873 and 1874, respectively, as institutions independent of the general Lutheran body. The free-church
spirit characterized both of these groups, and in 1885 in the
home of A.L. Skoog in Chicago, they merged to form the
Swedish Evangelical Mission Covenant Church of America.
At this time the membership consisted of nearly fifty churches
with thirty-eight pastors.

There is no close organizational tie with the Missionsförbund in Sweden, although E.A. Skogsbergh advocated a

similar type organization for the American Covenant. The
Evangelical Covenant Church, as it is now known, has grown
into a denomination similar to size to the Swedish Baptist group.

From primary sources consulted for this study, one is
forced to conclude that the Pentecostal churches of Sweden,
Norway, and Denmark do not have their counterpart as such
among the Scandinavians in America. This is also true of
the Norwegian Misjonsforbund and the Danish Missionsförbund.
Evidently immigrants from among these denominations found
their way into other Scandinavian denominations in America
or their American equivalents. At least no formal denominational organizations are in evidence among these groups at
the present time.

Hymnals of the Scandinavian Free-Churches
In America

Until comparatively recent years, many of the Scandinavian free-church congregations used their native language
in their services. Much to the dismay of the older members
who cherished the native tongue, English has now quite generally supplanted the old languages in public services of worship. The ties with the mother countries have been maintained, however, through the use of the favorite hymns with
their memories of bygone days in the native land.

Scandinavian Baptist Hymnals

Among the Swedish Baptists in America, Pilgrims-Sånger,
published by the Palmquists in Sweden in 1859, was a favorite
for many years. It was used in America until the close of
the nineteenth century.

As far as can be ascertained, Sions Basun, published
in 1876, was the first hymnal to be published for use among
Swedish Baptists in America. Prepared by John A. Peterson,
it was a "collection of spiritual songs for public use and private edification of God's children on the way to the heavenly
Zion," according to the inscription on the title page. The
foreword to the book states the purposes for its publication:

Many who love the truth have felt a great need to
truth-consonant songs suitable for special occasions,

like baptismal services, the Lord's Supper, etc. In
view thereof the publisher has been urgently requested
by a number of brethren to undertake this task. But
a collection of only such songs as those mentioned
above would be of far too limited in content to become
of general service and edification. Therefore, the
publisher and his advisors in the matter thought it
best to compile a songbook which could be used, not
only on special occasions but also in public services
and in circumstances of every kind. The editor has
therefore endeavored to make it as rich in subject
matter and varied in content as scope has allowed
and his ability has made possible. About 100 songs
are new, some are translated from English, and the
rest are a selection of the most spiritually rich songs
that have been available in the Swedish language.[1]

Second in order of publication for the Swedish Baptists
was the hymnal Nya Pilgrims Sånger, edited by A.P. Ekman
and published in Stromsburg, Nebraska, in 1887. As the
name indicates, it was meant to be a supplement to Palmquist's
Pilgrims-Sånger. In 1888 Eric Wingren, editor of the Swedish
Baptist organ Nya Wecko-Posten, compiled and published Fridsbasunen, which served the congregations for several years.

Pilgrimens Lof, edited by Olof Bodien and Frank Peterson, was published in 1894. Both men were pastors of Bethlehem Baptist Church of Minneapolis at one time. The purpose
for its publication in set forth by the editors in its preface:

A special need of a book with only well known and
good songs has prompted the publication of this songbook. No claim for originality is made. The endeavor
has been to select only such songs as by the public
have long been well known, and have been loved and
appreciated by God's children in many nations and
languages.

Nearly half of the number of selected from the immortal
Pilgrim Songs which in earlier days in such an es-
sential way have contributed to the progress of the
Baptist work.

These songs have become so integrated with our emotions and experiences that they cannot without great
loss be left aside in our meetings.

The second half compromises a selection from "Gospel
Hymns." These are now known nearly over the whole
world, and have been a means through the Holy Spirit
to produce the world's greatest revivals. Most any
preacher or song leader is amazed when he realizes
how few are the songs that are put to use during
the year--perhaps headly fifty in number.

The melodies in this book are generally known and
when the songs are taken from sources already indicated the music is readily available.

At the meeting of the Ministerial Association in Minneapolis in November, 1893 this song collection was
scrutinized by a committee appointed for that purpose
and unanimously approved and recommended for publication. [2]

The American Baptist Publication Society published the
next two hymnals for use among Swedish Baptists in America.
Valder Hymner was released in 1896 and Triumf-Sånger in
1900. Their respective forewords indicate the intent and purpose for their publication.

"Valda Hymner" is turned over herewith to the respected public. Since it has been of concern to us
to obtain as good songs as possible with appealing
melodies easily sung, we have endeavored to select
songs that will in those respects fulfill such requirements.... A large part of these have been selected
from Swedish song books kindly placed at our disposal,
while others are from the outstanding American authors,
like W.H. Doane, Robert Lowry, D.B. Towner, Ira D.
Sankey et. al., to whom we are exceedingly grateful
for their letting us use the songs. For the excellent
translation of the songs Prof. Hjalmar Edgren is surety.

With an ardent wish that the Lord's blessing may
attend the singing of these songs in church, Sunday
school and home "Valda Hymner" is herewith sent
forth in our common Master's Name to be sung for
His glory. [3]

Triumph Songs makes its appearance with one claim,
namely that it will, at least to a small extent, fill a

widely felt need for a song book suitable for our Sunday schools and young people's meetings. With exception of a few originals and some songs borrowed
from Swedish song books published at earlier dates,
this collection constitutes a careful selection from
various song books in the English language....

If Triumph Songs are intended in the first place for
Sunday school and young people's meetings, we are
nevertheless convinced that they can also prove a
blessing when used in family worship, at prayer-
meetings and on any occasion when God's people come
together for worship.... [4]

The first publication of any magnitude undertaken by
the Swedish Baptists in America was the hymnal Nya Psalmisten, issued in 1903. The book contains 675 hymns of both
the old and new variety; of the former type many were included which had provided spiritual inspiration to the early
Baptist pioneers. Many Swedish-American authors are represented such as A.L. Skoog, Nils Frykman, and Olof Bodien.
The purpose for its compilation and the scope of its contents
are presented in its foreword:

The song book Nya Psalmisten is herewith made over
to the public. The need of a song book for our
churches has been felt for a considerable time. The
dear old "Pilgrims-sångerna" accompanied us when we
came to this country. The tunes of those old songs
re-echoed throughout the soul ever since childhood.
Other collections of songs, most of them from English,
were tried out. Private persons and societies edited
and published song books which served us during the
course of years. All these well-known collections of
songs have proved a great blessing to the Christian
church in its spiritual work. The Swedish Baptist
churches of America stood ready to lay plans for the
observance of its fifty years of existence as a denomination and now deemed the Conference mature
enough to publish a song book of its very own.

In the selection of songs the Committee felt itself
obliged to comply with the strong wish generally expressed by the rank and file and try to recover for
our use the old pithy songs in our Swedish language.

In the next place it has been our concern to choose
from the songs translated from other languages,--songs
that during many years have been cherished by our
song-loving people. Furthermore, we have introduced
translations from English not sung in Swedish by our
people before.[5]

The book met with hearty response from the whole denomination and was used until recent years when the Swedish
language was abandoned in the public services of worship.
It went through several editions and also proved itself successful as a business enterprise.[6]

A small hymnal called Fridröster was published in 1910,
intended especially for use in revival and prayer meetings,
Sunday school, and the home. Edited by Olof Bodien, G.
Arvid Hagstrom, and Olof Hedeen, it contained 278 hymns
including a brief supplement of English hymns. The inroads
of the English language among the Swedish Baptists is alluded
to in the preface.

> Fridsröster is a new song selection which is now
> placed in the hands of the Swedish general public.
> It is meant, in the first instance, for use in young
> people's meetings, Sunday schools, and revival meet-
> ings, but is also suitable for spiritual devotional
> meetings in a more general way.
>
> During recent years a considerable number of valuable
> and popular songs have appeared in the English lang-
> uage, which songs have heretofore been published in
> Swedish dress, and of those that have been put forth,
> the Swedish array of many have only been sorry per-
> versions of our beautiful mother tongue, not to speak
> purely practical requirements.
>
> The undersigned, who at the behest of the Swedish
> Baptist General Conference of America were entrusted
> with the task of gathering and publishing of these
> songs have taken pains to select the best and most
> popular new songs in English available, even though
> quite high prices had to be paid for permission to
> use them. "Padding material," which is so common,
> even in song books, we have carefully steered clear
> of. Most of the translations have been performed by

the Swedish writer, Ader, well known even on this
side of the Atlantic, who, we believe has succeeded
in rendering the songs in flowing Swedish, while at
the same time retaining the poetic flight of the original. Beside these translations, which constitute
the greater number in the book, a considerable number of familiar songs, which in our view ought not
to be left out, have also been included in the selection. A few songs, specifically composed for Fridsröster have also been included. For the excellent
arrangement of the music the well known name of
A.L. Skoog is a sure guaranty. We have also found
it expedient to include a number of songs in English
since especially our Swedish-American youth and our
Sunday schools love to vary the singing with using
the language of our country. [7]

In 1925 the Swedish Baptists published the New Hymnal,
which was a first attempt at an English song book. The most
important successor to Nya Psalmisten was the Gospel Hymnal
published in 1950. This was accomplished through the help
and cooperation of the Rodeheaver Hall-Mack Company, which
supplied plates which had been used previously in the publication of an interdenominational hymnal. Twenty-six translations of well-known and best-loved Swedish hymns were
inserted into the previous publication, and thus the Gospel
Hymnal actually became a revision of the earlier one. The
mechanics of compilation and publication were known to few
of the constituency, and this volume became practically the
official hymnal of the Baptist General Conference for a time.
Several other denominations adopted it for use in their churches, although its contents left much to be desired as far as
quality is concerned.

The Norwegian Baptists have used the following hymnals
which are listed in chronological order:

Psalmer og Aandelige Sange was published by L.J.
Hauge in 1867, containing 543 hymns.

Missionsharpen, containing 530 songs, was published
in 1870.

Den Syngende Evangelist, compiled by H.A. Beishen-
bach in 1877, contained 150 songs.

Harpetoner, contained 115 songs, some of which were
in English. It was published in 1887 by Rev. P.H.
Dam.

Salme og Sangbok published in 1887 became the first
official hymnal of the Norwegian Baptists. It contained 645 songs and remained the official hymnal
for many years.

Several smaller hymnals of private publication were
forthcoming in succeeding years. Among these were
the Vakkelsharpen of O.H. Skotheim published in
1888, and Sangens Tid published in 1925 by Rev.
O. Breding.

Evangelisten, the official hymnal of the Baptists in
Norway was in use by Norwegian-American Baptists
until the close of World War I.[8]

In the beginning of Baptist work among the Danish-
speaking people, several hymnals from Denmark were used
among the congregations. These included Brorson's Troens
Rare Klenodie, Honningblomsten by Peter Sorenson, and Kob-
ner's Troens Stemme. As the need grew for songs peculiar
to the Danish-American tradition, the following hymnals were
issued:

Psalmer og Andelige Sange (Psalms and Spiritual
Songs) by L. Jorgensen (1867)

Missionsharpen (The Mission Harp), a large hymnbook with 530 songs, edited by N.P. Lange, O.C.
Jensen, H.A. Reichenbach. A revised edition was
published in 1873.

Gospel Hymns and Sacred Songs (Moody and Sankey)
translated by P.H. Dam.

Den Syngende Evangelist (The singing Evangelist)
by H.A. Reichenbach. This was a very popular
song book; it was published in five editions.

Salme og Sangbog (Psalms and Songs), containing
645 hymns, was compiled by an officially appointed
committee.... The first edition of this hymn book
appeared in 1887.[9]

The first official hymnal of the Danish Baptists in America was Psalme og Sangbog published in 1887. Practically all

of the churches made use of this hymnal over a period of
many years. The account of its compilation is gleaned from
the foreword to the hymnal.

> Under the steady progress made in the Mission among
> our people in this land during the course of the last
> thirty years, we have constantly grown away from
> the psalm books which have been given out among us
> and have made use of newer songs translated from
> English, a situation due to a general longing for the
> old more kernel-filled and powerful psalms, which
> are more suited as expression of various experiences
> of Christians as well as to the different phases of
> general worship....
>
> As the book now lies finished, containing 645 psalms
> and songs which--with the exception of a certain num-
> ber, written or translated for the book, most of them
> by H.A. Reichenbach--practically all have been taken
> from the following to us well-known Psalm and song
> collections, viz: "Troesstemmen," "Missions-Harpen,"
> "Hosanna," "Harpetoner," "Den syngende Evangelist,"
> "R. Nielsens Salmebog" and P.H. Dam's translation
> of Gospel Hymns. A considerable number of songs
> taken from the other books taken is unchanged, except
> for some unimportant grammatical and stylistic correc-
> tions or elimination of stanzas.[10]

The last hymnal of the Danish Baptists was published
in 1916, in answer to the need for a smaller song book which
could be used in evangelistic meetings. The foreword indicates the assignment made in the committee and the hymnal
which resulted.

> In the year 1887 was issued "Salme og Sangbog,"
> the first song book with notes among the Danish Bap-
> tists. Both to content and arrangement it represented
> an honest attempt to satisfy the continually growing
> demand among us for such a book. It has served our
> denomination these many years and will continue to
> do so for the future, especially as church song book.
> But there has for a long time been a desire among us
> for a smaller song book especially for use in our so
> called "Evangelistic meetings," one that could more
> easily be carried from place to place and be sold

at a lesser price.   In the execution of this assignment
the Committee has had in view the selecting of songs
with genuine Evangelical content, in good Danish language and with appropriate melodies.[11]

Hymnals of the Evangelical
Covenant Church

During the early years of the Mission Friends, no hymnals were used because of the poor financial status of this
young denomination.   Some churches used Ahnfelt's Sånger
and Lammets Lof, as well as the Baptist hymnal Pilgrimssånger.
One of the early publications by the Mission Synod was Samlingssånger issued in 1876.   In 1887 the Swedish Andeliga
Sånger merged with Samlingssånger and bore the double title
of both books.

The first hymnal of significance in the Covenant church
was the Evangelli Basun published for the first time in 1880
by E.A. Skogsbergh and A.L. Skoog.   The editors borrowed
freely from the old Swedish hymnals, such as Joel Blomqvist's
Sabbathklockan and Fridstonerna.   Several selections were
taken by permission from Rutström's Sions Nya Toner, as
well as other popular Swedish authors.

The largest hymnal to date among the Swedes was the
collection known as Sionsharpan, published in 1890 by the
Missions Friends' Publishing Company.   This became the standard hymnal of the Covenant churches to a greater or lesser
degree.   It contained 700 numbers arranged according to title
and content.

Jubelklangen, published by Skoog and Hultman in 1896,
is one of the several private hymnal publications by members
of the Covenant denomination.   It was designed primarily as
a youth hymnal and for use in the Sunday schools.   The popularity of the guitar is seen in the insertion of symbols to
aid in the accompaniment of the songs.

The Svenska Söndagsskolans Sångbok of 1908 was published by the Eastern Sunday School Association for use in
the Covenant Sunday schools.   N.J. Rossell's Nya Sånger
for Söndageskolan was purchased by the editorial committee
and became the nucleus for the new hymnal.   Arrangements
were made to include well-known songs by Skoog, Hultman,
Frykman, and others.

Since the organization of the Covenant Church in 1885, there have been what may be considered eight official hymnals. The first of these publications was the Sions Basun collection of 1909, compiled in celebration of the silver anniversary of the denomination. Such well-known composers and hymnists as Nils Frykman, A.L. Skoog, and J.A. Hultman were on the editorial committee. It contained over 700 hymns, one-fourth of which were written by Swedish-American Covenanters and 123 by Nils Frykman. Approximately one-fourth of the hymns were from Covenant authors and sources from Sweden.

De Ungas Sångbok, issued in 1914, contained many songs from Sions Basun as well as other well-known and well-liked Swedish and American song books. It was intended for use not only by young people but also by primary children, for whom appealing songs were included also. It numbered 264 songs, forty of which had English texts.

Missions Hymns of 1921 was the result of the desire of the Covenant church for its own English hymnal. In spite of factions which developed concerning a purely English collection, the hymnal was prepared under the editorship of A.L. Skoog. In the total of 223 hymns, thirty were translations from the Swedish language. The hymnal met with enthusiastic response and during the first year of publication sold 11,000 copies.

In 1931 the Covenant Hymnal was published under contract with the Hope Publishing Company. It contained 476 hymns; of this number, thirty-six were translations of Covenant hymns from America and Sweden. A number of hymns were written by younger members of the American Covenant. It was enthusiastically received in the denomination at large.

At the annual meeting of the Evangelical Covenant Church of America in 1944, it was recommended that a revision of the 1931 hymnal be attempted. A standard of selection was set up by a rather large editorial committee, and of the nearly 2,000 suggested hymns, 600 were chosen for inclusion. The format of the hymnal plus careful editing account for its appeal to the denomination. The first edition of the new Covenant Hymnal was issued in 1951 with a sale of 25,000 copies, followed by a second edition in 1951. In the early years of its use, over 70,000 copies were sold.

In 1973 the Evangelical Covenant Church of America

published a monumental hymnal for use by that denomination.
The 1951 hymnal had been in use for over twenty years, and
the time was ripe for a new tool for public worship. Known
as The Covenant Hymnal, it contains a wide variety of the
rather old and the rather new hymns. The preface to this
new publication describes its contents and the arrangement
of the materials.

> Each new generation responds to God in its own way
> and looks for new or different modes of expression
> in its worship. While The Hymnal (1950) has served
> us well for over twenty years, it is appropriate that
> a new hymnal be published--one that reflects the
> changing times. This is not to say that The Coven-
> ant Hymnal (1973) is entirely new; a little less than
> two-thirds of the songs in the present hymnal are
> retained, and many other traditional hymns from
> various sources have been included. In short, the
> Hymnal Commission has aspired to a volume containing
> the best from the past along with something new and
> fresh. The work was facilitated by the recent ap-
> pearance of several excellent new hymnals and by
> the publication of the Hymn Society of America.

> All texts were carefully examined by the editorial
> committee of the Commission. In some cases altera-
> tions were made to improve the lyrical quality and
> clarify the meaning. Several of the new texts were
> written or translated by Commission members. Most
> of the translations from the Swedish have been re-
> tained--with slight revisions--and several more have
> been added. It seems that the Covenant has become
> the custodian of this rich heritage.

> Some of the familiar texts have been given new or
> different melodies. Many of the contemporary texts
> have familiar tunes though some have new settings.
> Several of the new tunes have been composed by mem-
> bers of the Commission's music committee. Other
> musical settings have been reworked or reharmonized,
> and in some cases transposed to lower, more singable
> keys. When a tune appears more than once, two dif-
> ferent keys have been given in most cases. In order
> to increase the book's usefulness, notations have been
> provided on many pages referring to alternate tunes

and different keys or harmonizations. Several unison
settings have been included as well as descant arrangements.

Attention is directed to the enlarged section of service
music which provides a wide variety of old and new
material suitable for choral and congregational introits
and responses. At the beginning of this section there
is a supplemental list of hymns also suitable for use
as service music.

It is believed that the expanded section of Worship
Aids will enhance the usefulness of the hymnal as
a worship book, and will therefore commend itself to
pastor and laymen alike. Although the emphasis is
on biblical selections, both historic and contemporary
materials are included. The main divisions of this
section are as follows: Scripture Readings, Other
Worship Resources, and the Lectionary.

Historically, Covenanters have valued freedom and
variety in worship while also recognizing the need
for an order which is "reverent, festive, and beautiful." In keeping with this tradition, the Worship
Aids Committee has re-affirmed the principle of freedom by refusing to move in the direction of liturgical
uniformity. It has furthermore re-affirmed the need
for good order by providing a variety of materials
which will allow both pastor and congregation to develop ways of worshipping that will be edifying to
the whole body. [12]

For those interested in Scandinavian hymnals, there is
to be found in the new Covenant Hymnal a rich treasure of
hymns from all of the Scandinavian countries. About forty
Scandinavian poets and composers are represented in its contents with numerous selections, translations, and musical
settings. The number of Scandinavian hymns in the 1973
Covenant Hymnal is indicative of the interest maintained by
the Evangelical Covenant denomination in its rich Scandinavian
heritage in hymnology.

Hymnals of the Swedish Methodists

The Swedish Methodists used as their first hymnal the

Church Book of the Church of Sweden, supplemented by songs
by Rutstrom, Ahnfelt and others. This was eventually replaced by a collection of hymns of Victor Witting.[13] Psalmer
och Sånger compiled by Jacob Bredberg was the second collection of their very own used by the Swedish Methodist congregations. Published in 1862, it contained 700 hymns, among
them translations from the regular Methodist hymnal and familiar Swedish hymns. The hymnal of 1884, the Metodist Epis-
kopal Kyrkans Svenska Psalmbok consisted of 662 selections,
including several translations. A second edition, somewhat
revised, appeared in 1892.

The last official hymnal of the Swedish-American Methodists, known as the Psalmbok, was published in 1904 and remained the hymnal of the denomination until its dissolution in
1936. The foreword to the hymnal states its intended use
and presents a description of its contents.

> Herewith is presented to the Swedish Methodist chur-
> ches and its individual members a new Psalm and Song
> Book, designed for their use to serve in guidance
> and edification at public and private occasions of
> worship ...

> Of the six hundred psalms and songs found in this
> edition about one half of them come from the psalm
> book published in 1884 and are now revised in greater
> or lesser degree. The rest are partly new songs by
> Swedish authors, not published before, partly selec-
> tions from formerly published collections, and partly
> translations from the English language of songs which
> to the melodies are being sung even today by millions
> of Christians in all parts of the world. The transla-
> tions and selecting has been done by brethren suit-
> able thereto, who have spared no effort to satisfy
> every reasonable demand.[14]

In addition to the church hymnals, the Methodists issued
several song books for use by the Sunday school and youth
groups. In chronological order the list includes:

David's Harpa, 1887
Herde Stämman, 1893
Jubel Sånger, 1902
Unga Röster, 1909
Evangeliska Sånger, 1916[15]

Miscellaneous Collections

The following is a list of hymnals arranged in chronological order of publication which has been made available
for this study. Many of them are of private origin and were
compiled to meet the needs of all groups in the free-church
tradition.

Andeliga Sånger--(Ahnfelt), 1881
Cymbalen (Jultman), 1885
Sånger till Jesu Ära--(Witting), 1886
Herde-Rösten--(Davis), 1892
Nya Sånger For Söndags-Skolan, (Russell), 1892
Bornenes Harpa, 1899
Fridsbasunen, 1899
Svenska Söndagsskolans Sångbok, 1908

The foreword to Sions Seger-Sånger, published in 1911
by Evangel Publishing Company of St. Paul Park, Minnesota,
expresses the general sentiment of many of the publishers of
these collections:

Among the saints in the evening time of this reformation a keen need has been felt for a song book
containing only such songs as can be sung with the
spirit and with the understanding (I Cor. 14:15).
Therefore God has laid it upon the hearts and conscience of a few brothers and sisters to collect, translate, and compose these songs, new and old from song
treasures....

"Sions Seger-Sånger" is herewith offered to the public with a prayer to God that its evangelical messages
may reach many a lost child and bring same to the
Father's house, and that all God's dispersed children
may through its joyful sound be led away from Babel
and home to Zion--God's assembly. [16]

The final phase of this study of Scandinavian hymnody
involved a perusal of the hymnals of some of the major denominations in America, as well as those of inter-denominational
vintage. These hymnals were examined in order to determine
to what extent Scandinavian hymns of both the state-church
and free-church traditions have been selected by the editorial committees of American hymnals. Both texts and musical
settings have been included in this particular phase of the
study.

American Lutheran hymnals have drawn most heavily
on hymns of Scandinavian origin. The Hymnal and Order of
Service of the Evangelical Lutheran Augustana Synod published in 1925 contains a significant number of Swedish texts
and tunes. This is a reflection of the denomination's strong
Swedish background. From among the state-church hymnists,
thirty-three authors are represented, with the hymns of J.O.
Wallin numbering thirty. The pietistic, free-church contributions include three hymns each by Mrs. Berg, Mrs. Posse,
Rosenius, and Rutström. Two texts from Ahnfelt's Sånger
have been included. Musical settings and melodies include
five by Ahnfelt and one from his Sånger, as well as entries
by Blomqvist, Gustaf Düben, Prince Gustaf of Sweden, Haeffner, F.G. Hedberg, Peter Johnson, Israel Kolmodin, J.F.
Lagergren, and Lindeman, in addition to a sizable number
of other original settings and arrangements of Scandinavian
folk songs.

The Concordia Hymnal of 1932, which was used primarily by the Lutheran Free Church congregations, contains
a number of selections of Scandinavian origin. In the general category of hymnists, including American Scandinavians,
forty-three authors are listed in the index. Composers number eighteen with Ludwig Lindeman represented by thirty-
four musical settings. Thirteen original poems by Grundtvig
are included among the contents of this hymnal. Among the
pietistic and free-church authors, Brorson is represented by
ten original texts and two translations. One text each from
Mrs. Berg, Mrs. Posse, and Hans Hauge and three poems by
Rosenius were chosen for this collection. Three of the tunes
of Ahnfelt have been used as musical settings.

The Service Book and Hymnal of 1958 which was compiled for use by eight Lutheran Church bodies contains fifty-
four entries from both state- and free-church sources. These
include forty-two poems by Scandinavian authors, as well as
twenty-four melodies either of folk variety or by native composers. Only a few texts are by pietistic or free-church
authors such as Mrs. Berg and Hans Brorson. J.O. Wallin's
hymns are five in number.

The Lutheran Book of Worship of 1978 contains 10 hymns
from the Norwegian tradition and 12 selections from Swedish
hymnody. While there are considerably less entries in this
latest Lutheran hymnal than in the 1958 publication, the interest in Scandinavian hymnody has still been maintained.

The latest Methodist Hymnal of America contains only one song of Scandinavian origin, the well-known "Children of the Heavenly Father" by Mrs. Berg.

The Presbyterian Hymnal of 1933 includes one text by Laurentius Laurenti: "Rejoice, Rejoice, Believers" and two by J.O. Wallin: "We Worship Thee, Almighty Lord" and "Where Is the Friend For Whom I'm Ever Longing?" The Danish three-fold "Amen" is also contained in this hymnal.

Christian Worship, the hymnal of the American Baptists and the Disciples of Christ, contains only two selections from Scandinavia: Christian Ostergaard's "That Cause Can Neither Be Lost Nor Strayed," with its corresponding tune of Danish folk-song origin, and Ingemann's "Through the Night of Doubt and Sorrow."

American hymnals, particularly those with a preponderance of nineteenth-century "gospel songs," have contained Scandinavian hymns of the free-church variety in increasing numbers in recent years. Favorite Hymns of Praise, published in 1967 by the Hope Publishing Company of Chicago, contains the ever-popular "How Great Thou Art" by Carl Boberg and "He the Pearly Gates Will Open," written by Fred Blom. In other hymnals of this type, one is likely to find one or two selections of similar character from the Scandinavian countries.

The Foursquare Service Hymnal of 1957 contains one musical setting by Lindeman and a text by J.O. Wallin. It would seem that since T.B. Barratt received his inspiration for the Pentecostal movement in Norway from Aimee Semple McPherson, several of his hymns should appear in this collection. Such is not the case.

Crusader Hymns, published in 1966 by the Hope Publishing Company, includes quite a concentration of Scandinavian hymns. Compiled by Donald Hustad and Cliff Barrows musicians with the Billy Graham team, it represents a trend toward the use of more hymns and gospel songs from Scandinavia, particularly Sweden. For clarity, the hymns with their authors, composers, or sources are listed:

> "He the Pearly Gates Will Open"--Fred Blom and Elsie
> Ahlven-Sundeen

"In Heaven Above"--Laurentius Laurentii Laurenius
(Norwegian Folk Melody)

"Thanks to God"--August Storm and J.A. Hultman

"How Great Thou Art"--Carl Boberg (Swedish Melody)

"No Other Plea"--(Norwegian Folk Melody)

"Children of the Heavenly Father"--Lina Sandell Berg
(Swedish Melody)

"I With Thee Would Begin"--Translation from the
Swedish by Samuel Wallgren; musical setting by
W. Theodor Boderberg

This trend is to be seen in more recent publications
in American hymnody such as: Hymns for the Family of God,
a recently published nondenominational hymnal, includes within
its contents about ten selections from Scandinavian sources.
These include both texts and melodies. Hymns for the Living
Church, a 1974 nondenominational hymnal contains about twelve
texts or melodies from the past, as well as from one or two
contributors still living.

NOTES

1. Sions Basun, ed. John A. Peterson (Minneapolis: Tryckt
        i "Budstikkens" Tryckeri, 1976), from the foreword.
2. Pilgrimens Lof, ed. Olof Bodien, Frank Peterson (Min-
        neapolis: Svenska Baptist Literatur sallskaps Forlag,
        1894), from the foreword.
3. Valda Hymner (Philadelphia: A.J. Rowland, 1896), from
        the foreword.
4. Triumf-Sånger, ed. Henry Nelson, G.A. Hagstrom (Phila-
        delphia: The American Baptist Publication Society,
        1900), from the foreword.
5. Nya Psalmisten (Minneapolis: Skoog and Selander, 1903),
        from the foreword.
6. Adolf Olson, A Centenary History (Chicago: Baptist Con-
        ference Press, 1952), p. 510.
7. Fridstroster, ed. Olof Bodien, G.A. Hagstrom, Olof He-
        deen (Minneapolis: DeLander Music Printing Co.,
        1910), from the foreword.
8. Peter Stiansen, History of the Norwegian Baptists in Amer-
        ica (Philadelphia: The Norwegian Baptist Conference

of America and The American Baptist Publication Society, 1939), p. 304.

9. Seventy-Five Years of Danish Baptist Missionary Work
    in America (Philadelphia: The Danish Baptist General
    Conference of America, The American Baptist Publi-
    cation Society, 1939), p. 271.
10. Salme-og-Sangbog, N.P. Jensen, et al. (Chicago: 1887)
    from the foreword.
11. W.J. Andreasen, et al., ed. Missions Sange (Philadelphia:
    ed. The Danish Baptist General Conference of America,
    1916), from the foreword.
12. The Covenant Hymnal (Chicago: Covenant Press, 1973),
    from the preface.
13. Stephenson, op. cit., p. 259.
14. Svenska Psalmbok, ed. Henry W. Warren, et al. (New
    York, Cincinnati: The Methodist Book Concern,
    1904), from the foreword.
15. Hjortsvang, op. cit., p. 81.
16. Sions Seger-Sånger, ed. August Davis (St. Paul Park,
    Minn.: Evangel Publishing Co., 1911), from the
    foreword.

• CONCLUSION

From the time of the Reformation to the present day, the history of hymnody in Scandinavia parallels the history of the Church. The Church in Sweden can trace its hymnody from the contributions of Olavus Petri in the early years of the Reformation to the modern-day hymnists such as Wendell-Hansen of the Baptists, and Carl Boberg, the Mission Covenant poet. Other leaders, both within the State Church and the pietistic, free-church groups, have contributed to the total hymnody of Scandinavia through the last several centuries. As the free-church denominations came into being, there developed an intense interest in producing a body of hymns peculiar to each group which would enhance corporate and private worship.

As has been previously mentioned, hymns of the smaller denominations found their way into many state-church hymnals. Pietistic influence may be seen in the hymns of State-church hymnists such as Kingo, Brorson, and Grundtvig in Denmark and most significantly in the hymns of Wallin and Mrs. Berg in Sweden. The interpretation of the basic Christian doctrines similar to the pietistic, free-church groups, and the emphasis on the mystical element in Christianity and personal piety are reflected in the hymns of those writers who never left the confines of the State Church.

Not only have the free-church emphases appeared in the hymns of state-church hymnists, but as Chapter V has pointed out, there has been considerable reciprocal borrowing between the two branches of the Church in Scandinavia. The free churches in particular have availed themselves of the rich heritage of state-church hymns for use in their particular, official hymnals. The Danish Baptists, for instance, borrowed quite extensively from state-church hymnists in the compilation of their hymnal, while the Mission Covenant hymnal

of Denmark contains only a token number of hymns from
state-church sources other than Brorson, Grundtvig and
Ingemann.

Progress marks the present status of hymnody of the
major free-church groups as well as the state-church in the
Scandinavian countries. The fact that new hymnals have
appeared in comparatively recent years among these denominations lends credence to this assertion. Many of these hymnals
are of considerable size and proportion, and a considerable
number of selections of the "Gospel Song" type from American
poets of the nineteenth and early twentieth centuries are contained in several of them. Texts from British authors such
as Cowper, Newton, Watts, and Wesley have been used in
significant numbers.

Herren Lever in Sweden and Ny Sang in Denmark attest
to the interest in the Free Churches in the more contemporary
"congregation oriented" hymns for public worship. The Psalm
och Visor supplements to the State-church hymnal of Sweden
indicate the same trend. There are indications that other
denominations in Norway and Denmark are in process of producing similar hymnals to those published recently in Sweden.

As the Scandinavian denominations of the free-church
tradition became established in America, the development of
hymnody among them and the publication of a variety of hymnals followed naturally. Each of the major denominations has
had its traditional hymns of Scandinavian and Scandinavian-
American origin, particularly in the early years of its history.
The Baptist and the Mission Covenant denominations developed
a strong hymnody and showed a continuing interest in its use.
As the dates of publication show, the Methodists seem to have
lost interest in having a denominational hymnal early in the
present century.

The only group in America which has maintained a
strong interest in its heritage in hymnody is the Evangelical
Covenant Church. While the Baptist General Conference has
produced no official hymnal, distinctly its own, since 1925,
the Evangelical Covenant denomination has published two
within the last twenty-two years. This denomination at the
present time is the only one of the Scandinavian-American
origin which is carrying on an official traditional hymnody of
its own. One reason for this might be that the Evangelical

Covenant Church has maintained a moderately strong interest
in the use of the Swedish language, whereas the Swedish
Baptists have moved away almost entirely from the use of
the mother tongue. Whether the Swedish Baptists in America
will ever witness a real revival of interest in their hymnody
remains to be seen.

It is difficult to ascertain whether Scandinavian hymnody
will penetrate further into the contents of American hymnals.
Hymns of the type of "Children of the Heavenly Father" and
"How Great Thou Art" have become increasingly popular in
the last two decades in non-Scandinavian circles. Although
there has been an increase in the number of Scandinavian
hymns in American hymnals in the last decade, there is still
much work to be done in exploring the possibility of including
more of them in future publications. There is no justifiable
reason why Scandinavian hymnody should not share equal
honors with the rest of the countries where religious reforms
have produced a treasury of sacred verse and music.

APPENDIXES

förtappas j then ewinnerlig dödh / war
off barmhertigh .

A solis ortus

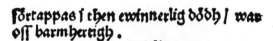

Är gladh tu helga Christen=
heet / och prijsa gudz barm
hertigheet / gott haffwer
han bewijsat tich / han är
tich godh ewinnerligh /

Itt vnder här på iorderich / lät han off
skee sää millelig / then som gudh fadhers
wijsdom war / wartt här j mandom op=
penbar /

Maria modher skäär och reen / födde
en son forutan meen / ingen haffuer wist
eller tenkt / at iomfru födde oforkrenkt /

Een ny menniskia föddes här / thñ som
gudz eenda sonen är / hä wart vthgiffuin
off til tröst / och haffuer alla återlöst .

Aff Adäs synd kom off then nödh at
off stodh före ewig dödh / och kom thm mz
j samma sund / forbannelse sä marghe=
lund / .

Thet togh han bort som helsan är / Je
sus Christus wåår brodher käär / wåår
synd och plicht drogh han på sich / wartt
pijnt och plåghat iämmerligh .

heluetit synd och dödzens krafft / som
oss hadhe för fångar hafft / wan han öff
uer i sin mandom / hans dödh war oss
san lälkedom.

Tess ware priiss i ewigheet / fadhrens
stora barmhertigheet / så thz hadhe beslu
tet så / och wille dödhen nidherslå.

Then femtiynode Psalmen
på latin Miserere mei
deus zc,

Orbarma tich gudh öffuer
mich / för thin stora barmher
tigheet / Och för then nådh
som är i tigh / tagh bort mijn
oretferdigheet / twå aff min synd och gör
mich reen / ty min brist iach wel kēna kan /
moot tich haffuer iach syndat aleen / ath
thin ordh skole bliffua sann.

See gudh i synd är iach aflat / i synd
afladhe modher min / see sannind haffuer tu elskad / thin hēligheet gaff tu mich
in / stenk mich medh heelsosam Jsop som
snid warder iach huijt och reen / låådt mich
höra glädhi och hopp / så frögdes mijn

THEN SVENSKA PSALMBOKEN OF 1695

Editions Available for This Study

The following editions are a cross-section of those published. All indicate on the title page authorization by the king.

1727	1851
1740	1863
1755	1875
1803	

Contents

Most of the editions are divided into two parts. The first section contains the 413 hymns which would indicate that for approximately 150 years these selections remained constant and intact. A spot check of numbers in the 1727 and 1875 editions bears this out. The following table of contents indicates the scope of subjects covered:

Catechisms Versified
King David's Psalms Versified
Advent Psalms
Incarnation Psalms
Christmas and New Year Psalms
Suffering and Death of Christ
Burial and Ressurection
Ascension
The Holy Spirit
The Holy Trinity
Holy Angels
All Saints' Day
Apostle Days
Psalms over Sunday Evangels
Fall and Restoration
God's Word and Church
The Lord's Sabbath Day
Prayer Psalm before and after Sermon
Anti-Christ
God's Eternal Protection
God's Grace and Forgiveness of Sin

Psalms of Penitence
Christian Walk
Patience and Trust in God
The Ways of the World
Psalms of Sorrow and Testing
Psalms of Petition
Psalms of Praise and Thanksgiving
Psalms under Various Circumstances
Psalms for Different People
Psalms for Various Occasions

The second section concerns itself for the most part with various items for instruction, devotion and corporate worship. To mention a few, there are included in this section:

The Gospels and Epistles
The Athanasian Creed
Scriptures on the Life of Christ
The Litany
The Swedish Mass
David's Penitential Psalms

In the editions available, one or two variations are to be found in regard to the second section of the hymnal. The edition of 1740 contains no second part, merely the regular hymns of section one. It is entirely possible that this omission could have been effected in rebinding. Of even greater significance is the make-up of the 1875 hymnal. The second part of this edition is a reproduction in its entirety of Sions Sånger, the Herrnhut hymnal of the pietistic group. Two observations are in order at this point. It is noteworthy that the Gamla Psalmboken, as this book later became known, was still being printed long after the 1819 book of J.O. Wallin had been published. Furthermore, the inclusion of the Herrnhut hymns indicates to this writer the strong influence of the Herrnhut group on that of the State Church. There are some strong implications in this arrangement.

Authors Represented

Even in some of the new hymn books from Scandinavia, there is a scarcity of names of the authors. Evidently these were not thought to be important. However, in examining the contents of the 1695 Psalmboken, the following observations are of significance regarding the authors. This outline of selected subjects indicates the contribution of prominent men among the several items in part one:

The Ten Commandments
Martin Luther
Olavus Petri
Laurentius Petri

Then Swenska

Med the stycker som ther til höra /
och på föliande blad vptcknade
finnas /

Vppå Kongl. Majtz.
nådigste befalning

Af thet wyrd. Predikoämbetet
Åhr M DC XCIII.

Med flit öfwersedd / förbättrad
och förmehrad /
Och Åhr 1694. i Stockholm
af tryckct vtgången.

Stockholm /
Vt thet af K. Majtt. privilegerade Burchardi
tryckieri / af Joh. Jacob Genath Faa.

Title page from

the 1694 Psalmboken

The Credo
  Martin Luther
  Ambrosius
  Augustinus

The Lord's Prayer
  Several renderings by Martin Luther

The Lord's Supper
  John Huss
  Martin Luther
  H. Spegel
  Johann Rist

David's Psalms (in meter)
  D. Becker
  L. Petri
  J. Swedberg
  J. Arrhenius
  M. Luther
  John Huss

Although the singing of metrical psalms was strikingly peculiar
to Calvin's Reformation, the presence of nearly 100 psalms in meter
in this book indicates their more than casual use in the Lutheran
Church of that day.

Representative Hymns in Translation

1. Bless us, Father, and protect us
        From all harm in all our ways;
    Patiently, O Lord, direct us
        Safely through these fleeting days;
    Let Thy face upon us shine,
    Fill us with Thy peace divine;
    Praise the Father, Son, and Spirit,
    Praise Him, all that life inherit.
                              --J. Swedberg

According to Ryden, this simple stanza by Swedberg became
a favorite "doxology of the church of Sweden." J.O. Wallin incor-
porated it into one of his own hymns, "O my soul, on wings ascend-
ing," which is the final hymn in his Psalmbook.[1]

2. The lilies, nor toiling nor spinning,
        Their clothing how gorgeous and fair!
    What tints in their tiny orbs woven,
        What wondrous devices are there!
    All Solomon's stores could not render
    One festival robe of such splendor
        As modest field lilies do wear.
                              --Haquin Spegel

Haquin Spegel, one of those who collaborated with Swedberg in the preparation of the rejected hymn book, was the more gifted poet of the two. It was he who by his hymns fixed the language forms that subsequently became the model for Swedish hymnody. Although Spegel never stooped to subjective sentimentality, his hymns breathe a spirit of personal faith and fervent devotion.[2]

> 3. Jesus is my Friend most precious,
>   Never friend did love as He;
>   Can I leave this Friend so gracious,
>   Spurn His wondrous love for me?
>   No! nor friend nor foe shall sever
>   Me from Him who loves me so;
>   His shall be my will forever,
>   There above, and here below.
>   --J. Arrhenius[3]

Music of Den Psalmboken

The tunes used in the singing of the "psalms" from this book must have been well known to the people of that day. In the copies examined, no music is printed. The tune to be used for a particular "psalm" is indicated as the one used for another supposedly familiar one. This is true even in the Sions Sånger section of the edition of 1875.

The companion to the 1695 hymnal was the Koralbok of 1697, edited and published by Swedberg and Vallerius. (The latter was an authority on Gregorian Chant.) It was a collection of texts and melodies with figured-bass accompaniments and scored as a pattern for subsequent collections. The influence of the German style is to be seen in the musical treatment of this collection as well as later ones. According to Lundholm the book was still popular among Swedish people at the time of his study in 1937, although the melodies do tend to be consistently in the high range.

Influence of the Swedberg Psalmbok

The influence of Swedberg's monumental work is seen even in the present century. According to Ryden:

> ... the final form in which Swedberg's hymnbook was published was still so impregnated by his spirit that a noted critic has called it "the most precious heritage he left his native land." The fact that the latest Swedish Psalmbook (1937) contains no less than thirty-three hymns and translations credited to Swedberg, in part or in whole, testifies eloquently to the enduring mark he has left on Swedish hymnody.[4]

NOTES

1. Ryden, op. cit., pp. 171, 172.
2. Ibid.
3. Ibid., p. 173.
4. Ibid., p. 171.

Andeliga

Wijsor/

Om

Swargehanda

MATERIER,

Och

Wid Atskilliga

Tilfällen,

[handwritten inscription]

Title page of the Radical Pietist Hymnal

162

effter följa, Emedan sådan af Gud blir,
Wårkat i henne innerlig, At hon Guds
stänckte blifwer, Som landet all, besittia
stal, vti friden, och i tiden, Som och sedan,
När som wandring stier vr tiden.

9.

The fromma skola thet och se, och vti
glädie frögda sig, At ondstan blir bortta-
gen, Så skola de och märcka här, Wäl-
gierningar som Herren kiär, bewisat och
andragen; Ty bör jag helan dag Tack
lofsiunga, Anda tunga, wärck och handel
At alt blir til helig wandel.

67

I.

! Vnderbare Gud, Som låter mig
här skåda, De ting som jag, Til-
förne aldrig sett, Jag wil ditt lof
med tack samt hierta båda, För all den
nåd, Mig är af dig betedt, Om du mig
här, eii hade nådigt kallat, Jag wiser-
ligen had i gropen neder fallit?

2.

Synd, död och diefwulen, Med all
des anhang leda, samt alt det som för-
skräcligt wara må, De månde för min
Siäl ett yncligt fall tilreda, Vppå den
stig/

stig, Jag ändtlig skulle gå, Men du o! JE-
su! Som mig hafwer styrckt och lisat, skal
för din godhet all, I ewighet bli prisat.

Joh. Bunjan

Kan siungas som:

Store Jmmanuel:nådigste skåda 2c

6 2.

I.

RUdgummen kommen, Skynbar,
Ehr alla, Til Bröllops waker, Si
JEsus är här, Han sänder röster
och låter er kalla, Skynder er Salig den
som redo är, Bruden är tilred, Och skal
snart hemföras, Allting är redo ty röster-
na höras.

2.

Vpp och er skynder at mörkret betäcker,
Ei edra Siälar vtl ewig tid, JEsus mild
ropar och Siälen vpwäcker, Til biuder al-
lom sin nåde och frid, Warer då redo och
dröijer ei länger, Jnnan Gud dören til him-
melen stänger.

3.

I som med macht emot lambet dierfft
striden, Lägger ner wapnen för hielten
med hast, Faller til sota och tigger om fri-
den,

163

Page from the Radical Pietist Hymnal showing the signature of John Bunyan

DEN SVENSKA PROF PSALMBOKEN

During the eighteenth century, new trends in religious poetry began to be in evidence and from certain quarters came demands for a new and improved hymnal. In response to these demands, the Celcius Psalm Proposal was issued in two sections in 1765 and 1767, respectively. The following table of general contents indicates, by the titles contained therein, the influence of Pietism and Herrnhutism. Much of the poetry was "uninspired and devoid of spiritual content," according to the estimate of Lövgren.

First Collection, 1765

God's Laws and Commandments

The First Table

God's Holy Law in general
God's Ten Commandments in general
Love to God
The first commandment
The second commandment
The third commandment
The observation of Sunday
Before the Sermon
At the close of the service

The Second Table

Love for neighbor
Love for enemies
Fourth commandment
Fifth commandment
Conciliatory attitude
Sixth commandment
Marital purity
Seventh commandment
Eighth commandment
Nineth commandment
Tenth commandment
The Law's decisions
Faith-rewards for the true
The Conscience

Purposed sins and sins in weakness
Partaking in the sins of others
Necessity of the Law
Good deeds

Concerning the Apostolic Faith

God and His attributes
Christian thoughts in regard to God's attributes
The Holy Trinity
Creation
The angels
God's image
Man's fall and restoration
God's providence
Psalms of praise and gratitude
Christ's incarnation
Christ's self-humiliation
Preparation for Christmas
Christmas psalms
New Year psalms
Jesus' name and works of mercy
Jesus rideth into Jerusalem
Jesus' pain and suffering
The beginning of Jesus' last suffering
Jesus washes his disciples' feet
Jesus suffers in the garden
Jesus is taken prisoner
Jesus suffers in the palace of Caiaphas
Peter's fall and tears
Judas' sin and perdition
Jesus questioned before the council
Jesus is sent to Herod
Jesus is scourged
Jesus is dressed in purple, crowned with thorns, reviled
    and brought forth to the people
Jesus condemned to death
Jesus bears his cross
The difference between the two robbers who were crucified
    with Jesus
Jesus suffers on the cross
The seven words of Jesus
The death of the faithful with Christ and life in his death
Jesus' death and burial
Christ's exaltation and ministry
Easter psalms
Christ's ascension
The last judgment

DEN SVENSKA PSALMBOKEN OF 1819
AND ITS ANTECEDENTS

The Revision of Swedish Psalms of 1807

This volume, the work of Michael Choreaus and J.O. Wallin, was issued in two parts in 1807. Choreaus, whose works appeared posthumously, was considered to have been quite liberal in theology in comparison to the rather conservative Wallin.

The Psalms of 1809

J.O. Wallin contributed fourteen originals to this collection. In no other volume before or since this one do the neologistic and new-styled psalms appear. He is very naturalistic in his teachings about God in this book.

The Psalms of 1811

After much dispute concerning the work of the committee of 1809 appointed by the Riksdag, Wallin suggested that a hymnal be published which would be the work of one man, and, in turn, offered to the committee such a proposal. The neo-romantic movement in Sweden suggested to Wallin that a hymnal, in addition to its service to the church, should foster an aesthetic in his country among all people.

Wallin himself had been under severe criticism, which criticism moved him in a positive direction of improvement. In the introduction to the 1811 collection, he acknowledges the weaknesses of his earlier poetry. The Psalms in this collection mark a decided rise in quality over previous poetry of Wallin, but he was yet to attain greater heights in subsequent books.

The Prof-Psalmer of 1812

This hymnal was issued jointly by Franzen and Wallin. Several of the best hymns by Franzen are to be found among those in this collection. A second edition was published in 1813, containing the work of these two poets.

Förslag till forbattrade Kyrke-Sånger 1814
(Proposals for Improved Church Songs)

This proposal was the work of a committee appointed in 1811. In 1812, when the proposal was nearly ready to be issued, an appeal was made for new songs to fill in the gap. Many were submitted which were of relatively little merit. In the spring of 1814 the committee, assisted by Wallin, scrutinized these songs, and the collection was accepted and printed under the above title. Wallin was not pleased with the final results, mainly because the general scheme was so similar to the old psalmbook.

Förslag till Svensk Psalmbok 1816

While previous psalmbook proposals had been the joint effort of committees and individuals, Wallin's proposal for the "Svensk Psalmbok" of 1816 was entirely his own. He had worked persistently on it and did not feel bound to the opinions of others. He presented his plan to the Committee in 1815 and after that sought no help or suggestion. This hymnal became the pattern for the 1819 volume, which adhered quite closely to it in its form. The number of psalms was increased to 500 in this collection.

Wallinska Psalmer 1817-18

The Psalm Book Proposal of 1816 was well received and approved by the committee and the general public, although not without some criticism. Wallin himself was his strongest critic. He continued to write a number of new psalms which he published in religious papers during 1817-18, or used in connection with sermons. In 1817 he published a sermon on the errors of the times, in which he included his hymns "O Thou Who Seest Every Heart." Another was written for use in the dedication of a cemetery in Vasterås in 1818.

The Psalmbok of 1819

After a period of intense work from the year of 1811, the committee approved Wallin's proposal in 1818. It was legalized by the king on January 29, 1819, and became the official hymnal for the church of Sweden. Wallin's contribution was the greatest although many other poets of note were among its contributors. The book became very popular not only among the state-church constituency but also among the pietistic and free-church congregations.

Olson has analyzed the contents of this psalmbook from which the following titles and descriptive phrases have been selected:

Psalms for special occasions
Philosophic and abstract psalms
Political psalms
Jesus' teaching on mercy and simplicity
Psalms of pietistic contrition
Pedogical and pastoral psalms
Separation from the world
Homesickness for heaven
Children's psalms[1]

The Svensk Psalmbok After 1819

Even concerning works of note and popularity disagreements
arise, and the Psalmbok of 1819 was no exception. Most of the opposition came because of the neology expressed in many of the psalms.
J.H. Thomander and Peter Wieselgren published a revised book in
1849 to meet the demands of those who desired such a revision.
Further revision was discussed in 1868 but the work proceeded slowly.
A large number of private scripts were submitted, some of which are
worthy of mention:

Proposal for the Revision of the Svenska Psalmboken, by
C.A. Cornelius (1879)

Psalmbok Proposal by some Psalmbok Friends (1882-83)

Proposal for the Revision of the Svenska Kyrkopsalmboken,
by Severin Cavallin (1882)

In 1889 an official proposal was published and rejected, and
a later revision of 1896 was turned down. Many private and several
official proposals followed, which were unofficially received and used.
These led to the supplement of 1921. Known as the Nya Psalmer,
it restored to use many psalms of the 1695 book, which Wallin had
omitted. Swedish originals from private collections as well as many
free-church psalms were included in this supplement. Foremost
among the contributors to Nya Psalmer was John A. Eklund (1867-
1945) who translated and edited twenty-eight selections, in addition
to his many originals. These are considered to be the best in the
Swedish language.

At the behest of the king a new proposal was worked out by
Eklund in 1934. He revised psalms from the seventeenth century
and translated many from Danish, German, and English sources of
the eighteenth and nineteenth centuries. A private proposal was
issued by Paul Nilsson in 1936. Official proposals were coming in
February and September of 1936. These became more decisive.
After the official church meeting had worked over these proposals,
the new Svenska Psalmboken was legalized by the king in 1937.

Since 1950 there has been further agitation for a new hymnal

292296

which would meet the requirements of the day regarding contents
and the language. A hymnological institute has been formed to
undertake the task of revision over a long period of time. At the
present time there is also an effort to revise the Choral Book, with
the purpose of restoring to use many of the old chorales in their
original rhythmic forms.

NOTE

1. Olson, op. cit., pp. 57-60.

V?. S~,

C.~.̇. ~o~ .

)a. ̇

1843

Samling

af några

Andeliga Sånger.

✹❀✹

Talande emellan eder i Psalmer,
och lofsånger, och Andeliga wisor;
sjungande och spelande Herranom
uti edor hjertan. Ephes. 5: 19.

Götheborg, tryckte hos Sam. Wahlström 1843.

Title page of F.O. Nilsson's Psalmbok

SELECTED PAGES FROM DILLNER's <u>PSALMODIKON</u>

Melodierna

till

Swenska Kyrkans Psalmer;

Noterade med ziffror, för Skolor
och Menigheten.

STOCKHOLM,
Tryckt hos P. A. Norstedt & Söner, 1830.

Det Swenska
Presterskapet.

Eder, Wördade Fäder och älskade Bröder! egnas
med rördt hjerta den späda förstlingen af ett wåg-
samt nit, som wille aldrig upphöra att, efter för-
mågan, tjena Församlingen och Eder.

I Christo Jesu,

Eder i lif och död tillgifne

wördnadsfulle medtjenare
JOHANNES DILLNER.
Hofpredikant och Kyrkoherde i
Östra Ryd af Upsala Stift.

114

1	2 3	4 2	3 4	2
De	ſkola	doċ en	dag för-	gås,
1	2 3	4 2	3 4	2
Och	ſåſom	gräs till	jorden	nås,
5	5 4	5 3	2	1
Och	wißna	och för-	tram-	pas.

N:o 233.

Eß+2+3+6+7.

1	3 4	5		
Haf	tåla-	mod,		
6	4 5	3		
War	from och	god,		
5	6 2	4 3	2	1
Och	efter-	följ Guds	wil-	ja.
1	3 4	5		
Den	detta	hör,		
6	4 5	3		
Och	detta	gör,		
5	6 2	4 3	2	1
Skall	Gud ej	från ſig	ſkil-	ja.
1	5 5	3		
Ett	himla-	bröd		
3	6 6	×5		
I	jordiſk	nöd		
×5	6 7	8 7	6	5
Dig	tåla-	mod.et	gif-	wer.
5	3 3	4		
Af	denna	ſpis		
4	3 3	2		
Du	lugn och	wis,		

MUSICAL EXAMPLES FROM <u>PSALM OCH SÅNG</u>

German Chorale Settings:

Example I   "Ein' Feste Burg"
Example II   "Lobe Den Herren"

American Gospel Songs:

Example III   "He Leadeth Me"
Example IV   "The Old Rugged Cross"

Representative Swedish Gospel Songs:

Example V   "Med Gud och Hans Vänskap"
Example VI   "Tryggare Kan Ingen Vara"
Example VII   "Tack, O Gud, För Vad Som Varit"

12. Vår Gud är oss en väldig borg

M. Luther, 1529
Olaus Petri, 1536
P.A. Sondén, 1816
J.O. Wallin, 1816

Mkl 298

M. Luther, 1529

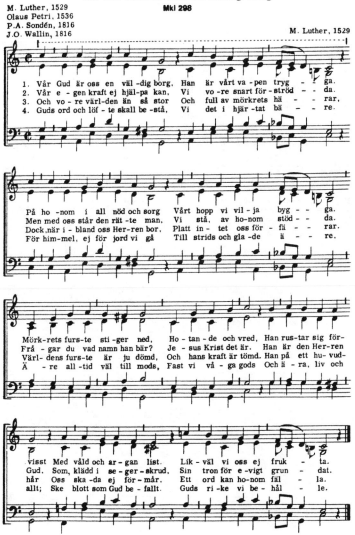

1. Vår Gud är oss en väl-dig borg, Han är vårt va-pen tryg - ga.
2. Vår e - gen kraft ej hjäl-pa kan, Vi vo -re snart för - ströd - - da.
3. Och vo - re värl-den än så stor Och full av mörkrets hä - - rar,
4. Guds ord och löf - te skall be -stå, Vi det i hjär -tat bä - - re.

På ho -nom i all nöd och sorg Vårt hopp vi vil - ja byg - - ga.
Men med oss står den rät -te man, Vi stå, av ho-nom stöd - - da.
Dock,när i - bland oss Her-ren bor, Platt in - tet oss för - fä - - rar.
För him-mel, ej för jord vi gå Till strids och gla -de ä - - re,

Mörk-rets furs-te sti -ger ned, Ho - tan - de och vred, Han rus-tar sig för-
Frå - gar du vad namn han bär? Je - sus Krist det är. Han är den Her-ren
Värl- dens furs-te är ju dömd, Och hans kraft är tömd. Han på ett hu-vud-
Ä - re all -tid väl till mods, Fast vi vå - ga gods Och ä - ra, liv och

visst Med våld och ar-gan list. Lik - väl vi oss ej fruk - ta.
Gud. Som, klädd i se - ger - skrud, Sin tron för e -vigt grun - dat.
hår Oss ska -da ej för - mår. Ett ord kan ho-nom fäl - la.
allt; Ske blott som Gud be - fallt. Guds ri -ke vi be - hål - le.

EXAMPLE I

479. Kommen för Herren
Miki 80

P. Nilsson, 1908   Tysk mel., Stralsund, 1665

1. Kom-men för Her - ren med tack - sam-het, gam-la och ung - å,
2. Här-li - ga verk ha-va fram-gått ur Ska-pa-rens hän - der:
3. Gud har gjort un - der och rik - ligt väl - sig - nat vår mö - da.
4. In - nan jag ro - pat om nåd, är han re - do att sva - ra.
5. Kom-men, I folk, och för - nim - men, att Her-ren är nä - ra.

Kom-men med fröjd att vår Fa - der av hjär-tat lov - sjung - a.
Som-ma - rens ym - nig-het ströd-de han kring vå - ra strän - der,
Väx -ten han gi - vit, och jor-den har bu - rit sin grö - da.
Sa - ligt det är i hans he - li - ga tem-pel att va - ra.
Sjung-en, I him - lar och jord, den Alls-mäk-ti-ges ä - ra.

Vid - ga dig, bröst, Lyft dig mot him - len, min röst,
Syn - da - res jord Du - kar han lik - som ett bord,
Än me - ra gott, Ri - ka - re gå - vor jag fått,
Han i sitt ord Mät-tar sin hung - ran - de hjord,
Hjälp oss i dag, Fa - der, att dig till be - hag

Jub - la Guds ä - ra, min tung - a!
Man - na av him - me - len sän - der.
Sjä - len till fäg - nad och fö - da.
Le - der till käl - lan den kla - ra.
He - li - ga tack - of - fer bä - ra.

EXAMPLE II

444. Han leder mig
Mkl 241

J.H. Gilmore, 1859
E. Nyström, 1876
Bearb. 1962

W.B. Bradbury, 1864

1. Han le - der mig. Vad himmelsk tröst Den lju - va tan - ken ger mitt bröst.
2. Lär mig, o Gud, att slu - ta in Med tro och hopp min hand i din,
3. Och när min vand-ring här är slut Och jag i tron har käm-pat ut,

Var - helst jag går, på all min stig, Min Fa-der stän - digt le - der mig.
Nöjd med den nåd jag får av dig, När med din hand du le - der mig.
Jag räds ej då för dö-dens bud, När jag är ledd av dig, o Gud.

Han le - der mig, han le -der mig, Hur nå -de -fullt han le -der mig.

Så må jag vand-ra glad den stig, Där Her-ren Gud själv le -der mig.

EXAMPLE III

107. På en avlägsen höjd
Mkl 303

G. Bennard, 1913
A. Aleby, 1925

G. Bennard, 1913

1. På   en   av - läg- sen höjd   Stod ett grovt, dys-tert kors,   Sym-
2. O   det ur - gam-la kors Är   till-dra - gan-de blott,   Fast
3. I   det ur - gam-la kors, Av   Guds blod fär-gat rött,   En
4. För det ur - gam-la kors Vill jag tro - gen och glad   Nu

bo - len av smär-ta och skam.____   O jag äls - kar det kors, Där vår
höljt ut - av världens för- akt,____   Sen Guds he - li - ga Lamm, Som till
un - der- bar skön-het jag ser.____   Ty det är på det kor - set Han
bä - ra båd skymf och för-akt,____   Tills han kal - lar en dag Mig till

Her - re för oss Blev till dö - den en smär-tor-nas man.____
Gol - ga- ta gått, På sar- ga - de skuld-ror det lagt.____
li - dit och dött, Han som fräls-ning-ens nåd åt mig ger.____
him - me-lens stad För att de - la hans ä - ra och makt.____

Jag vill äls-ka det ur-gam-la kors,____ I dess kraft skall jag seg-ra till slut.__ Jag om-

EXAMPLE IV

236. Med Gud och hans vänskap
Mkl 166

C.O. Rosenius, 1851
Bearb. 1937   O. Ahnfelt, 1851

1. Med Gud och hans vän-skap, hans   An-de och ord   Samt bröders gemen-skap och
2. I   stor-mi - ga ti - der, bland töc-ken och grus, En   ska-ra dock skri-der mot
3. Den kors-märk-ta dräk-ten med smädnamn jag tar, Om   ing- en i släk-ten det
4. Den molnstod oss höl - jer och   le - der vårt tåg, Den klip-pa oss föl-jer med
5. Se, här är   nu grun-den för   lyc- ka och frid I   hårdas-te stun-den av
6. O   Je -sus, bliv när oss, bliv   när oss allt fort Och   sköt oss och bär oss,som

nå-de-nes bord De o -sed-da da -gar vi mö- ta medtröst: Oss föl-jer ju Her-den,
himmelens ljus. Dess hopp och dess här-lig-het världen ej ser, Men Herren går för dem,
namnet ock har, Och föl-jer med gläd-je, I käm-par,med er, Som tågen till ä - ra,
springkällans våg,Ar Kristus,hans kär-lek och re -nan-de blod. Där lever vårt hjärta,
kval och av strid.Om mig än för-smäk-ta min kropp och min själ,När dig blott jag haver,
all-tid du gjort.Ja, a -men,din tro-het skall bring-a oss fram. Lov,pris,tack och ära,

oss föl - jer ju Herden, Den tro-fas- te Her-den, Vi kän - na hans röst.
men Her - ren går för dem, Ja, Her-ren går för dem Med se - gerns ba - ner.
som tå - gen till ä - ra, Till o -vansk-lig ä -ra Vid kor - sets ba - ner.
där le - ver vårt hjärta, Där fröj-das vårt hjär-ta, Där li - vas vårt mod.
när dig blott jag ha-ver, När dig blott jag ha -ver, O Gud, är allt väl.
Lov,pris, tack och ä-ra, Lov, pris,tack och ä -ra Vår Gud och vårt Lamm!

EXAMPLE V

308

557. Tryggare kan ingen vara

Mkl 21

Lina Sandell-Berg, 1855

Svensk folkmel., känd från 1874

1. Tryg-ga-re kan ing-en va - ra   Än Guds lil - la bar - na - ska - ra,
2. Her - ren si -na trog-na vår - dar   Ut - i Si - ons hel - ga går - dar.
3. Ing - en nöd och ing -en lyc - ka   Skall ut - ur hans hand dem ryc - ka.
4. Gläd dig då, du lil - la ska - ra.   Ja - kobs Gud skall dig be - va - ra.
5. Vad han tar och vad han gi - ver,   Sam-me Fa - der han dock bli - ver,

Stjär-nan ej på him-la - fäs - tet,   Få - geln ej i kän-da näs-tet.
Ö - ver dem han sig för-bar - mar,   Bär dem up - på fa -ders-ar -mar.
Han, vår vän för and -ra vän - ner,   Si - na barns be - kym-mer kän-ner.
För hans vil - ja mås-te al - la   Fi - en - der till jor-den fal - la.
Och hans mål är blott det e - na: Bar-nets san - na väl al - le - na.

521

EXAMPLE VI

467. Tack, o Gud, för vad som varit
Mkl 222

A. Storm, 1891   J.A. Hultman, 1908

1. Tack, o Gud, för vad som va-rit, Tack för allt vad du be-skär,
2. Tack för vad du up-pen-ba-rat, Tack för vad jag ej för-står,
3. Tack för him-mel klar i li-vet, Tack för moln du strött där-på,
4. Tack för ro-sor-na vid vä-gen, Tack för tör-net i-bland dem,

Tack för ti-der-na som fa-rit, Tack för stun-den som nu är,
Tack för bön som du be-sva-rat, Tack för vad jag ic-ke får,
Tack för sol-ljus av dig gi-vet, Tack för mörk-ret li-ka-så,
Tack för res-ta him-la-ste-gen, Tack för e-vigt tryg-gat hem,

Tack för lju-sa, var-ma vå-rar, Tack för mörk och ku-len höst,
Tack för li-vets hem-lig-he-ter, Tack för hjälp i nö-dens stund,
Tack för pröv-ning-en och stri-den, Tack för hopp som upp-fyllts väl,
Tack för kors och tack för plå-ga, Tack för him-melsk sa-lig-het,

Tack för re-dan glöm-da tå-rar, Tack för fri-den i mitt bröst.
Tack för nåd som ing-en mä-ter, Tack för e-vigt frids-för-bund.
Tack för nå-den, tack för fri-den, Tack för hopp som sla-git fel.
Tack för var be-sva-rad frå-ga, Tack för allt i e-vig-het.

440

EXAMPLE VII

• BIBLIOGRAPHY

General Works

Aaberg, J.C. Hymns and Hymn Writers of Denmark. Dee Moines:
The Committee on Publication of the Evangelical Lutheran Church
of America, 1945.

Bergendoff, Conrad. Olavus Petri and the Ecclesiastical Transformation in Sweden (1521-1552): A Study in the Swedish Reformation.
New York: Macmillan, 1928.

Blomqvist, Axel, ed. Svenska Pingst Vackelsen Femtio År. Stockholm: Forlaget Filadelfia, 1951.

Brorson, A. Winding. Nogle Af Salig Biskop Hans Adolph Brorsons
Psalmer. Kjobenhavn: Andreas Seidelin, 1823.

Bucke, Emory Stevens, et al. The History of American Methodism.
Vol. II. New York, Nashville: Abingdon Press, 1964.

Davies, James P. Sing with Understanding. Chicago: Covenant
Press, 1966.

Dillner, Johannes. Psalmodikon. Cedarholm: 1830.

Erickson, J. Irving. Twice Born Hymns. Chicago: Covenant
Press, 1976.

Fredmund, I., ed. One Hundred Years of Danish Baptist Missionary
Work in America (1856-1956). Reprint of the Watchman, Danish
Baptist General Conference.

_____, et al., Seventy-Five Years of Danish Baptist Missionary
Work in America. Philadelphia: The Danish Baptist General
Conference of America and the American Baptist Publication So-
ciety, 1939.

Grimm, Harold J. The Reformation Era, 1500-1650. New York:
Macmillan, 1965.

Jensen, Arne. Baptisternes Historie i Danmark. København: Baptisternes Forlag, 1961.

Latourette, Kenneth Scott. A History of Christianity. New York: Harper and Brothers, 1953.

_____. The Nineteenth Century in Europe. Vol. II. New York: Harper and Brothers, 1959.

Lövgren, Oscar. Psalm och Sånglexikon. Stockholm: Gummessons Bokforlag, 1964.

_____. Våra Psalm-och Sångdiktare. 3 vols. Stockholm: Tryckeri Aktiebolaget Thule, 1939.

Norgaard, Johannes, et al. Baptist Work in Denmark, Finland, Norway and Sweden. Stockholm: Westerbergs, 1947.

Norton, H. Wilberg, et al. The Diamond Jubilee Story of the Evangelical Free Church of America. Minneapolis: Free Church Publications, 1959.

Nyvall, David, and Karl A. Olsson. The Evangelical Covenant Church. Chicago: Covenant Press, 1954.

Olson, Adolf. A Centenary History: As Related to the Baptist General Conference of America. Chicago: Baptist Conference Press, 1952.

Olson, Arnold T. Believers Only. Minneapolis: Free Church Publications, 1964.

Olson, Oscar N. The Augustana Lutheran Church in America: Pioneer Period 1845-1860. Rock Island: Augustana Book Concern, 1950.

Olsson, Karl A. By One Spirit. Chicago: Covenant Press, 1962.

Ryden, E.E. The Story of Christian Hymnody. Rock Island: Augustana Press, 1959.

Selander, Sven-Åke. Den Nya Sånger. Lund: CWK Gleerup Boxforlag, 1973.

Stephenson, George M. The Religious Aspects of Swedish Immigration: A Study of Immigrant Churches. Minneapolis: The University of Minnesota Press, 1932.

Stiansen, Peter. History of the Norwegian Baptists in America. Philadelphia: The Norwegian Baptist Conference of America and the American Baptist Publication Society, 1939.

Waddams, H.M. The Swedish Church. London: Society for Promoting Christian Knowledge, 1946.

Westin, Gunnar, et al. De Drikyrkliga Samfunden i Sverige Stockholm: Svenska Missionsforbundets Forlag, 1934.

_____. Den Kristna Friförsamlingen i Norden. Stockholm: Westerbergs, 1956.

_____. The Free Church Through the Ages. Translated from the Swedish by Virgil A. Olson. Nashville: Broadman Press, 1958.

Dictionaries and Encyclopedias

Johnson, Samuel Macauley, ed. The New Schaff-Herroz Encyclopedia of Religious Knowledge. Vol. IX. Grand Rapids: Baker Book Horse, 1953.

Julian, John, ed. A Dictionary of Hymnology. London: John Murray, 1925.

Articles and Periodicals

Hallenberg, Aron. "Church Music on the Swing." Translated from Vecko-Posten, March 17, 1966.

Liedgren, Emil. "The History of Free Church Songs." Translated from the Standaret, June 26, 1934.

Osbeck, C.R. "Old Acquaintances in New Garb." Translated from Svenska Standaret, February 12, 1924.

Pietisten. Vols VI-XVIII. Stockholm: Tryckt Hos Rudolf Wall, 1947-1859.

The Danish Baptist General Conference of America. Twenty-Eight Conference Report. 1956.

Hymnals

Andeliga Sånger: Dels Samlade, Dels Bearbetade Samt Utgifna af Oscar Ahnfelt. Chicago: Engberg and Holmbergs Forlag, 1881.

Børnenes Harpe: Andelige Sange for Sondagsskolen og Hjemmet. Privately printed, 1899.

Christian Worship, A Hymnal. Philadelphia: The Judson Press, 1941.

Concordia: A Collection of Hymns and Spiritual Songs. Minneapolis: Augsburg Publishing House, 1925.

Bibliography 313

Crusader Hymns: For Church, School, and Home. Chicago: Hope
Publishing Co., 1966.

Cymbalen: Andliga Sånger Utgifna af J.A. Hultman. Chicago:
"Missions-Vannens" Expedition, 1885.

Den Swenska Psalm-Boken: Med de Stycken, Som Dertill Hora-Uppa
Konglmaj: ts Nadiga Befallning ar 1695. Kalmar: Tryckr Hos
O. & A. Westin, 1951. (Also edition of 1780, 1755, 1803, 1863,
1875.)

Den Svenska Psalmboken of ar 1819. Ofversedd af J.H. Thomander
och P. Wieselgren. Rock Island: Augustana Book Concern, 1884.

Den Swenska Psalmboken: Af Konungen Gillad och Stadfastad år
1819. Westerås: Tryckt Hos D. Torfzell, 1845.

Den Svenska Psalmboken: Af Konungen Gillad och Stadfastad år
1819. Svenska Bibelsällskapets Edition. Stockholm: Svenska
Krykans Diakonist Tyrelses Bokforlag, 1923.

Ecumenical Praise, Carol Stream, III.: Agape, 1977.

Enchiridion Eller Then Swenska Psalmboken: Sampt Andra Wanligha
Handbocker. Aff. M. Petro Joh. Rudbeckion. Tryckt aff Oloff
Oloffsson, 1627.

Evangeli Harpe: Et udvalg af Salmer og Aandelige Sange. Chicago:
Evangelisten Publication Society's Forlag, 1906.

Evangelie Toner: Samlet til Glaede og Opmuntring for Guds Folk.
København: Korsets Evangeliums Forlag, 1956.

Evangeliska Sånger: for Söndagsskolan, Hemmet och Evangeliska
Möten. Chicago: Svenska Bokhandelsforeningen, 1917.

Evangelisten. Salmer og Sånger til Bruk i Menighet og Hjem. Oslo:
Norsk Litteraturselskap, 1953.

Förbundstoner: Andliga Sånger och Psalmer till Offentligt och Enskilt Bruk, Utgivna av Helgelseförbundet. Stockholm: Nya
Tryckeri-Aktiebolaget, 1912.

Församlings-Sångbok: Andeliga Sånger for Gemensam och Enskild
uppbyggelse. Stockholm: P. Palmquists Akriebolag, 1878.

Foursquare Hymnal. Los Angeles: The International Church of
the Foursquare Gospel, 1957.

Fredsbasunen. Minneapolis: Skoog and Delander Music Printers,
1899.

Frids-Basunen: Andliga Sånger. Text och Musik. Chicago: Er-
halles Hos Nya Wecko-Postens Expedition, 1888.

Fridsröster: Sangbok för Väcxelsemöten, Bönemöten, Ungdomsmöten,
Songdagsskolan och Hemmet. Chicago: The Swedish Baptist
General Conference of America, 1910.

Gospel Hymnal. Chicago: Baptist Conference Press, 1950.

Hemlandssånger. Rock Island: Augustana Book Concern, 1892.

Herde-Rosten: en Samling af Kårnfriske och Lifliga Sånger. Minneapolis: Privately printed, 1892.

Herren Lever. Falköping: Gummessons Tryckeri, 1978.

Hymnal for Church and Home. Blair, Neb.: Lutheran Publishing
House, 1953.

Hymns for the Family of God. Nashville, TN: Paragon Assoc., 1976.

Hymns for the Living Church. Carol Stream, Ill.: Hope Publishing,
1974.

Jubel Klangen: Andliga Sånger. Minneapolis: Privately printed
by A.L. Skoog and J.A. Hultman, 1896.

Ludv. M. Lindemans Koralbog: Med et Tillaeg samlet og ordnet af
Oluf Glasoe. Special American edition. Minneapolis: Augsburg
Publishing House, 1916.

Maran Ata: Samlet av T.B. Barratt. Oslo: Filadelfiaforlaget a/s,
1955.

M.B. Lanstads Kirkesalmebok. Oslo: Andaktsbokselskapets Forlag,
1956.

Missions Sånger. W.J. Andreasen et al., eds. Privately printed by
the Danish Baptist General Conference of America, 1916.

Mose och Lamens Wisor. Stockholm: Tryckt Hos Joh. L. Horrn,
1717.

Ny Sang. Holbaek: S.M. Olsen, 1976.

Nya Pilgrimssånger. Stockholm: P. Palmquists Aktiebolag, 1891.

Nya Psalmisten: Sånger for Allman och Enskild Uppbyggelse. Privately printed, 1903.

Nya Sånger for Sondags-Skolan. Chicago: N.J. Russell and Son,
1892.

Pilgrims Lof: Sånger for Enskild och Allmän Uppbyggelse. Minneapolis: Svenska Baptist Literatursallskaps Forlag, 1894.

Pilgrimstoner: Andliga Sånger till Enskildt och offentligt. Orsa:
Fribaptistsamfundets Forlag, 1915.

Pilgrimstoner: Andliga Sånger för Enskilt och Offentligt Bruk.
Habo: Fribaptistsamfundets Forlag, 1957.

Psalm och Sång: For Enskild Andakt och Offentlig Gudstjanst.
Falköping: Svenska Baptistsamfundet, Örebromissionen, 1966.

Psalmer och Visor 71. Stockholm: A.B. Tryckmans, 1971.

Psalmer och Visor 76. Lund: Berlings, 1981.

Psalmer och Visor 82. Arlov: Berlings, 1982.

Psalmisten: Gamla och Nya Kristliga Sånger. Stockholm: Expedieras
af Palm & Stadling, 1880.

Salmebog for Kirke og Hjem. København: Faas I P. Hasses Boghan-
del, 1927.

Salmebog for Metodistkirken I Danmark. København: Kurer-Forlaget,
Metodistkirkens Forlag, 1953.

Salms og Sangbog. N.P. Jensen et al., eds. Chicago: Private
publication of the Danish Baptist Conference, 1887.

Salme og Sandbog. Holbaek: Dansk Baptist Forlag, 1916.

Salme og Sangbog for de Danske Baptister. Privately published in
1928 by the Dansk Baptist-Forlag.

Salmer og Sange. København: Missionsforbundets Forlag, 1954.

Salmer og Sanger. Drammen: Det Norske Misjonsforbund, 1961.

Sånger för Söndagsskolan och Hemmet. Teodore T. Truve, ed.
Chicago: Nya Wecko-Postens Förlag, 1886.

Sånger Till Herrens Lov. Minneapolis: Privately printed by A.A.
Holmgren, 1911.

Sånger Till Jesu Ära: For Hemmet, Bonemotet och Söndags-Skolan.
Edited by V. Witting. Chicago: Tryckt Hos W. Williamson, 1886.

Service Book and Hymnal. Minneapolis: Augsburg Publishing House,
1958.

Sionsharpan: Andeliga Sanger till Guds Forsamlings Tjanst. Chicago: The Mission Friends Publishing Co., 1890.

Sions Harpe: En Samling Evangeliske Sanger og Leilighetssanger.
Oslo: Norsk Forlagsselskap, 1949.

Sions Sånger: Bagge Samlingarne. Stockholm: n.p., n.d.

Sions Seger Sånger. August Davis, ed. St. Paul Park, Minn.:
Evangel Publishing, 1911.

Sionstoner: Sångbok för Den Kristliga Andakten Utgifwen af Evang.
Fosterlands-Stiftelsen. Stockholm: Ev. Fosterlands-Stiftelsens
Forlags-Expedition, 1901.

Solglimtar: 100 Andliga Sånger Tillegnade Barn och Ungdom.
Edited by J.A. Hultman. Worcester: Utgifvarens Forlag, 1916.

Svenska Psalmbok. New York, Cincinnati: The Methodist Book Concern, 1904.

Svenska Söndagsskolans Sångbok. Boston: Tryckt Hos Carl Asp-
lind, 1908.

The Concordia Hymnal. Minneapolis: Augsburg Publishing House,
1932.

The Concordia Hymnal. Minneapolis: Augsburg Publishing House,
1948.

The Covenant Hymnal. Chicago: Covenant Press, 1973.

The Hymnal. Philadelphia: Presbyterian Board of Christian Education, 1933.

The Hymnal and Order of Service. Rock Island: Augustana Book
Concern, 1925.

The Lutheran Hymnary. Decorah, Iowa: Lutheran Publishing House,
1913.

Then Swenska Prof: Psalmboken: Som efter Hans Kongl. Maj:ts
Radigsta Befallning, Bor Utgifivas, Forsta Samlingen. Stockholm:
Tryckt Hos Lorens Ludvig Grefing, 1795.

The Swenska Psalmboken: Med the Stycker som Ther Til Hora och
pä Foltjiande Sida Upteknade Finnas. Uppa Kongl Majestäts Na-
digsta Befallning, Ahr 1695. Gotheborg: Tryckt Hos Joh.
George Lange, 1755. (Also editions of 1727, 1740, 1803, 1875.)

Triumf-Sånger: En samling af Sånger för Söndagsskolan och Ungdomsmoten. Philadelphia: American Baptist Publication Society, 1900.

Troens Rare Klenodie: og Befordet til Tryffen, af A. Winding Brorson. København: Trykt og Forlagt af Andreas Seidelin, 1823.

Valda Hymner: Sangbok for Enskild och Allman Uppbyggelse. Philadelphia: A.J. Rowland, 1896.

Zions Basun: En Samling af Andliga Sånger. Minneapolis: n.p., 1876.

Chorale and Tune Books

Den Danske Koralbog. Jens Peter Larson og Mogens Woldike, eds. København: Wilhelm Hansen, Musikforlag, 1954.

Den Svenska Koralboken. Stockholm: Svenska Kyrkans Diakonistyrelses Bokforlag, 1939.

Koralbog Indeholdende Melodier til Salmebog For Luterske Kristne i Amerika. Minneapolis: Augsburg Publishing House, 1916.

"Maran ata" Sånger: Noter till 200 Sånger (Nr. 301-499). Oslo: Filadelfiaforlaget a/s, 1946.

Melodier: Psalmebog For Kirke og Hjem, Udgivne ved V. Bielsfeldt. København & Leipzig: Wilhelm Hanse, Musik-Forlag, 1901.

Melodibok Till Evangelisten. Oslo: Det Norske Baptistsamfunn, 1947.

Melodier Til Lanstads Salmebog: Ordnede og Harmoniserede af Ludv. M. Lindeman. Christiana: J.W. Capp Cappelens Forlag, 1875.

Melodier Till Metodistkyrkans Psalmbok. Stockholm: Nya Bokforlage Aktiebolaget, 1958.

Melodier Till Sions Harpe. Oslo: Norsk Forlagsselskap, 1953.

Menighedens Melodier Til Brug i Kirke og Hjem. Vols. I & II, Udignet af L. Birkedal-Barford. København: Wilhelm Hansen, Musik-Forlag.

Musik Till Andliga Sånger. Örebro: Örebro Missionsförenings Förlag, 1931.

Musik Till Psalmisten. Stockholm: Trycknings Kommitteens Forlagsexpedition, 1904.

318   Scandinavian Hymnody

Psalmisten: Baptistamfundets Sångbok.   Stockholm: B-Mis Bokförlags
A.-B, 1946.

Musik Till Samlingstoner.   Stockholm: B.-Mis Bokförlags A.-B.,
1921.

Psalm och Sång.   (Music edition).   Falköping: Svenska Baptistam-
fundet, Orebromissionen, 1966.

Salmer og Sanger.   (Music edition).   Oslo: Det Norske Misjonsforbund, 1952.

Sånger och Psalmer.   Stockholm: Missions-Forbündets Förlag, 1951.

Svenska Psalm-Boken Förenad Med Koral-Bok.   J.H. Thomander &
P. Wieselgren, eds.   Rock Island: The Lutheran Augustana Book
Concern, 1892.

Svenska Psalmbokens Melodier och Sånger: Skrefne Af Eric Wasberg.
Strengnås: MDCCIXXV.

Unpublished Material

Cartford, Gerhard M.   "The Contribution of Ludwig M. Lindeman
to the Hymnology of the Norwegian Church."   Unpublished Master's thesis, Union Theological Seminary, 1950.

Daquin, Henry.   "Pietism and the Traditional Worship Practices of
the Lutheran Church."   Unpublished Master's thesis, Concordia
Seminary, 1955.

Hjortsvang, Carl T.   "Scandinavian Contributions to American Sacred
Music."   Unpublished Ph.D. Dissertation, Union Theological Seminary, 1951.

Lundholm, Brynolf.   "An Analysis of the Swedish Chorale."   Unpublished Master's thesis, Eastman School of Music, 1937.

Newquist, Reidun.   "The Hymnody of the Evangelical Mission Covenant Church of America."   Unpublished paper prepared for the
University of Minnesota, n.d.

Olson, Lee Olof Gustaf.   "History of Swedish Church Music."   Unpublished Ph.D. Dissertation, Union Theological Seminary, 1945.

Personal Correspondence

Knut Andersen, Oslo, Norway.

E. Wendel-Hansen, Stockholm, Sweden.

Trygve Hoglund, Uppsala, Sweden.

Gällno Ingemar, Solentuna, Sweden.

Gunnar Kvist, Brønderslev, Denmark

John Magnusson, Örebro, Sweden.

Simon Oberg, Huddinge, Sweden.

K. Kyrø-Rasmussen, Copenhagen, Denmark.

Erik Ruden, Stockholm, Sweden.

• INDEX

(Initial articles in titles have been
used for alphabetizing.)